Praise for *The Fall of the Euro*

"Despite diminished concerns about the immediate instability of the eurozone, the ultimate fate of the euro common currency regime lingers as one of the great unresolved—and potentially cataclysmic—issues on the minds of market participants. *The Fall of the Euro* offers readers an exceptional opportunity to understand and evaluate the technical elements and the practical market realities of what the future holds. Jens Nordvig is one of the most insightful and brightest minds in the industry on these matters, and throughout the evolution of the events in Europe, I have come to depend on his interpretation of the evolving story. Nordvig brings to this book both his tremendous market experience and fundamental economics training, as well as his passion to see those in Europe—and across the global economy—successfully navigate the unsettled waters that lie ahead for the euro."

—Curtis Arledge, Chief Executive Officer, BNY Mellon Investment Management; Vice Chairman, BNY Mellon

"Jens Nordvig's book artfully combines a master economist's framework, a seasoned market participant's advice, an historian's far-reaching perspective, and a European citizen's passionate case for an open discussion of the way forward for the world's largest economic bloc. As a European living in the United States and working for a Japanese financial institution, Nordvig is able to provide a singularly unique perspective that should be read by investors, policymakers, and the average man on the street."

—Scott Bessent, Chief Investment Officer, Soros Fund Management LLC

"*The Fall of the Euro* offers a bold, concise, and thoughtful perspective on the conditions and compromises that triggered the euro crisis, the political and economic dynamics that have hindered policy response, and the range of plausible scenarios that may trace the uncertain road ahead. Jens Nordvig brings a keen insight into markets and economics that he ably combines with a brisk, no-nonsense narrative. This is essential reading for market players, investors, and prognosticators of the future of the eurozone."

—Richard Clarida, C. Lowell Harriss Professor of Economics and International Affairs, Columbia University; Global Strategic Advisor, Pimco; Former Assistant Secretary of Treasury for Economic Policy

"Jens Nordvig has delivered a primal scream about his Europe. Describing the great democratic deficit and failure of the Eurozone experiment, *The Fall of the Euro* is riveting in its discussion of the euro's history and its present, and most importantly in the prescriptions that Nordvig provides. There is anger in the streets. Voters must and will be heard. *The Fall of the Euro* needs to be read by all those demanding brave policy from Europe's timid elite."

—Tom Keene, Editor at Large, Bloomberg Television & Radio; Host of Bloomberg Surveillance

"In this bold, highly readable book, Jens Nordvig beautifully high-lights the tensions between the politics and the economics that are at the heart of the euro crisis. A must read for anyone who cares about the future of Europe."

—Anil Kashyap, Professor of Economics and Finance, University of Chicago Booth School of Business

"This excellent book combines a clear understanding of the euro's past with an insightful economic analysis of its inherent flaws. Nordvig calmly explains how a breakup might work, dispelling many popular myths along the way. I learned much from *The Fall of the Euro* and I thoroughly recommend it."

—Simon Wolfson, CEO of Next plc and sponsor of the Wolfson Economics Prize

"Jens Nordvig has always stood out from the crowd as a market economist. He has the imagination to ask the hardest questions on the subject of political economy and was one of the first to analyze the economic, legal, and political consequences of the euro splitting asunder. Whether or not you share his pessimism about the future of the euro project, Nordvig's guide to the crisis is a compelling and essential read."

—Gavyn Davies, Chairman of Fulcrum Asset Management LLP, former Goldman Sachs Chief Economist, and *Financial Times* columnist

THE FALL
OF THE EURO

THE FALL OF THE EURO

Reinventing the Eurozone and the Future of Global Investing

JENS NORDVIG

New York   Chicago   San Francisco   Athens   London
Madrid   Mexico City   Milan   New Delhi
Singapore   Sydney   Toronto

1 2 3 4 5 6 7 8 9 10 QFR/QFR 1 9 8 7 6 5 4 3

ISBN 978-0-07-183057-7
MHID 0-07-183057-X

e-ISBN 978-0-07-183119-2
e-MHID 0-07-183119-3

Library of Congress Cataloging-in-Publication Data
Nordvig, Jens.
  The fall of the euro : reinventing the eurozone and the future of global investing / Jens Nordvig.
    pages cm
  ISBN 978-0-07-183057-7 (hardback)—ISBN 0-07-183057-X (hardback)
1. Euro. 2. Eurozone. 3. Europe—Economic integration. 4. Monetary policy—European Union countries. I. Title.
  HG925.N668 2013
  332.4'94—dc23   2013025279

The views expressed in this book reflect the personal opinion of the author and do not necessarily reflect the official view of his employer.

To my parents:
Inge and Per

Contents

Preface   ix

Acknowledgments   xiii

Introduction   xv

PART I   **The Euro: The Early Years**   **1**

CHAPTER 1   The Premature Celebration   3

CHAPTER 2   The Birth of the Euro:
A Grand Political Bargain   13

CHAPTER 3   The Euro's Honeymoon Years   33

CHAPTER 4   The Euro Crisis:
Waves of Escalating Tension   49

PART II   **European Integration: The Difficult Path**   **73**

CHAPTER 5   The Big Choice:
More or Less Integration?   75

CHAPTER 6   The Revenge of Realpolitik:
Europe's Dilemma   83

CHAPTER 7   An Involuntary Gold Standard:
The Economics of Inflexibility   99

CHAPTER 8   Where's the Growth?:
The Cost of Deflation   109

CHAPTER 9   Europe's Political Fragility:
The Seeds of the Next Crisis   123

PART III   The Mechanics and Implications of Breakup   141

CHAPTER 10   When a Currency Splinters   143

CHAPTER 11   The Devil's Guide to a Eurozone Breakup   153

CHAPTER 12   What's the Worst-Case Scenario?   163

CHAPTER 13   Who Should Stay and Who Should Go?:
The Economics of Exit   175

PART IV   The Future Euro: Investment Implications   191

CHAPTER 14   Europe at the Center:
Europe's Effect on Global Financial Markets   193

CHAPTER 15   A Road Map for the Future Euro   203

Afterword   221

Data Appendix:
The Breakdown of Eurozone Debts   227

Bibliography   229

Notes   235

Index   249

Preface

I wrote this book because I care about Europe. I feel both sad and angry about the situation in the eurozone and how it has been handled.

I feel sad because so many innocent European citizens are now victims of a devastating economic crisis. Young, bright graduates in Madrid, Rome, and Lisbon are having a very hard time getting a decent job—not through any fault of their own, but because of ineffective economic policy. It is unfair. And it is not only about youth unemployment. Many other groups around the eurozone are unfairly feeling the pain from years of economic mismanagement.

I feel angry because of all the misinformation about the euro: what it is doing to the eurozone countries and what can be done about it. For a long time, the "religion" of the common currency has precluded any debate about alternative policies. European policy makers have been schooled to think about the euro in a certain way, and overconfidence and tunnel vision have made it almost impossible for them to think creatively about new solutions. Misinformation leads to bad decisions, and bad decisions lead to bad outcomes. Millions of people are suffering as a result.

I grew up in Denmark. As a child, I traveled with my parents though France, Spain, Italy, Portugal, and Greece on long vacations; as a teenager, I went to summer school in Germany; while I was studying economics in university, I spent time in Spain; and my first real job was as a markets economist based in London, focusing on Central and Eastern Europe. Through these experiences, I saw the European integration firsthand.

I moved to London in 2000. I immediately felt the city's diversity and energy. The fact that London is such a cultural melting pot is not solely a function of the European integration process, but free movement of labor within the European single market has given the city's diversity a further boost. When I moved to the United Kingdom, all I had to do to start a career there was to catch the first plane and go to the local council's office in East London to get a national insurance number.

Because of the European Union's single market, I had the right to work anywhere I wanted within the EU. My older siblings had not had the same freedom when they graduated some years before me. It was a new European freedom to cherish and celebrate.

In those years, a lot of things in Europe seemed to be going in the right direction. The single market was working (allowing goods, capital, and people to move freely). The EU had played a key role in securing peace in the former Yugoslavia. The euro had been launched successfully. Finally, 10 Central and Eastern European countries joined the European Union in 2004. Europe was successfully integrating along multiple dimensions.

By 2010, it was all falling apart. How could it come to this? Over the last four years, I have spent hours upon hours thinking about it all. I wrote dozens of papers and strategy notes in my capacity as head of currency strategy for Nomura Securities. In addition, I was the lead author on a large technical paper called "Rethinking the European monetary union," which was a finalist in the Wolfson Economics Prize competition in 2012. This book builds on this background material and on innumerable direct interactions with investors and policy makers.

The more I studied the history, the politics, and the economics, the more I wanted to scream: "Why did they do it?!" Creating the euro was such a reckless gamble. Many of the weaknesses in the euro's foundations were foreseeable, and had indeed been foreseen by many before the currency was launched. But those European leaders who were spearheading the creation of the common currency pushed away all arguments against it. They wanted the euro, regardless of its faults and risks.

The other components of European integration—including the common market within the European Union—had a 60-year track record of success, based as they were on a philosophy of gradualism. But the fast jump to a common currency created serious trouble only 10 years after the euro was born.

This book is about how Europe got into this mess—and what the ways out are.

Acknowledgments

Over the past four years, a great deal of my time has been dedicated to analyzing the euro crisis. My main motivation has always been to understand the underlying issues as well as possible, and perhaps help others understand these matters too. I am grateful to those who have offered insights and advice and, throughout the process, helped educate me.

In connection with this book, I want to thank Melissa Flashman at Trident Media Group. She immediately embraced the idea of a book about the euro crisis and guided the process of building a structure for the book.

Lauren Silva Laughlin deserves praise for her commitment and professionalism. Her input was invaluable, given a tight deadline. While she was editing the initial manuscript, she always kept track of the big picture (while tolerating my stubbornness).

Tom Miller at McGraw-Hill was excited about the idea from the beginning, and provided valuable input during the writing process. Thanks also to Alice Manning for a very diligent copy edit.

There are several people who have provided input to various parts of the book. Special thanks to Nikolaj Malchow-Møller and Thomas Barnebeck Andersen from the Department of Business and Economics at University of Southern Denmark, who provided insightful feedback throughout the process, often with remarkable speed.

Various other people provided input for parts of the book. I would like to thank Lewis Alexander, Alessio De Longis, Valerie Galinskaya, Mark Hsu, Irina Novoselsky, Athanasios Orphanides, Leif Pagrotsky, Karthik Sankaran, Bo Soerensen, Vadim Vaks, and Mads Videbaek.

Thanks also to Ankit Sahni and Charles St-Arnaud from Nomura's currency strategy team for help with data gathering and number crunching, and to other staff members at Nomura Securities who ·helped with many of the underlying research projects that have helped shape my thinking over the last few years.

Most important, I would like to thank my wife, Anna Starikovsky Nordvig, who continues to patiently support every crazy project I undertake.

Introduction

The euro crisis is morphing from a financial crisis to an economic and political crisis. Financial markets have calmed, but many eurozone economies continue to suffer from historically deep recessions. How unprecedented economic weakness will influence politics from north to south in the eurozone is the key to the future of the euro.

To understand the euro and the current crisis in the eurozone, you need to understand history and politics, and a bit of economics too. Politics was the main driving force behind the euro when the idea of a common European currency was conceived more than 20 years ago. Politics remains the key parameter today. The interplay of national politics in the 17 eurozone member countries will determine the specific form the euro will take in the future, including the possibility of it disintegrating.

Policy makers can attempt to circumvent the basic laws of economics, but over time, the core economic truths take their revenge. Uncompetitive countries will eventually experience an economic crisis. Overly indebted countries will eventually have to restructure their debts or default. The longer these imbalances are ignored and allowed to accumulate, the greater the ultimate cost of unwinding them.

The euro crisis has been about letting imbalances accumulate and not recognizing the euro's weaknesses before it was too late. European policy makers have finally woken up to the reality, but they are still playing defense. They are fighting to build new institutions, foster greater cooperation, stabilize markets, reignite economic growth, and maintain political stability.

It is an uphill battle. History suggests that a currency union without a political union is a vulnerable thing, and that some form of breakup is a high risk as long as independent countries are focused on their own interests. The optimal solution would be to create a political union in the eurozone and thereby centralize the decision making (as in the United States). But European policy makers have lost credibility, and euroskeptic sentiment is growing across the continent.

Currently, there is simply no public support for the idea of a United States of Europe—not in Greece, not in Spain, and not in Germany. Meanwhile, the economic reality of an inflexible currency union remains one of severe economic pain. This remains the case in large parts of the eurozone even after a period in which markets have been more stable.

How the eurozone evolves institutionally and how the euro behaves in coming years will affect the livelihood of millions of European citizens. The specific form the euro assumes in the future will have an impact on growth and employment across the eurozone and will also drive global financial markets. In line with how we have already seen the euro crisis drive global markets during the last few years, new shocks from the eurozone have the potential to dominate global asset markets, from equities and bonds to currencies and commodities.

This book is organized in four parts.

Part I, "The Euro: The Early Years," gives you the historical background for understanding the current crisis in the eurozone. It begins with the early stages of European integration in the 1950s, continues through the birth of the euro in 1999, and ends with the various eurozone-driven financial market crisis waves that rocked global markets during 2010–2012. The four main crisis waves eventually led to the fall of the euro in its original form. The euro as it was created in 1999 was not strong enough to endure a severe crisis. The euro crisis has forced policy makers to rethink the monetary union, giving the European Central Bank more power and pursuing greater economic cooperation. Only a strengthened version of the euro has the potential to survive in the longer term.

Part II, "European Integration: The Difficult Path," deals with the big choice that Europe is facing. It is a choice between closer integration and cooperation, on the one hand, and a form of breakup, on the other. In 2012, European leaders stared into an uncertain future that included the potential breakup of the currency. To avoid this, policy makers agreed on a new vision for a more mature and closer union.

But there is a difference between vision and reality. The eurozone lacks a political union, and there is no public support for creating one. This is a major obstacle to rapid and radical integration, and it will leave the eurozone in an incomplete and inflexible state for years to come. This is the realpolitik of Europe today. The common currency is still missing a mechanism to deal with economic crises in individual countries. There is no eurozone budget to help countries that are in dire straits.

In a manner similar to the way the gold standard operated almost a hundred years ago, the main adjustment mechanism in the eurozone is now deflation. Over the very long run, lower prices will bring about increased competitiveness. But during the adjustment phase, which could take many years, this is a very painful path for countries with high debt. The pain can be readily observed in historically weak growth and unprecedentedly high unemployment rates in several eurozone countries. This, in turn, creates a fragile political situation. The economic pain is increasingly feeding into political instability along various dimensions. This is sowing the seeds of a future crisis, one that is driven by political tension rather than market breakdown.

Part III, "The Mechanics and Implications of Breakup," confronts the topic of the breakup of the euro, an idea that remains taboo among most European policy makers. This is the scenario that European officials do not want to contemplate, even if the realities of the last few years have forced them to admit that various types of breakup cannot be ruled out entirely.

There are many myths about the implications of breakup, and some of these myths are kept alive for political reasons. This is an underresearched topic, and you should not believe everything you read. In this part, I try to debunk some of the myths about breakup and to provide a framework for thinking objectively about it—something that European officials have a hard time doing.

Two lessons are crucial. First, there are many different types of breakup, from the departure of a tiny country such as Cyprus to a full-blown breakup involving dissolution of the eurozone altogether. In addition, the implications of an economically weak country like Greece leaving are fundamentally different from those relating to a strong country such as Germany leaving. Each type of breakup has its own special considerations, and it is nonsensical to make any blanket statements about the consequences of them all.

Second, when thinking about breakup, there are important legal aspects that need to be taken into account. Economists often ignore or forget these factors, but any practical analysis needs to take into account the legal constraints associated with switching to another currency, something that is inherent in a euro breakup. Otherwise, it is just useless theory.

Part IV, "The Future Euro: Investment Implications," provides a framework for investment strategy in a new world of elevated uncertainty in the eurozone. Over the last few years, we have observed that news from the eurozone now carries unprecedented weight in global financial markets. The challenge for investors and individuals who are trying to protect their savings is that we still don't know the exact form that the euro will take in the future. It will depend on the interplay between politics in the core and the periphery of the eurozone.

Will the euro be a strong currency? Will it be a weak currency? Or will it break into pieces? How the current deadlock is resolved will shape the future of the euro, have a major impact on the lives of millions of European citizens, and drive the performance of many different financial assets around the world.

The Euro:
The Early Years

You cannot understand the euro without understanding its history. The euro was born out of a political desire for European integration. Economics played only a secondary role in the process. This is ironic, since giving up its currency is one of the most important macroeconomic decisions a country can make.

We start in Chapter 1, "The Premature Celebration," with the euro's 10-year birthday celebration in 2009. The fathers of the euro were celebrating their own achievements. They did not realize that the shaky foundations of the original euro would soon lead to a period of sustained and homegrown instability.

In Chapter 2, "The Birth of the Euro: A Grand Political Bargain," I outline the main phases in the history of European integration. The process culminated with the creation of the euro, and it was made possible through a grand political bargain centered on German reunification.

Chapter 3, "The Euro's Honeymoon Years," describes the eurozone's initial 10 years of perceived success. Growth was booming in most of the eurozone periphery, fueled by abundant credit from the core. But under the surface, severe imbalances were building.

In Chapter 4, "The Euro Crisis: Waves of Escalating Tension," I analyze the extreme instability in European and global financial markets during the euro crisis from 2010 to 2012. Each wave of the crisis had its own epicenter. But all these waves reflected the euro's fundamental flaws. The common currency would need to be fundamentally reinvented if it were to be viable in the long run.

The Premature Celebration

A great deal of mystery surrounds the concepts of money and currency. What constitutes money? How can a piece of paper be worth anything? What is the value of one currency relative to another?

Money derives its value from the common belief that people can always convert it into goods and services at will. It is the universal acceptance of the idea that money can be exchanged for something else at some time in the future that gives it value. Government actions underpin this acceptance. Certain laws, such as those that allow people to use money to pay taxes, help define the role of money in our society. Meanwhile, government control of the supply of money helps to ensure trust in the value of the currency. As a society, we have entered into this social contract.

Each country has its version of money. In the United States, money is called dollars. In the eurozone, it is euros. In Japan, it is yen. In each case, the currency has value because it can be used to facilitate transactions (buying and selling of goods) and to store wealth for the future.

THE PURPOSE OF A CURRENCY

But currencies serve a purpose beyond providing the ability to buy a carton of milk, sell a house, and accumulate savings conveniently. Governments that have control of their own currency have a powerful tool at their disposal. Having an independent currency allows a country to tailor its monetary and exchange rate policy to meet the specific needs of the economy. For this reason, currencies are often symbols of national power. During the nineteenth century, for example, at the peak of the British Empire, the pound sterling was the dominant international currency.

The relative values of currencies are determined in foreign exchange markets. For most major currencies today, market forces are allowed to determine exchange rates. The supply of and demand for a currency will dictate its price in accordance with economic and political developments at home and abroad. But the success of a currency cannot be judged from its nominal strength or weakness alone.

A currency's success should ultimately be evaluated based on its ability to deliver on the core objectives of the country's citizens. In many countries, this isn't limited to economic prosperity, but also includes basic values such as democracy, equal opportunity, and political stability.

The euro was created with such fundamental values in mind. Therefore, it should follow naturally that judgment on the euro's success should not be based solely on its value against the dollar, or against any other currency. Rather, the euro's success should be based on the currency's ability to deliver prosperity for all European citizens and its ability to reinforce the most treasured European values.

PREMATURE EURO CELEBRATIONS

The euro turned 10 years old on January 1, 2009. European officials used the occasion to celebrate their achievements. Past and present leaders—the people who had created the idea of the euro and watched it come into being—gathered at a high-profile conference in Brussels, Belgium. The European Union even launched a public website to celebrate the euro. The 10-year birthday website showcased the euro's success through a series of easy-to-understand (albeit fictional) stories from the various countries using the currency. A family from Greece was happy because of low interest rates on its mortgage. A line manager from Finland was happy because of strong growth and new business opportunities.

On the front page of the website, the top economic official of the European Union, Joaquin Almunia, captured the positive spirit of the moment in relation to the euro:

> Ten years on, it is a historic achievement of which all Europeans can be proud. Not only is such a currency union unprecedented in history; we can declare it a resounding success. Within the space of a decade it has clearly become the second most important currency in the world; it has brought economic stability; it has promoted economic and financial integration, and generated trade and growth among its members; and its framework for sound and sustainable public finances helps ensure that future generations can continue to benefit from the social systems that Europe is justly famous for.

At the time, the European currency was still viewed as a pillar of strength, a strong common anchor during a time of global financial turmoil. In previous crises, individual European currencies had fluctuated wildly, buffeted by global shocks or homegrown tensions. This time, the euro had been strong and relatively stable. The initial catalysts for the global financial crisis were concentrated in the United States, and the euro had actually gained versus the U.S. dollar in the early part of the crisis.

BACK TO REALITY

Just four years later, the reality is very different. Some eurozone countries are chugging along just fine; Germany is the best example. But others, like Greece, Spain, and Italy, have plummeted into unprecedentedly long and deep recessions.

In Greece, teachers are seeing their students doubled over with hunger pains during class. Like scenes straight out of Dickens, some children are even pawing through trash cans to try to find food or begging their classmates for scraps. In a story in the *New York Times* highlighting this issue, one of the teachers said, "Not in my wildest dreams would I ever expect to see the situation we are in. We have reached a point where children in Greece are coming to school hungry. Today, families have difficulties not only of employment, but of survival."

In Spain, more than 26 percent of the labor force is unemployed, up from less than 10 percent before the crisis. Meanwhile, youth unemployment has skyrocketed to more than 50 percent. People cannot pay their mortgages, are losing their homes, and have nowhere to turn. In February 2013, four people in one week committed suicide after being evicted from their properties throughout Spain.

In Italy, small businesses—in aggregate the biggest employer in the country—are struggling to pay their bills and are closing. According to the Italian business association Confindustria, the number of bankruptcies has doubled since 2007, and with credit conditions still worsening, there is no relief in sight. In May 2013, even the pope chimed in on Twitter: "My thoughts turn to all who are unemployed, often as a result of a self-centered mindset bent on profit at any cost." You know that the economic hardship is significant when the pope enters the debate.

Meanwhile, Europeans elsewhere, especially the more prosperous ones in the north, are getting tired of the woes of the poorer countries. They are growing weary of funding bailouts for struggling banks and sovereigns in the south. They have turned the screws on places like Spain and Greece by demanding severe government spending cuts and structural reform with the aim of bringing budgets into balance. But this is affecting funding for basic social services, including public hospitals in Greece. This exacerbates the situation for people in poorer countries at the worst possible time.

Recently, demonstrators took over a square in Madrid, shouting, "To fight is the only way!," according to a report on CNN. During demonstrations this year in Greece, Cyprus, and Spain, depictions of Angela Merkel dressed in a Nazi uniform have been shown. Both sides are fuming. The Germans are paying the bills, but they are getting blamed for the hardship. The common currency was supposed to bring Europe together. But in reality it is a source of disturbing political tension.

THE EURO'S CONGENITAL FLAWS

To the creators of the euro, their achievement looked strong and successful just a few years ago. But the euro's underlying flaws have now been exposed. Since the euro's 10-year birthday, the global financial crisis has morphed into a euro-specific crisis. The euro's flaws have been made evident through repeated waves of financial market turbulence and a trend of underlying economic deterioration.

The euro crisis started in Greece. The country was vulnerable after years of excessive government spending, and it underwent its own credit crunch when investors pulled back in late 2009. Then housing markets collapsed in areas that were previously booming, and Ireland and Spain descended into severe recessions. The largest eurozone banks teetered, not only in Ireland and Spain, but also in France and Italy. Individual European financial markets started to drift apart, reversing the trend of financial market integration that had existed for the previous 10 years. Finally, for the first time since World War II, a developed European country defaulted on its debt. Greece restructured its government bonds in March 2012.

Now, public finances in places such as Portugal and Spain look close to unsustainable. The anchor provided by the common currency has become dislodged, and confidence in European institutions and policy making has eroded. Today, few would agree with the statement that the euro has been a resounding success.

The euro was born out of a political desire for European integration. It was a noble idea, but it lacked a sound and resilient underlying structure. Countries that adopted the euro would be united through the common currency and a common monetary policy set by the European Central Bank (ECB). Each individual country that was part of the eurozone surrendered its ability to make its own monetary decisions, even in a time of crisis. Unified monetary policy implied that tools that could help save an individual economy during periods of severe stress were no longer available to the individual countries. Meanwhile, there was no centralized fiscal policy to provide an offset. Unlike the United States, the European currency union had no backing from a common federal government that was able to transfer funds between weak and strong regions. What's more, no European institution had any real ability to control an individual country's budget or spending habits. The monetary union was handcuffed in the event of a catastrophe.

These fundamental flaws have caused severe economic and financial stress in the eurozone since 2010. Over the last four years, major swings in global asset markets—across currencies, fixed income securities, and equities—have been driven by European events, a clear departure from patterns in recent history. In the past, Europe was one of the most stable parts of the global economy, and its typically minor economic fluctuations would have little bearing on U.S. equity markets, for example.

TRYING TO REINVENT THE EURO

Recognizing the incompleteness of the infrastructure supporting the euro, senior European officials eventually put forward a blueprint for a so-called genuine economic and monetary union of the eurozone countries. This change in thinking came about in the summer of 2012. The new vision for the euro involves closer coordination of public-sector budgets and common supervision of the region's banks. Some officials also hope to eventually put in place a common financing instrument, so-called eurobonds. This is a long-term vision.

But there are serious obstacles to moving toward a more mature monetary union.

First, short-term problems need immediate responses that a long-term vision won't provide. Large eurozone countries such as

Spain and Italy are currently facing high public-sector borrowing costs and negative growth, which threaten to make their debt burdens unsustainable.

Second, although the eurozone now has more ECB support, European treaties were written to categorically preclude central bank financing of public-sector deficits. While, astoundingly, many deals have been able to circumvent this seemingly clear legal directive, the ECB has been forced to attach at least some conditions and caveats to its interventions. For example, in order to get access to ECB support in the future, the Spanish government would have to submit to unpopular budget restrictions and supervision from the ECB. The lack of unconditional backstop from the ECB leaves public finance in an uneasy vacuum of uncertainty while policy makers struggle to make progress on the longer-term integration process.

Third, the political reality is that voters across the eurozone have lost their appetite for further European integration. Even if European leaders are willing to sign up, European citizens are skeptical that they can make good on their promises. Future elections and referenda may present significant and decisive setbacks to the integration process, and this uncertainty may feed into a growing sense of pessimism in the shorter term.

THE EVOLVING EURO CRISIS

The complexity of the euro crisis is derived from several main elements. The euro is an incomplete monetary union, incapable of dealing with shocks in specific eurozone countries. It has a conservative central bank that is unwilling to provide unconditional support for individual countries. And, perhaps most important now, European countries have diverging political views and cultural backgrounds, and European policies are rapidly losing credibility. A severe decline in public trust in European institutions across the entire eurozone makes significant further integration extremely challenging.

To put it bluntly, *the eurozone cannot survive without further fundamental reform, and if further integration is not feasible, some form of breakup is inevitable.*

In the early part of the euro crisis, any mention of a breakup of the eurozone was regarded as speculative paranoia in European policy circles. But new political realities in Greece and Cyprus have opened up a space for such conversations. European policy makers have finally admitted that some types of exit from the eurozone are a possibility. You could even argue that a form of breakup has already taken place when severe capital controls were imposed on Cyprus in 2013, limiting the movement of money into and out of the country. President Nicos Anastasiades of Cyprus admitted the same in an interview with the New York Times on July 9, 2013. "Actually, we are already out of the eurozone", he said.

At the same time, policy makers are still trying to pretend that other forms of breakup—such as those involving the departure of Spain, Italy, or even Germany from the euro—remain inconceivable. But this position may change over time too.

THE POLITICS OF THE FUTURE EURO

Still, European policy makers have invested immense amounts of time and energy, not to mention political capital, in the euro project, and they are not about to give up easily. They are pursuing gradual further integration to save the common currency, and they may even have gained confidence from a degree of financial market stabilization since the last intense crisis wave in the summer of 2012.

To be viable in the long run, Europe's currency union needs to be underpinned by more closely integrated economies. Member countries need to move toward fiscal and political union; and the ECB needs to assume direct responsibility for protecting the currency by assuming an explicit role as the lender of last resort.

Just a few years ago, European policy makers were celebrating the euro as a "resounding success," and markets were assuming minimal government default risk across the entire eurozone. But the euro is failing to deliver on the core objectives of European citizens. Markets are no longer collapsing, but confidence in European institutions is. Weak growth and years of broken policy promises are combining to create unprecedented euroskepticism, both in peripheral countries and in the very core of the eurozone.

EUROPE'S NEXT CRISIS IS POLITICAL

This book will provide a new framework through which readers can understand the key indicators that are of longer-term importance for the future of Europe and global financial markets. Investors should learn the danger of premature celebrations and position themselves for a new investment environment in which *political risk* in Europe plays a potentially dominant role.

2

The Birth of the Euro: A Grand Political Bargain

It was never a secret that the euro was a political project. But the extent to which politics have dominated economic considerations has not always been fully known or appreciated. The historical context and political considerations have repeatedly trumped any economic cost-benefit analysis. This is a central feature of a multi-decade European integration process. These historical, cultural, and political factors concerning how Europe works will remain a crucial element of the crisis resolution and the chosen path for coming years.

A PROJECT FOR PEACE

The roots of the eurozone can be traced back to around 1950. The most devastating war that the world had ever seen had ended just five years earlier, and Europe remained severely wounded and shaken.

Entire cities had been bombed to rubble, millions of people had been displaced, families had been torn apart, and transport and communication had broken down. Starvation was commonplace. Europe was in a debilitated condition, both economically and socially.

In order to heal and recover, the nations that had been at war needed to secure lasting peace by encouraging cooperation. This cross-border integration became an overarching political goal.

France and Germany, because of their size and their historical influence, had to be at the core of this peace process. But memories of the atrocities of the Third Reich were still fresh. Other European nations were still fearful of potential German power, and the vanquished country was in no position to assume political leadership. East Germany was controlled by the Soviet Union. Meanwhile, West Germany was divided into three zones, supervised by the United Kingdom, France, and the United States.

The postwar climate meant that Germany could take part in, but could not lead, a movement toward greater European cooperation. It was no coincidence, therefore, that French policy makers assumed leadership of the first integration efforts.

The French minister of foreign affairs, Robert Schuman, described the grand vision in a speech in Strasbourg in 1949:[1]

> We are carrying out a great experiment, the fulfillment of the same recurrent dream that for ten centuries has revisited the peoples of Europe: creating between them an organization putting an end to war and guaranteeing an eternal peace.

To turn that vision into reality, Schuman spearheaded an idealistic initiative whereby France and Germany would pool the key resources required for the postwar rebuilding effort. The result was a proposal that sought to eliminate cross-border tariffs on steel and coal, the resources that were most essential for economic revival at the time. It was a small initial step, but it signified a broader political movement of historic proportions.

The idea was formalized in 1951, when Belgium, France, Italy, Luxembourg, the Netherlands, and West Germany created the European Coal and Steel Community (ECSC). Another French policy maker took the helm of this first supranational European body. Jean Monnet became the president of the High Authority that governed the ECSC. Later, in a letter to U.S. President Eisenhower in 1953, Monnet painted with visionary strokes the ideal behind the ECSC:[2]

> Our Community is not an association of coal or steel producers: it heralds the beginning of Europe .... Europe has enough raw material and energy resources, and all the necessary resources in

the form of labour, the will to work and inventiveness, to achieve a prosperity comparable to that of America, provided it reverses the course of events that, born of divisions, led it into war and threatened its decline. It is by uniting its peoples, widening its markets, creating and respecting the new institutions it has set up, that Europe will create the conditions for progress and peace.

The specific mission of the community may have been fairly narrow, but its broader political importance was immense. The creation of the European Coal and Steel Community set in motion a *gradual integration process* that lasted more than 60 years and is still ongoing. The basic building blocks were made from coal and steel. The goal was to build a house for peace.[3]

In 1957, the six founding European countries signed the Treaty of Rome. This initiated a more ambitious forum for cross-border cooperation, which was called the European Economic Community (EEC). The main goal of the EEC was the gradual elimination of tariffs on all goods and services traded between the community's member countries. Like the ECSC, this second leg of integration also centered on increased economic cooperation in specific areas. The scope of the EEC was broader, but the lofty political goal remained the same—to secure lasting peace in Europe after centuries of repeated violence.

The 1950s and 1960s were a period of rapid European growth. German industrial production in particular grew at an extremely fast pace (comparable to China's in recent decades). The Volkswagen Beetle was a symbol of the German economic miracle. From 1950 to 1968, more than 11 million of the unusual-looking vehicles were produced and exported around the world. It was by far the most popular car in the world. Trade between the different European countries increased sharply as a result of reduced tariffs and an environment that supported cross-border cooperation.

By 1968, the initial stage of the economic integration process was complete. The six founding members of the EEC had eliminated all import and export tariffs and had built a comprehensive European customs union.

The entire project of gradual economic integration was a cover for increased political cooperation—and it worked. Most people would have agreed that Schuman's prescient vision from 20 years earlier had been highly successful in binding Europe together.

BRANCHING OUT

The next step in the European integration process was the enlargement of the EEC's membership. The group first expanded in 1973, when the United Kingdom, Denmark, and Ireland joined, increasing the membership from six to nine countries. Outside countries now considered participation in the customs union to be economically advantageous, and they wanted a seat at the table in an increasingly important European decision-making process.

The group continued to grow in 1981, with the addition of Greece, and in 1986, with the addition of Portugal and Spain. Membership was now 12. The driving force throughout this process was again political. By joining the EEC, these three countries, which had emerged from dictatorships in the 1970s, were now cemented on their democratic trajectory. Spain had suffered under the brutal dictatorship of General Franco from 1936 to 1975, Portugal had been under authoritarian rule from 1940 to 1974, and Greece had been ruled by a military junta from 1967 to 1974. As members of the EEC, the southern European countries were suddenly anchored to a club of well-functioning democracies.

Still, for the new countries, the economic benefits of membership surely played a role. Economic carrots included entrance into the large EEC market and access to EEC funds for economic development. Transfers from the EEC central budget to the community's poorer regions were designed to speed up economic convergence, and they provided an extra incentive for membership. It was a mechanism that was consistent with the European ideal of equality. Meanwhile, the existing member countries were encouraged to expand the community by their political desire to support democracies in the south. This happened both for idealistic reasons and as part of a more calculated foreign policy aimed at cementing political stability in the region during the Cold War.

The fast-tracking of Greece's EEC membership in 1981 (ahead of Portugal and Spain) was a blatant example of politics dominating economics. Only seven years earlier, Greece had been under a military dictatorship, and its GDP per capita was just half of the EEC average. It was hard to find a good economic reason why Greece should be allowed into the community before Spain.

But European and global leaders feared that an escalating conflict between Greece and Turkey could unsettle an already unstable region on the southeastern edge of Europe. Greek EEC membership was agreed upon with considerable speed, leaving Spain and Portugal outside the EEC for five more years.[4] Chart 2.1 shows the increase in the number of countries in the EEC and its predecessor and successor institutions (the ECSC and the EU) from its formation to the present, and also the number of countries using the euro.

Another gradual step toward integration was taken in 1987 when a new European treaty was signed. The initial phases of integration had been based on cooperation between national states, each with its

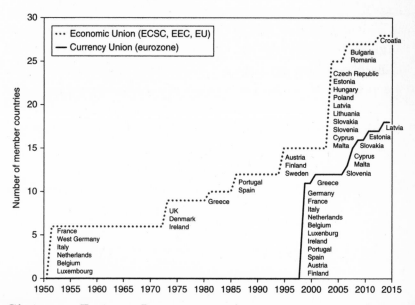

Chart 2.1   European Integration, 1950–2014

own incentives to protect local industries. The Single European Act replaced the Treaty of Rome of 1957 and envisioned creating a *single market* in Europe, with free movement of goods, services, capital, and people. The EEC had been successful in eliminating explicit barriers to trade, such as tariffs, but implicit barriers still existed in the form of various national regulations and restrictions. The idea was to remove control of European markets from the protective national bureaucracies and empower supranational institutions to harmonize and enforce European regulation. To create a truly common market, supervision and regulation were increasingly centralized within European institutions in Brussels and Luxembourg, including the European Commission, the European Parliament, and the European Court of Justice.

A huge shortcoming, however, was that banking regulation was not included in this reform. About 20 years later, when a serious banking crisis arose, European policy makers would come to severely regret the fact that bank supervision was still in the hands of local regulators with conflicting national agendas.

Before the single market was created, multinational companies had often targeted only the largest European markets. For example, General Electric might have big operations in Germany, France, and the United Kingdom, but the complicated, country-specific regulations in the smaller European countries made it cumbersome to do business in the entire region. Why bother with frustrating red tape in a bunch of small European countries? With common regulation in place, the cost of entering all markets within the member countries was dramatically reduced, helping to increase competition, boost trade, and lower prices.

EUROPEAN CURRENCY TENSION

Currency policy was not a main focus during the initial phases of the European integration process. From the end of World War II to the 1970s, European currencies were tightly controlled as part of the globally agreed-upon Bretton Woods system. This new global financial architecture was developed during an international monetary conference in Bretton Woods, New Hampshire (perhaps the most famous tiny village in the world) toward the end of the war.

The Bretton Woods system fixed other countries' exchange rates relative to the dollar. It was a globally coordinated system, managed through the International Monetary Fund in Washington, DC. All major currencies, including the various European currencies, participated in the system. The German mark (the so-called deutsche mark or D-mark) was fixed relative to the U.S. dollar, as was the French franc. When market forces caused exchange rates to depart from the agreed-upon objectives, central banks would intervene and supply currency as needed to bring market rates back to the target. By construction, exchange rates between European countries were also fixed, except when there was international agreement that an exchange-rate adjustment was warranted on fundamental grounds.[5]

In the 1960s and 1970s, increasing global capital flows strained the Bretton Woods arrangement. As part of the broader trend of opening international markets, borders were also softened to allow a freer flow of capital into and out of countries. Maintenance of agreed-upon target exchange rates required increasingly large interventions by European central banks.

Adjustment of central parity rates, which involved the devaluation of weaker currencies, turned out to be necessary on a regular basis. Weaker European countries saw repeated periods of exchange-rate tension that led to an agreed-upon devaluation versus the dollar. Meanwhile, the German mark remained strong versus the dollar.

During various currency crises in the 1960s and 1970s, policy makers used the term "gnomes of Zurich" to describe a supposed group of evil currency speculators hiding behind bank secrecy laws in Switzerland. Politically, it was more convenient to project the blame for economic instability onto rich, selfish speculators than to admit to failed domestic economic policies.[6]

In the 1970s, the Bretton Woods system broke down after a period of financial market instability. President Nixon announced in August 1971 that the United States would sever its longstanding link between the dollar and gold. After a few years of unsuccessful attempts to revive the Bretton Woods system, the global monetary system moved toward freely floating exchange rates between major economies. By 1973, the U.S. dollar, the Japanese yen, the British pound, and the German mark were generally freely floating against each other, with their values being determined on a day-to-day basis by supply and demand in the market rather than by government-dictated parity rates.

UNACCEPTABLE CURRENCY FLEXIBILITY

The global shift toward floating currencies left European policy makers in a predicament. A system of market-determined exchange rates was not an acceptable situation in Europe. The countries in the European Economic Community had moved toward close integration of goods markets. Highly volatile exchange rates between these countries were viewed as a serious problem, especially because many European officials viewed currency speculators as among their worst enemies. The thinking was that large shifts in relative production cost resulting from currency movements would affect the profitability of exporters and importers, potentially bankrupting certain companies in the process. Corporations and policy makers preferred stable export revenue and predictable production cost. Managing currencies was a way to secure this stability.

Meanwhile, at the country level, the Germans feared that freely floating currencies would allow the dramatic devaluation of other European currencies versus the deutsche mark. In that scenario, German producers would become uncompetitive, at least for a period of time. The French, on the other hand, wanted to achieve currency stability, partly to support the political notion that they were equals with the Germans in economic matters.

In response to persistent tension in currency markets, European leaders established their own system of managed exchange rates.

Initially, the system was called the "currency snake," and it allowed currencies to fluctuate against each other only within narrow bands (hence the name). In 1979, the framework evolved into the European Exchange Rate Mechanism (ERM), with a similar goal of reducing exchange-rate volatility.

But the system of managed floating exchange rates failed to deliver any lasting stability. In fact, both the currency snake and the ERM suffered repeated crises. The European countries had reduced capital controls during the 1960s and 1970s, and maintaining fixed exchange rates became increasingly difficult. The official interventions needed to keep a fixed exchange rate in place were too big to stomach. The United Kingdom famously lost around $40 billion worth of foreign currency reserves in about a month when the pound came under an intense attack during the fall of 1992. This figure amounted to roughly 4 percent of U.K. GDP, illustrating how free capital mobility made currency intervention an uphill battle for governments and central banks. The United Kingdom was eventually forced to leave the ERM and allow the pound to depreciate. A similar fate befell the Italian lira, which left the ERM the same day.

Mario Monti, at the time an academic economist at the University of Bocconi, told the newspaper *La Stampa*, "This is a grave defeat for Italian economic policy."

Meanwhile, other weak European currencies, including the Spanish peseta, the Portuguese escudo, and the Irish pound, were forced to devalue over the course of several tumultuous months.

Periods of currency instability often culminated in late-night emergency meetings of European leaders concerning adjustments of exchange rates. The system was a source of ongoing political tension, a negative component of an otherwise generally collegial and productive process of increased cross-border European cooperation.

For example, Chart 2.2 illustrates how the French franc was regularly devalued during the 1970s and 1980s relative to the German mark.

It was against this background of market instability that the idea of a common currency was born. It was not a new idea. Various

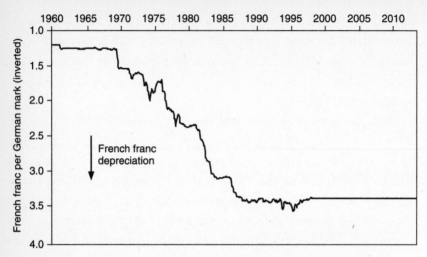

Chart 2.2   French Franc Versus German Mark Exchange Rate

Source: Haver

European politicians had fantasized about a common currency for decades. But French European Commission president Jacques Delors gave the idea credibility. The so-called Delors Report, published in April 1989, outlined a three-stage plan for building an Economic and Monetary Union (EMU) within a 10-year period.

However, there was a fundamental disagreement standing in the way of the plan. The French wanted to use the common currency as a means of driving political union in Europe and avoiding German dominance of European affairs. The Germans, on the other hand, viewed political union as a precondition for a common currency. There was little movement on either side. The specific sequence was crucial to both the French and the Germans. Neither side was willing to compromise.

A GRAND POLITICAL BARGAIN AND A CURRENCY UNION

For several years, there was little political momentum behind the idea of a common currency. But things changed dramatically when developments in Eastern Europe during 1989 suddenly forced the issue of German reunification. The fall of the communist regimes in Central and Eastern Europe ended the Cold War era and opened the way for reuniting West Germany and East Germany.

For Germany, reunification trumped all other political considerations. The country had been artificially split at the end of World War II and had remained violently separated by the conflicting ambitions of the Soviet Union on the one side and the Western Allies on the other. The brutality of the division was most clearly demonstrated in Berlin. In 1963, a concrete wall, with barbed wire on top as in a prison, had been erected to divide the city. The Berlin Wall was built to separate the socialist east from the capitalist west, and to prevent East German citizens from fleeing to better economic conditions and political freedom in the West. Against this backdrop, reunification of Germany was the sole focus of the German political leadership. Economics and broader foreign policy issues were secondary.

In autumn of 1989, German chancellor Helmut Kohl famously devised a radical 10-point plan for unification. The plan was announced just a few weeks after the Berlin Wall had unexpectedly fallen. Kohl saw the unification of Germany as an inevitable outcome of the fall of the wall, and this historical project completely dominated policy making.

Kohl's 10-point plan was created in haste, without consultation with Germany's international partners or German economic experts. It was a political plan that was aimed at achieving fast-paced integration of the two parts of Germany, with little regard for the economic cost. Other European leaders, especially French president François Mitterrand, feared that German unification would cement German supremacy in Europe. While East Germany—or the DDR, as it was officially known at the time—had a population of only 16 million, adding this to West Germany's more than 60 million would make the united Germany the clearly dominant economy in Europe. Its combined population would effectively dwarf France's population of 57 million.

To counterbalance a stronger, united Germany, Mitterrand wanted Germany to give up its currency, the deutsche mark, and agree to a common European currency. The common currency would be a way to reduce Germany's economic dominance and allow other countries to gain influence over European monetary policy, which had previously been dictated by the Bundesbank in Frankfurt.

The compromise was all about politics. German chancellor Helmut Kohl was determined to deliver German reunification to the German people. Other European leaders, including French president Mitterrand, U.K. prime minister Margaret Thatcher, and Soviet leader Mikhail Gorbachev, were opposed to German reunification if it were done solely on German terms.

It took intense pressure from Mitterrand to secure the crucial concessions from Germany. Mitterrand threatened to isolate Germany, and said that Germany would be acting in opposition to an alliance among France, the United Kingdom, and the Soviet Union if it went ahead with reunification without accepting broader European integration. By this means, Germany was strong-armed into signing up for a common European currency in exchange for support for its reunification plans.[7]

For about 20 years, Europe had dealt with repeated periods of currency-market instability, but it had never been able to agree on the parameters of a common currency. Germany's unification provided a historic opportunity for a grand political bargain. In 1990, an official timetable for adopting a common European currency by the end of the decade was agreed upon. It was a political compromise. As usual, economic cost-benefit analysis played only a secondary role.

PREGNANT WITH A COMMON CURRENCY

Once the idea of a common currency had achieved political backing from the major EEC countries, the process had its own self-sustaining momentum, and there was no turning back. In 1991, European leaders signed the Maastricht Treaty, which formalized the process for adopting a common European monetary policy. A timetable for the launch of the common currency by the end of the decade had been pinned down.

The first step was ratification of the new treaty, country by country. I was living in Denmark at the time, and, as a young voter, I felt compelled to study the subject carefully and vote responsibly. Ahead of the public referendum on the new treaty in June 1992, the Danish government made the full text of the Maastricht Treaty available in libraries and other public spaces, free of charge. It was a dense document, printed on 59 pages of cheap recycled paper. I forced myself to read the entire ugly pamphlet. For an average citizen without legal background, the content was very nearly incomprehensible. It was the full legal text of the treaty, with no explanation or interpretation. Almost nobody was able to fully absorb it.

For some European leaders, the euro project was almost a religion. When the Danish population rejected the Maastricht Treaty and thereby voted against adopting the euro, the news was received angrily in Paris. In an internal meeting, Jean-Claude Trichet, then the head of the French Treasury, expressed the view that an "insignificant country" should not be allowed to delay the European integration process.[8] The politicians at the center of the euro project wanted the euro so badly that other considerations (economic analysis and respect for democratic principles) were relegated to the background.

During the 1990s, it was taboo to talk about postponing the launch of the euro either in policy circles or in the public debate (similar to the way discussion of the possibility of a euro breakup was taboo during the first waves of the euro crisis).

Still, some countries had good reason to sign on. In the south, democratic institutions and government had less credibility, given their shorter histories and less impressive track records, and the populations were less concerned about relinquishing sovereignty. Similar to joining the EEC (which morphed into the European Union [EU] in 1993), membership in the eurozone implied an anchor to a more reliable and controlled democratic system. Hence, public support for the euro was quite strong in the south at the time.

But in the richer countries in the north, public support for the concept of a common currency was more limited. They had a nostalgic attachment to their old crowns, marks, and pounds. Moreover, since the northern European countries had democratic institutions with a long track record, there were more concerns about giving up precious national sovereignty to European institutions. The debate there focused more on whether the economic benefits of a currency union were meaningful.

The focus on economic costs and benefits was strongest in the United Kingdom. In fact, the United Kingdom was one of the few countries where euroskepticism was part of the debate. Neither the public nor the country's political establishment had a strong desire to join the common currency. The United Kingdom had a different history from other major European countries, as evidenced by its late entry into the EEC.

Margaret Thatcher was against the common currency—often called the EMU in policy circles—right from the start. In 1990, as the debate about monetary union was starting, she made the following comments to the U.K. Parliament: "EMU is really the backdoor to a federal Europe, and we totally and utterly reject that." (Watching her speech on YouTube more than 20 years later, I cannot help thinking, "She could not have been more right.") Thatcher's stance was clear, and unlike many of her fellow European leaders, she did not try to hide her belief that giving up your currency means giving up a key component of your sovereignty.

The official U.K. policy stance also reflected this more skeptical sentiment. The U.K. Treasury did detailed cost-benefit analysis in the form of five economic tests in 1997 (and again in 2003). The first paragraph of the document, titled "UK Membership of the Single Currency" and written by Gordon Brown in his capacity as chancellor of the exchequer, said: "The decision on a single currency must be determined by a hard-headed assessment of Britain's economic interests." The conclusions of the report were mixed: there was no clear economic case for adopting the euro. Hence, the United Kingdom's stance was broadly consistent with the analysis of most academic economists. There was an inherent skepticism about the economic merits of adopting a common currency and giving up monetary independence, and in the United Kingdom, as opposed to most other countries, this consideration was given considerable weight.

Meanwhile, the Swedes, who had joined the EU in 1995, used a delaying tactic to stay out.[9] However, the reluctance of a few countries at the perimeter of the EU had little impact on the momentum of the core European countries. The United Kingdom had been late in joining the EEC in 1973 and was repeatedly the "odd one out" in setting European policy.[10] Hence, the United Kingdom's reservations were not sufficient to stall the overall momentum.

In Germany, the public did not support giving up the deutsche mark. During the 1990s, more than 60 percent of the German population responded in surveys that they did not trust the common currency.[11] However, no public referendum was held on the matter. Helmut Kohl stuck to the bargain he had made with other European leaders during the reunification process, pushing through plans to implement the common currency by the end of the decade.

CAMPAIGNING FOR THE EURO

To support their political efforts to create a common currency, European policy makers and officials were creating a simple narrative on the benefits of the euro. This "propaganda" was used to win over the public and secure successful referendum results. They argued that a single currency would reduce transaction costs, improve the logistics of travel and foreign trade, and create more integrated and more efficient financial markets.

The official narrative was told in semiacademic official working papers and in a more populist format in informational material sponsored by the EU and national governments. Happy-go-lucky Europeans were pictured in pamphlets describing the advantages of lower transaction costs, easier cross-border trade, and stable exchange rates in making the case for the euro.

But in these marketing materials, there was no mention of how the system would fare during a crisis; no analysis of the cost associated with fixed exchange rates in the face of adverse economic shocks; and no discussion of how adjustments would take place in the future, when important macroeconomic shock absorbers had been disabled.

Few countries had a rigorous debate about the economics of joining the currency union. Most of the debate was focused on the more sentimental issue of giving up sovereignty, and the limited economic input to the debate was confined to more or less arbitrary estimates of the potential growth benefit the euro would generate.

A SUBOPTIMAL CURRENCY AREA

Meanwhile, in academic circles, doubts bubbled. A number of prominent economists highlighted the deficiencies in eurozone institutions well before the euro's creation. They argued that the euro was a suboptimal currency regime for a set of diverse economies that were not bound together by a strong political union. Nobel Prize–winning economist Milton Friedman was one of the skeptics. He argued that the euro would not survive its first serious crisis. But the opinions of outsiders did not feature very prominently in the debate.

More generally, there was an entire branch of economics that highlighted the costs associated with adopting a fixed-exchange-rate regime. The reality was that the countries that made up the European Union had strong cultural and macroeconomic differences. Economic divergence, which would render a common monetary policy inefficient, was a risk. Language barriers, among other things, meant that labor mobility was relatively low. When dealing with shocks, the reduced flexibility inherent in a fixed-exchange-rate system could be hugely negative.

The costs associated with an inflexible currency arrangement were well documented in academic research done on the subject. Most studies found no evidence that Europe was an optimal currency area.[12] Indeed, even the central banks at the core of Europe, including the German Bundesbank, were skeptical that the common currency was a good idea on economic grounds. The staff at the Bundesbank made this case in internal working papers, but the political decision had been made. Helmut Kohl overruled the economic opinion of the experts at the Bundesbank. To him, political considerations took precedence.

In reply, some argued that even if the eurozone economies had not entirely converged before they adopted the euro, they would converge fully once they were within it, meaning that the poorer countries would become wealthier and more productive with the help of others. This theory was popular within the pro-euro political establishment. But it was just one theory among many, and it did not have any particular widespread backing in the academic profession. For example, Paul Krugman, the Nobel Prize–winning economist, provided aggressive arguments against the theory.[13] But it was too late; the euro, ready or not, was about to be born.

THE INVITATION LIST

The dominance of political considerations was abundantly clear when it came to determining which countries would adopt the euro in 1999. Candidate countries were evaluated on their economic performance during 1997 and 1998. The European Monetary Institute, the predecessor to the European Central Bank, was in charge of the process.

The evaluation was based on five criteria for economic convergence spelled out in the Maastricht Treaty. The criteria were tangible and relatively easy to evaluate. The basic requirements were low inflation, low government budget deficits, moderate government debt, a stable exchange rate, and long-term interest rates that were close to the average in other euro candidate countries.

The goal of the criteria was to screen countries in order to ensure that the economies adopting the euro had sufficiently converged.

But politics took over the process, and the opportunity to apply an objective economic screening process was missed. The Maastricht criteria were overruled almost more often than not. For example, Italy had a public debt level that dramatically exceeded the defined limit of 60 percent of GDP. In the official convergence report from 1998, the Italian government debt-to-GDP ratio stood at 122 percent, and there was no clear trend of decline. Belgium was not far behind. But both countries were allowed to adopt the euro.

Several candidate countries (including Germany) used creative accounting, involving ad hoc revenue figures to massage their fiscal deficits to less than the 3 percent fiscal deficit limit. But knowledge that this manipulation of the key figures was taking place had no real influence on the evaluation of the countries' readiness to join the euro.[14]

Temporarily tight fiscal policies in the run-up to euro evaluation helped push inflation below the permitted limit (as did certain technical measures, such as reductions in goods taxes). The Maastricht criteria may have been satisfied mathematically, but true convergence had hardly been achieved. All these violations of the Maastricht criteria did not matter in the end.

Not everybody rejoiced in this process. Dutch officials were highly skeptical of Italy's readiness, for example. In a letter to senior German officials in early 1998, they argued:[15]

> Without additional measures on the part of Italy to provide credible proof of the longevity of the consolidation, Italy's acceptance into the euro zone is currently unacceptable.

The only applicant country that was not allowed to adopt the euro in 1999 was Greece. Greece had failed all five of the Maastricht criteria by a wide margin (but was nevertheless allowed to enter the common currency in 2001, after a delay of just two years).

All told, 11 countries ended up entering the eurozone at the outset in 1999. Their objective economic readiness for the common currency was a secondary consideration relative to subjective political considerations.

A POLITICAL CURRENCY

The objective of European integration was given priority over an open debate and a robust economic analysis. The political nature of the selection process was just the final indication of the entirely political nature of the process leading to the creation of the euro.

Therefore, the euro was born prematurely. European leaders hoped that it would facilitate a continued process of economic integration and convergence, with the result that the inherent flaws of the euro would gradually be overcome.

But the sheer political will behind the project, even if impressive, was not sufficient to alter the basic economic reality. The economic risks associated with the euro project remained, although they would come to the surface only later.

Ironically, time would tell that the premature and incomplete currency union would itself become a source of severe economic tension among the eurozone countries and also the impetus for anti-European political movements across the continent. Rather than achieving its founding intentions, the common currency would end up risking increased political instability in Europe.

It was also ironic that the German leader at the time the euro was launched, Gerhard Schröder, had very different views about the currency union from those of his predecessor, Helmut Kohl, who had pushed aggressively for the single currency.

In an interview with *Berliner Zeitung* before the launch of the euro in 1999, Gerhard Schröder characterized the euro as a *kränkelnde Frühgeburt*. In English, this translates into a "sickly premature baby"—hardly a ringing endorsement of the common currency. But even Schröder accepted that Europe was about to have a common currency. There was no turning back on the euro at that point.

3

The Euro's Honeymoon Years

T he euro was launched on January 1, 1999. Initially, it was a hybrid system: the euro was used for electronic transactions, but the physical notes and coins of the 11 European legacy currencies were still used for cash transactions. Retail prices were quoted in both euros and the old currency of the country in question. But at this point, the flexibility between eurozone currencies had stopped. No matter what the look of the coin or the picture on the currency note might be, the exchange rate was fixed and the underlying currency was the same. The common currency had been born.

THE SUCCESSFUL EURO LAUNCH

The initial phase of the transition to euros went remarkably smoothly. Financial institutions managed the changeover without serious hiccups, shoppers were becoming acclimated to seeing prices quoted in euros, eurozone financial markets functioned well, and the euro was relatively stable versus other global currencies. (The exchange rate versus the dollar was 1.18 when the euro was launched, and in its first year of trading, the range was 1.00 to 1.20.)

With a common currency came a common monetary policy. Interest rates were set by the European Central Bank in Frankfurt based on aggregate economic developments in the overall region. Each country in the eurozone named a member to the ECB's governing council, which together with the ECB president set interest rates for the entire eurozone.

The ECB was a brand new institution, but it was modeled on the German Bundesbank, which had a reputation as a steadfast guardian against inflation. In fact, the ECB was indeed successful in keeping aggregate inflation under control. From 1999 to 2008, the ECB achieved average inflation of 2.2 percent, compared to a rate of 2.8 percent in the United States. The small overshoot relative to its "below, but close to, 2 percent" target was arguably the result of rising global commodity prices over the period, rather than any policy mistakes of its own.

After a three-year transition using the hybrid system, the next phase of the currency shift took place. In 2002, the process of exchanging physical money into euros started. From then on, people were encouraged to exchange notes and coins of the legacy currencies to euros. Cash machines would provide only euros, for example. Soon eurozone citizens would carry euro notes and coins in their wallets. Marks, francs, lira, pesetas, guilders, schillings, pounds, and escudos were gradually removed from circulation (although some people held on to their old currency for nostalgic reasons). From then on, travelers no longer had to bring different currencies when taking a trip from Frankfurt to Paris or from Vienna to Milan.

Initially, the unified currency appeared to create a relatively favorable growth environment in most countries. The average real growth rate in the eurozone in the first 10 years of the euro was 2.3 percent. This was not as high as the growth rate in the United States, which achieved a 3 percent average during the period, but the discrepancy was accounted for by demographic trends. In GDP per capita terms, there was no major difference.

In the aggregate, the eurozone appeared to be achieving stable and balanced growth. But under the surface, each country had its own special story.

THE EUROZONE'S BULLS

During the euro's early years, I was working for Goldman Sachs as an international economist. A key part of my job was advising corporations and banks around the world on how to manage risk in global currency markets.

On one of my regular business trips to Spain, I met with Banco Santander, continental Europe's largest bank at the time based on market capitalization. We were meeting with senior risk managers and senior traders, presenting our latest analysis and currency forecasts. There was nothing unusual about the meeting itself. But the surroundings were startling.

Normally, a bank's corporate headquarters is located in the financial district of a major city. You enter through a formal lobby area with high ceilings, expensive, shiny marble, and a stern security guard.

But Banco Santander was different. The bank had moved outside Madrid because its growth during the boom years had been so vibrant that there was no longer enough space for it in the center of Madrid.

The new headquarters was located a 45-minute drive outside Madrid. It was called Santander City. It was a sprawl of modern buildings that occupied an entire section of the countryside and was designed to reflect the progressive and international image of the rapidly expanding bank. It looked more like a modern apartment complex, and the traditional marble had been replaced by functional and progressive concrete.

At the entry to Santander City, there was a checkpoint. Visitors had to show their identification, then the Santander minibus would take them to the right location within the compound. Seven thousand bank employees were working in Santander City, which included several restaurants, gyms, hairdressers, and even an 18-hole championship golf course for the executives. Santander City was a sign of Spain's vibrancy and the growth momentum behind some of Spain's major corporations.

Santander's expansive suburban sprawl was the poster child for a nationwide phenomenon. It was an example of the boldness with which unprecedented amounts of new construction were being undertaken in Spain in those honeymoon years.

In Barcelona, high-rises were transforming the city's historic skyline. Throughout the country, thousands of kilometers of

EU-sponsored highways were built. In Andalusia in the south, the mountains were covered with holiday homes as far as the eye could see. In the major cities, condo buildings mushroomed. Across the country, new office towers and other bold commercial real estate projects were changing the landscape, epitomizing a new era of Spanish energy and confidence.

Housing prices marched steadily higher. From the early 1990s to their peak around 2007, the cumulative rise was nearly 200 percent. Developers were building about 600,000 houses annually, twice as many as in previous years. It was a real bonanza, even relative to what was happening in other countries. In 2006, construction as a percentage of GDP peaked at more than 12 percent. In Germany, the equivalent figure was below 4 percent, and in the United States, the peak during the period was not above 6 percent, according to data from the UN's Economic Commission for Europe.

Rising prices and historically low borrowing rates created confidence in the real estate sector. In the mid-1990s, before Spain adopted the euro, mortgage interest rates had typically been around 10 percent. After the country adopted the euro, interest rates in Spain were indirectly determined by the ECB in Frankfurt, and mortgage interest rates quickly dropped to below 5 percent. Borrowing costs had never been that low before. Meanwhile, Spain remained a net recipient of EU funds for investment purposes. The EU's cohesion funds helped fund infrastructure and other construction activity, adding further to investment.

THE CELTIC TIGER

Another eurozone bull story was Ireland. The country's economic history had been troubled, and there had been waves of large-scale emigration to escape economic hardship on the island. But Ireland grew strongly in the 1980s and 1990s, earning the nickname the "Celtic Tiger" because its growth was on a par with the super-fast-growing Asian Tiger economies. Competitive exports were a key driver of the growth during the tiger years. In the 2000s, however, real estate speculation and a major construction boom took over as the key sources of expansion.

Real estate development became a veritable frenzy. Between 2000 and 2006, house prices more than doubled, and leverage in the system was building fast. In 2007, credit extended by Irish banks to the private sector reached 200 percent of Irish GDP, double the level in countries such as Germany, France, and Italy.

A few rapidly expanding Irish lenders accounted for most of the credit expansion. Anglo Irish Bank (AIB) was among the most aggressive participants in the Irish real estate El Dorado. AIB was founded in 1964, and it initially grew fairly slowly. At the outset of the real estate boom in 2000, AIB had €11 billion in assets. By 2008, which marked the abrupt end of the boom years, its total assets had grown almost tenfold to an astonishing €101 billion. The large majority of the expansion came from lending to real estate projects. By comparison, Irish GDP was then around €160 billion.[1]

Construction activity in Ireland was almost as elevated as that in Spain. It peaked at 10.7 percent of GDP in 2006. This hyperbuilding resulted in a large overhang of unoccupied homes. In 2006, the Central Statistics Office Ireland identified 266,000 empty residential properties, equivalent to 15 percent of all homes in the country.

Leaving aside the statistics, the excess was readily visible in communities around the perimeter of Dublin. In the boom years, many of these suburban residential properties had been sold to investors who were looking for rental properties or a quick flip. But as that demand slowed, entire communities became unoccupied and were labeled "ghost towns."

Country-specific forces, including favorable demographics, came into play in the construction booms in Spain and Ireland. But these countries also benefited from historically low interest rates associated with the common monetary policy. Moreover, as financial markets in the eurozone became more integrated, banks and investors in Frankfurt, Paris, and London differentiated less among the eurozone countries. This allowed borrowers in Spain and Ireland to obtain much more credit than they could have obtained before the euro was created. Local banks took advantage of this newfound flexibility, and some expanded at an unprecedented pace by borrowing in liquid interbank markets and by issuing billions worth of unsecured bank debt. In its own way, Europe played a prominent role in the global credit boom.

THE GOOD YEARS IN GREECE

Greece also experienced strong growth in the early years of eurozone membership. Despite its failure to meet certain financial criteria, Greece had been admitted to the Eurozone in 2001, after a two-year delay relative to the first 11 countries. Before entering the euro, Greece had managed to lower its fiscal deficits and temper inflation in order to satisfy the euro entry criteria temporarily. After its entry, Greece experienced a period of strong growth and increased optimism. Reversal of fiscal austerity also helped. Real growth fluctuated around 4 percent in the early 2000s, and the unemployment rate was heading lower. For a change, it felt good to be Greek. Each year, the European Commission conducts a comprehensive survey of public opinion in the European Union (EU). In the 2005 survey, 65 percent of Greeks responded that they were either very or fairly satisfied with their lives (by 2012, that number had dropped to 32 percent).

Greek households took advantage of better economic conditions and started making some expensive purchases. Passenger car registrations jumped from a level generally below 150,000 a year before eurozone entry to above 250,000 in the years after eurozone entry. The proportion of households owning a car increased sharply, from around 50 percent in 1999 to 67 percent in 2005. Greece's economic standing was finally catching up with the rest of the eurozone. Some improvements in social programs were also implemented. For example, pension payments were raised during the early 2000s.

But Greece had plenty of problems, too. The Athens Olympics in 2004 was just one example. The event was meant to symbolize the return of Greece to the peak of Western civilization. The budget for the event was large, and the planned improvements included a new airport, a subway system, and a new ring road around Athens. In the end, the outlays were twice the budget. The total cost, not including the airport and the subway, was €9 billion, or 5 percent of Greece's GDP. The large overshoot epitomized the chaotic nature of the Greek budgeting process.

Meanwhile, revenue remained very low by European standards, in part because of poor tax collection. Fiscal deficits had been kept close to the 3 percent limit in the years just before euro entry (1999 and 2000). After euro entry, however, fiscal policy was relaxed and deficits quickly moved higher. By 2003, the deficit was 5.7 percent of GDP, and in 2004, it jumped to 7.4 percent of GDP, in part because of unexpected costs related to the Athens Olympics.

Strong GDP growth helped to keep the debt-to-GDP ratio relatively stable, and Greece's fiscal performance was not a major focus in a world where Greece lived under the eurozone umbrella.

Before the euro, market participants would have raised their eyebrows over Greece's excessive government spending. There would have been concerns in financial markets about an increasing risk of insolvency and potential currency depreciation. But Greece's exchange rate was now fixed, and people thought it inconceivable that a "proper" eurozone country would not honor its debts.

Deceptively robust headline economic performance combined with a buoyant global credit cycle to fuel complacency. International investors started to view Greek bonds as merely another type of eurozone government debt rather than stand-alone sovereign debt with its own credit characteristics. As an element of this, in the years leading up to and immediately after Greece's entry into the euro, the major credit rating agencies were busy upgrading Greek sovereign debt. Fitch Ratings upgraded Greece four times between 1999 and 2003, and Moody's sovereign credit ratings upgraded Greece three times between 1996 and 2002. By 2003, both agencies ranked Greece just four notches below their top AAA rating.

CONVERGENCE OPTIMISM

There was a sense of optimism across the continent, especially in previously lagging regions that were now catching up with their richer cousins in Germany and France.

Spanish and Irish citizens were finally getting the investment home of their dreams. Meanwhile, residents of Athens were tooling around their historic streets in new cars. Whatever the specific benefits, there appeared to be a common trend of convergence in income levels within the eurozone.

GDP per capita in Greece, Portugal, Spain, and Ireland grew rapidly in the early days of euro membership. From 1998 to 2008, Greece's GDP per capita almost doubled, from €10,700 to €20,900. This was much faster than the growth observed in Germany. As a result, there was a convergence in income levels. In 1998, Greece's GDP per capita was just 45 percent of Germany's. In 2008, it was 69 percent.

Convergence of income levels took place in most peripheral eurozone countries. Spain moved from 57 percent of German GDP per capita in 1998 to 79 percent of the German level in 2008. Portugal moved from 46 percent of the German level in 1998 to 54 percent in 2008. Ireland was the most extreme example. It started at 89 percent in 1998, and by 2008 it had surpassed the German level by a wide margin, with a level of 134 percent.[2]

This was how the economic and monetary union was supposed to work. The poorer countries were expected to benefit from free trade, access to liquid financial markets, and historically low interest rates. Meanwhile, the EU budget (albeit limited in size for the region overall) channeled additional capital into what were supposed to be productive investments in infrastructure, healthcare, and education. For some of the smallest countries, such as Greece, the structural funds from the EU budget were a significant contributor to growth in the years after entry into the eurozone. In a research report, the European Commission estimated that this increased GDP by 2.8 percentage points from 2000 to 2006.[3]

EUROPEAN OPTIMISM

Greater optimism and increased confidence in previously depressed peripheral regions manifested itself in many ways. Every year since 1985, a European city has been designated European Capital of Culture of the year. The purpose was to increase awareness of different cultures and their historical heritage and to foster a common European identity.

In the euro's early honeymoon period, the cities of the fast-growing periphery dominated the list of cultural capitals. In 2000, Santiago de Compostela in Spain was selected. In 2001, Porto in Portugal was named. In 2002, it was Salamanca in Spain. In 2005, Cork in Ireland was chosen, while Patras in Greece won the honor in 2006. There were 15 EU member countries at the time. But during this period, it was more common than not for the cultural capital of Europe to be located in one of four countries on the periphery: Spain, Portugal, Ireland, and Greece.

While most southern European countries and Ireland enjoyed fairly strong real growth, the eurozone countries that were toward the center of the currency union enjoyed a boom in the financial sector. In particular, banks in Germany and France took advantage of new lending opportunities. Previously, markets in Greece, Portugal, and even Spain had been viewed as risky and exotic. But they now entered the mainstream of many banks' business model. The common currency framework eliminated currency risk and was often perceived as reducing other risks, too. For the banks, it looked like a safe way to take advantage of markets with stronger growth than on the home turf.

Banks in Germany and the Netherlands channeled excess domestic savings to credit-hungry countries like Spain and Ireland. And if no large pool of excess savings existed, as in France, international wholesale funding markets offered readily available cash for banks that were looking to expand their balance sheets. By 2007, German and French bank exposures in the so-called PIIGS countries (Portugal, Ireland, Italy, Greece and Spain) had ballooned to well above €1 trillion.

The increased cross-border lending within the eurozone was viewed as a sign of success. Financial integration appeared to be playing out as the founders of the euro had hoped it would.

THE EUROZONE'S LAGGARDS

Growth was not strong everywhere. In Italy, the euro honeymoon was very short-lived. Immediately following Italy's entry into the eurozone, growth picked up somewhat, as fiscal policy was relaxed and interest rates dropped. But from 2002 to 2007, the Italian economy grew at a minimal pace of just 1 percent on average.

The weakness had multiple causes. For example, some Italian industries, such as textiles, faced fierce competition from emerging market countries, which were steadily gaining global market share. The rise of China as a global manufacturing powerhouse played a key role here. Meanwhile, the housing market in Italy was more mature than that in Spain, and prices remained broadly stable, despite a decline in borrowing cost for mortgages resulting from the common monetary policy. Hence, Italy did not enjoy the growth support from strong credit growth and buoyant construction, as Ireland and Spain had.

Then there was Germany—the country that was funding much of the expansion elsewhere through its cash-rich banks. Its business cycle had been shaped by German reunification. Reunification involved large-scale fiscal and monetary transfers to the former East Germany.[4] This resulted in a period of higher inflation and deteriorating German competitiveness. The hangover was felt in the years immediately following the adoption of the euro, where Germany's loss of international competitiveness showed up in relatively weak overall performance.

GERMANY PUSHES REFORMS

Most eurozone countries were content with their economic performance in the initial years of the euro. In most of the region, economic reforms and initiatives to boost efficiency and growth did not gain momentum. This was true of some of the largest member countries, such as France and Italy.

But Germany was different. In the early 2000s, in response to Germany's homegrown economic issues, Chancellor Gerhard Schröder initiated a wide-reaching and proactive reform program called Agenda 2010. Its main goal was to make the German labor market more flexible and to regain the country's lost competitiveness by 2010. The key elements of the program included wage restraint, more flexible work arrangements, and large-scale retraining programs for the unemployed.

The program was initially a drag on Germany's economic performance. While growth was booming across southern Europe, German growth was subdued, as many workers were facing declining real wages and lower disposable income. The effect was particularly visible between 2001 and 2005, when German growth averaged just 0.6 percent, lagging significantly behind the rest of the eurozone's average of 1.8 percent. It even became common to label Germany "the sick man of Europe," a term that had been used in previous decades to describe the troubled U.K. economy (and well before that to characterize the struggling Ottoman Empire).

Over time, however, the reforms had a positive impact on Germany's competitiveness. With wages steady and productivity rising, per unit production cost were lower, especially relative to those of other countries in the eurozone.

This eventually led to strong export growth. Germany was able to gain market share both in Europe and globally. In fact, by building on its strength in machinery, automobiles, and chemicals, Germany was particularly well placed to take advantage of strong industrial growth in emerging markets such as China. In addition, Germany derived a benefit from the reintegration of the Central and Eastern European economies into the broader European supply chain during the 2000s. Large German companies such as BMW, Siemens, and Volkswagen were quick to expand their supply chains in more cost-effective areas, such as the Czech Republic and Hungary. Germany's export engine was running at full power, partly at the expense of other European countries.

In many ways, the euro helped Germany chip away at other countries' competitiveness. In the past, before the euro was created, a German export boom would have created currency tensions. Strong German exports would have created devaluation pressure on other European currencies (or revaluation pressure on the deutsche mark). Because exchange rates were now fixed, however, there was not much debate about Germany's gains in relative competitiveness. In addition, many European countries had fairly strong domestic demand growth anyway, hiding any problems relating to exports. Over the years, Germany quietly gained market share, while other eurozone economies lost theirs. But this did not ring any alarm bells, as it would have done in the past.

IMBALANCES UNDER THE SURFACE

So on the surface, growth looked robust, financial markets appeared calm, and European institutions were building credibility. But under the surface, severe economic imbalances were starting to build. The policy divergences between Germany and the PIIGS countries (and to some degree France) were sowing the seeds for a future imbalance. This was not immediately visible in terms of monetary or exchange-rate tension. With a common currency, there were no market prices that could directly reflect the building tensions. But the lack of coordination of structural economic policies, including labor market reforms, would gradually become a source of imbalance within the currency union.

UNUSUAL NUMBERS

In the decade before their entry into the euro, Greece and Portugal had external deficits averaging slightly more than 2 percent of GDP. Total domestic demand exceeded total domestic production, but only by a moderate amount.

Following their entry into the eurozone, this changed. Current account deficits (a broad measure of net trade in goods and services with other countries) ballooned to well over 10 percent in some years during the honeymoon period. Each year, these countries imported much more from the rest of the world than they exported to it. Their current account deficits were financed by bank loans, bond sales, and foreign direct investment by companies. The flip side of the excess consumption was a large buildup in financial liabilities.

The average current account deficit for Greece and Portugal during the first 10 years of the euro was a staggering 9 percent of GDP, more than four times the deficits that had been in place during the previous 10 years. Spain was not far behind. Its current account deficit peaked at 10 percent in 2007 and averaged 5.8 percent in the 10 years following its entry into the eurozone.

The overall strength or weakness of a country's balance sheet can be summarized in its net foreign asset position, which is defined as the country's total external assets minus its total external liabilities. Before their entry into the eurozone, Ireland, Portugal, and Spain had net foreign asset positions that were in moderate deficit. External liabilities exceeded external assets by around 25 to 35 percent of GDP. By 2008, the liabilities had ballooned, and the gap had reached 70 to 95 percent of GDP. By comparison, emerging market countries (such as Turkey, Brazil, and South Korea) that had experienced currency crises over the previous 15 years typically had had only a negative net foreign asset position in the region of 30 to 40 percent at the time of their crises.

Greece held the record in terms of the largest amount of public debt, which had been sold to willing domestic and foreign investors. Spain held the record in terms of the largest amount of external debt, a large part of which was issued by private corporations and banks. Emerging market countries with such high debt ratios—public or external—would have faced intense market pressure and potentially a currency crisis. But the countries in the eurozone were given the benefit of the doubt.

Inflation trends were another sign of imbalances. Because the economies were growing strongly, inflation rates in Spain, Portugal, Greece, and Ireland were drifting well above the eurozone average. The Maastricht criteria for entering the eurozone stipulated that no country should have an inflation rate more than 1.5 percentage points above those of the three countries with the lowest rates. Nevertheless, in its first five years in the eurozone, Greece had inflation of around 3.5 percent, while German inflation was averaging closer to 1.5 percent. Over time, such differences in inflation rates and wage growth would create competitiveness problems. But the erosion happened slowly, and decent top-line growth masked the underlying weaknesses.

FORGOTTEN COUNTRIES

A close look at economic performance country by country would give you hints of the building imbalances. There were large differences in growth among the different eurozone countries. Inflation trends varied, and trade deficits had reached historically high levels in some countries. Greece won the prize for the most extreme deficit relative to the rest of the world. In 2007, its current account deficit reached an astonishing 14.6 percent of GDP. It was an extreme case of excessive spending.

While there had been elements of convergence of income levels, there was no overall structural trend toward synchronization of business cycles. Monetary policy had become unified (at least in terms of nominal interest rates), but structural policies differed from country to country. Importantly, during the early 2000s, when Germany embarked on major structural reforms, there was little effort to coordinate policy within the eurozone. The economists who had predicted convergence of business cycles as a result of the common currency were disappointed.

But since these countries were a part of the euro, this divergent economic performance seemed more forgivable. Most investors and observers did not care very much about the obscure details of economic development in small eurozone countries. Even economists ceased to be interested in the country specifics, but focused instead on analyzing eurozone aggregates. Very few economists looked at trade positions at the country level, for example.

I was working in the European research department of Goldman Sachs at the time and was focusing on Central and Eastern Europe. Tellingly, the research department had more macro analysts covering these European emerging markets than it had covering the eurozone, even though the size of the eurozone economy was much bigger.

European bond markets had been exciting for investors in the 1990s. In the run-up to entry into the eurozone, economic convergence in preparation for such entry was showing up in narrowing spreads and opportunities for large returns on bond investments in countries such as Spain and Italy.

But the economists covering the smaller economies, such as Portugal and Greece, had been laid off after the countries joined the eurozone. Investors were not focused on intra-eurozone differences. Similar to the way investors and analysts approached the United States, they now looked at the eurozone in the aggregate.

MARKET COMPLACENCY

In the 2000s, the various eurozone peripheral markets, such as Spain and Italy, had become relatively boring. Spreads between different countries were tiny and generally very stable. So whether you owned German government bonds (Bunds) or Italian government bonds (BTPs) hardly mattered. What mattered was whether you got the broader trends in the eurozone right, so that you could predict ECB policy and the implications for all the bond markets across the eurozone, which tended to move in tandem.

The regulatory frameworks also played a role. A sovereign default by any country in the eurozone was deemed unthinkable, and banks were not required to hold any capital against positions in sovereign bonds. This helped sovereign spreads stay very low across the board, with only marginal differences between yields in Germany and in other eurozone sovereign markets. From a regulatory perspective, Greek bonds were treated the same as German bonds, and this meant that banks were more than willing to assume the extra risk in the peripheral markets, even for a tiny additional yield.[5]

THE FINAL DAYS OF THE HONEYMOON

Countries developed rapidly during the euro's first decade. It was during this time—when markets were integrating and poorer countries were catching up—that optimism about the euro's prospects was greatest. There were academic papers about how the euro would soon take over as the world's leading reserve currency. In April 2008, Harvard economics professor Jeffrey Frankel (with coauthor Menzie Chinn) published a paper called "The Euro May over the Next 15 Years Surpass the Dollar as Leading International Currency."

This was just one example of the view that the euro might be a better store of value than the U.S. dollar, and therefore a preferable choice for global central banks that were looking to expand their foreign exchange portfolios.

In 2007 and early 2008, the euro traded at all-time highs against the dollar and against the Japanese yen. In March 2008, as the U.S. economy was suffering from a weak housing market and European growth appeared to be holding up better, the euro exchange rate rose to 1.60 (dollars per euro). This was substantially above the launch rate of 1.18 in January 1999 and nearly double the euro's value against the dollar in 2002, when it hit an all-time low.

It was around this time—at the peak of the euro's honeymoon period—that celebrities such as U.S. rap star Jay-Z and Brazilian top model Giselle Bündchen reportedly demanded payment in euros for their major assignments. The news media reported that they would no longer accept payment for major jobs in U.S. dollars.

Overall, the euro's rise to prominence and its potential challenge to the dollar as the dominant reserve currency was a remarkable development, given that the euro was an unprecedented construct and given that it had been in existence for only 10 years.

As is often the case following honeymoons, however, the euro's period of carefree bliss would soon come to an end.

CHAPTER

4

The Euro Crisis: Waves of Escalating Tension

I n 2008, the eurozone was in for a surprise. The global financial crisis shook people's confidence, put global banking systems on the edge, and triggered a synchronized recession in all the world's major economies. The eurozone could not escape its effects. However, at least for a while, the global nature of the crisis allowed European policy makers to place the blame on reckless policies in the United States and on the excesses of greedy bankers.

The European elite was confident that the euro was a sound currency and worthy of being honored. In January 2009, in the midst of collapsing economies and disorderly financial markets, the Europeans celebrated their achievements at a 10-year birthday party for the euro in Brussels. ECB President Jean-Claude Trichet commented, according to *EUobserver*: "The crisis has revealed fundamental weaknesses in the global financial system." However, there was not much soul-searching about what might have gone wrong at home.

The Europeans had been right in identifying the United States as the original epicenter of the crisis. But when the Greek crisis escalated in early 2010, just as the global economy was clearly recovering, the finger-pointing became counterproductive. Instead of thinking about a long-term answer for dealing with Greece and the shortcomings in the eurozone's structure, the policy makers tried to blame "irresponsible" rating agencies and shortsighted speculators for their troubles.

In reality, the Greek crisis was just the first wave in a euro-specific crisis. Between 2010 and 2012, while the global economy gradually recovered, the eurozone was mired in repeated waves of financial market instability and economic weakening. In the end, outside forces could not be blamed. The institutional structure of the euro was directly responsible for the underlying vulnerabilities.

For years, European policy makers were blind to the lack of sustainability of the euro's original architecture. Instead, they put patches on the structure during crisis after crisis, ruining the confidence of market participants, households, and companies. Instability escalated, with tremendous real costs. By the time a proper crisis-fighting bazooka was loaded during 2012, the eurozone's peripheral economies were in a downward spiral, heading for the deepest recessions in decades and putting local political and social stability at risk.

Here is the chronology of the four main waves in the euro crisis.

THE FIRST WAVE: THE INITIAL GREEK SHOCK

The initial wave of the euro crisis began in late 2009. The Greek socialist party (PASOK) won the election in October and formed a majority government. One of its first actions was to announce revised budget figures correcting previously misstated items. The numbers showed an extraordinarily large public-sector deficit of 14 percent of GDP for 2009. The number was so far above the generally agreed-upon ceiling on budget deficits for European Union (EU) member countries, 3 percent of GDP, that it essentially made a joke of the controls that were supposedly in place to avoid overshoots.

The much higher deficit figures meant that government debt levels were also substantially higher than had been previously reported. In response to the news, credit rating agencies quickly downgraded Greek government debt. Almost immediately, investors started to liquidate their Greek government bonds.

At the time, I was starting a new job as head of currency strategy for Nomura Securities, a global investment bank with headquarters in Japan. I was based in New York, but part of my time was dedicated to advising Japanese asset managers in Tokyo on their international investments.

Japanese investors don't get the same airtime in the financial press as the flamboyant hedge fund managers in London and New York. (When did you last see a Japanese portfolio manager on CNBC?) But Japan as a country has accumulated a very large pool of savings over the last few decades, and the amount of assets managed by Japanese institutions easily exceeds that of even the biggest hedge funds. The importance of Japanese money is particularly pronounced in global bond markets, and indeed, Japanese investors were the biggest foreign investors in many eurozone bond markets in 2009, with positions that were often multiples of those of U.S. investors.

An investors' meeting in Tokyo is different from a similar meeting in London or New York. Normally you sit close to the ground on leather couches around a low coffee table. A polite Japanese woman will serve you tea or coffee, then walk backward out of the room after doing so. You are supposed to go through your presentation meticulously, page by page, and the feedback you get is often confined to an approving nod, or perhaps a hard-to-interpret drawn-out "nnnn" sound. The typically middle-aged Japanese investment managers will rarely ask any questions at all. This reluctance comes from differences in culture and language. If there is a question, you know that it means trouble; it reflects a deep-seated and imminent concern. In one particular meeting, I received more than half a dozen questions on Greece alone. This was highly unusual. Fundamental beliefs had been shaken, and fresh decisions needed to be made.

The negative headlines out of Athens in late 2009 led to a rapid reassessment of risk. During December 2009, the Japanese investor community embarked on a wholesale liquidation of its Greek government bond holdings. It had taken institutional investors in Japan more than 10 years to accumulate a total position in Greek government bonds worth more than $10 billion (more than €7 billion). It took them just six months to liquidate the large majority of them (see Chart 4.1), and they were not looking to return to the Greek market any time soon.

Not all investors were as fast at getting out of Greece as the Japanese were. European banks and global insurance companies were slower, but liquidation from these sources also gathered steam

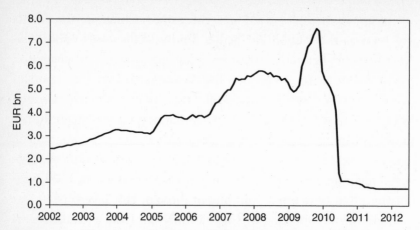

Chart 4.1 Japanese Holdings of Greek Debt Securities

Source: Nomura, IMF, MOF

in 2010 (except banks in Cyprus, which maintained large positions). Importantly, the realization that a member of the eurozone could potentially default on government debt was a tremendous shock to investor psychology.

For decades, markets had assumed, perhaps with good reason, that the risk of government default was negligible outside of emerging markets. Since the immediate aftermath of World War II, there had not been a single sovereign default in a developed market country: not in Europe, not in North America, and not in the Asia-Pacific region.[1]

Problematic defaults had happened in Russia in 1998 and in Argentina in 2001, and they had generated substantial global market volatility. But at the time, the global investment community did not regard these countries as developed, and global banks had only limited exposure to them. Hence, the impact of these defaults on the global banking system proved to be relatively short-lived and ultimately manageable.

The assumption of near-zero default risk in government bond markets in developed countries was now up for reassessment. It put in motion a broader wave of rethinking concerning investments in Europe. Global markets reacted violently to the new reality. Since major banks were heavily exposed to the assets in question, it seemed like a case of uncontrolled internal bleeding at the heart of the global financial system.

Bond markets in peripheral eurozone countries saw dramatic weakness and unprecedented volatility. Meanwhile, global stock markets took pronounced hits, and the euro dropped sharply against other major currencies, especially the U.S. dollar and the Japanese yen. The shock to confidence in eurozone financial markets was tremendous, and European leaders convened an emergency meeting in May 2010 to hammer out a deal that could support Greece and restore confidence to the eurozone financial system.

It was a race against time. Support for Greece was urgently needed to avoid a disorderly default and runaway contagion to the rest of the eurozone. However, the European Union was built around a "no-bail-out clause" that prevented member countries from assuming other countries' debt. Decisions had been delayed to the last minute, in part because German chancellor Angela Merkel did not want to appear "weak" ahead of a local German election the same weekend. Hence, actual negotiations could take place only on Sunday and late into the evening in Brussels.

This was the first time since the global financial crisis that an emergency weekend summit had been needed to avoid global market panic. And as had been the case in 2008, this meant that analysts and traders in the key financial centers of New York and London had to go to the office on Sunday. It was the one time you got to see your colleagues in plain clothes in front of their trading floor screens—not always a pretty sight. (I for one was wearing a bright red tracksuit similar to the one John McEnroe had sported in the 1980s.)

I was in my office on the twentieth floor of the World Financial Center in lower Manhattan, monitoring the various live newswire services. But the press conference continued to be pushed back, and it was a frustratingly long wait. European policy makers were negotiating until late in the evening in Brussels to reach an agreement.

We eventually got the news. Eurozone governments (with support from the International Monetary Fund) would provide funding for Greece amounting to €110 billion and set up a new €440 billion[2] bailout fund to support eurozone countries with financing difficulties in the future. The structure was not particularly logical. Why not use the bailout fund to support Greece? The explanation was simple: there was not enough time to get the fund up and running. The individual eurozone countries had to come up with the money within weeks if Greece was to make its next debt payment in time. In parallel with the announcement from political leaders, the European Central Bank (ECB) declared that it would intervene selectively in certain eurozone government bond markets to ensure orderly market conditions.

The worst-case scenario of disorderly default by a eurozone country had been avoided. As the news reached the Bloomberg and Reuters news screens on the trading floor, I was frantically writing a quick research note on the implications of the announcements. There was little doubt that markets would rally in the short term because of relief that an imminent disaster had been avoided. But bigger questions remained. What were the medium-term implications of the events? Was this the end of the euro crisis?

The measures succeeded in gradually reducing broader markets tensions over the coming months. We observed better trends in eurozone bond markets and subsiding tension in the European banking system, and the euro recovered about half of the losses it had incurred during the first wave of tension in the early months of 2010.

Part of the explanation for the market recovery, however, was that many assumed that Greece was a special case.

THE SECOND WAVE: TROUBLE MOVES BEYOND GREECE

The idea that the problems were confined to Greece was disproved less than six months later, when worries arose concerning other countries at the edge of the eurozone. Individual European countries' financial systems are as unique as those countries' cultures. Though crises soon arose in several other countries, all related to debt, each had its own idiosyncrasies.

The second wave of tension gathered momentum in the final months of 2010, and it hit Ireland the hardest. While many other countries had experienced housing bubbles in the run-up to the global financial crisis, the Irish case was the most extreme. By 2011, the cumulative house price decline had reached almost 50 percent, making it the worst housing crisis that had ever been seen in a developed market country.

The exceptional losses suffered by Irish banks were a function both of the extreme boom and bust in the housing market and of failed risk management in the burgeoning Irish financial sector (which was not subject to any centralized European regulation). Sound risk controls would have constrained the banks' exposure to the real estate sector. Instead, Irish banks were doubling down on essentially identical exposures in other frothy housing markets in the United Kingdom and on the East Coast of the United States. It was a huge bet on one single horse: a booming housing market in the Anglo-Saxon world.

During the most intense period of the global financial crisis in 2008, the Irish government had acted boldly—perhaps too boldly—by guaranteeing all Irish bank deposits and all debt of Irish banks.

In October 2010, yields on Irish government bonds were heading sharply higher as investors became increasingly concerned about the sustainability of Irish government debt. The process had an uncomfortable resemblance to the tension over Greek debt less than a year earlier, although the underlying cause was different. In Ireland, the weakness in the government bond market was the result of the public sector's rising contingent liabilities to the Irish banking system, not reckless fiscal spending. It was the fear of future debt, rather than past sins, that put pressure on Irish government bonds.

The guarantees that the Irish government had provided for banks in 2008 were called upon in 2010. By early 2013, the total bill had reached €64 billion, rounding to an astonishing 40 percent of

Irish GDP! The size of the bank bailout meant that the ratio of Irish government debt to GDP moved from being one of the lowest in the eurozone to being one of the highest.

During the autumn of 2010, Ireland's situation looked increasingly desperate, and markets were becoming skeptical that Ireland was just "another exception" (as Greece had been perceived six months earlier). After Ireland, who would fall next?

The markets turned to Portugal, which had been suffering from weak growth, poor fiscal performance, and rising debt for years. There were also doubts about Spain, which, like Ireland, was facing a housing market collapse and accumulating losses in its banking system.

As a result, eurozone equity and credit markets weakened, and the euro again depreciated against the U.S. dollar and the Japanese yen. But the price moves were more orderly this time. The markets were less surprised than they had been by the initial Greek shock, and the sentiment was that the worst case of disorderly default by Ireland could be avoided, given that the backstop from the bailout fund would be available if needed.

A bailout package for Ireland was negotiated and announced in November 2010 (another one of those Sunday afternoons in the office wearing clothes that were rather inappropriate for banking business). The bailout took the form of €68 billion in loans from the eurozone bailout fund and the IMF, enough to cover Irish funding needs for a three-year period. As it had been when the similar Greek announcement was made May, the market reaction was positive. The consensus among market participants was that Portugal would probably need support, but that such support was well within the capacity of the bailout fund, given the relatively small size of Portugal's economy. As it turned out, a bailout for Portugal would be announced several months later (in May 2011), and it never provided much of a negative impulse to the market, which had now become fairly confident that the bailout fund was equipped to handle tension in the smaller peripheral economies of the eurozone.

Meanwhile, during the winter of 2011, most investors viewed Spain as strong enough to stand on its own, a view that was supported by evidence that growth in Spain was slowly returning.

Furthermore, Spain's mortgage market was quite conservative in one respect: it had a full-recourse system. When a Spanish borrower is delinquent on a house-related loan, lenders have full recourse to all the borrower's assets. This is different from the United States, where lenders generally are limited in recourse to the collateral specifically provided for the mortgage loan. So delinquency rates on mortgages in Spain remained quite low several years into the crisis, even after house prices had started to drop notably.

During the first quarter of 2011, policy makers at the European Central Bank became so confident in the economic recovery and the stabilization of the financial markets that they started to think about monetary tightening. Germany reported an impressive 6 percent annualized GDP growth in the first quarter of 2011, and aggregate eurozone growth was also relatively robust at around 3 percent. The ECB was not overly concerned about much weaker growth in Greece, Ireland, and Portugal, since together they accounted for only 6 percent of eurozone output.

In April 2011, the ECB hiked rates by 0.25 percentage point, to 1.25 percent, and by another quarter point in July. This surprised most market participants and caused the euro to rally in the first half of 2011. Back in the United States, the Federal Reserve was moving in the opposite direction, looking for ways to ease policy further, even with rates at 0 percent. By the summer, things were looking up. The euro had more than recovered the losses generated by the Irish crisis wave.

There were six months of relative calm in early 2011. But the assumption that the crisis would be confined to small peripheral countries, for which bailout funds were certainly sufficient, would soon come into question.

THE THIRD WAVE: CRACKS IN THE CORE

In the summer of 2011, bond markets in Spain and Italy suddenly started to look shaky. A deteriorating political situation in Italy was one of the key catalysts.

The biggest problem was Prime Minister Silvio Berlusconi. Amid Italy's financial problems, he was tangled up in his own personal ones, among them being on trial for having sex with a minor. As a 2011 *Vanity Fair* article put it at the time:

> How is it that in France Nicolas Sarkozy is spearheading the efforts to oust Qaddafi, in Germany Angela Merkel is sorting out the European Union's debt crisis, and in Italy Berlusconi is not just bedding young women left and right but flaunting it publicly and giving them high-profile government posts? ... In any other Western democracy, a leader like this would have been pushed out long ago.

Berlusconi's mere presence at the helm caused a huge rift among EU leaders, which were being asked to pump money (through the ECB) into the country to keep the euro together. Berlusconi was reluctant to implement reforms. He had even suggested tax cuts in a desperate attempt to regain his lost popularity. Given Italy's very high debt level, uncertainty about the maintenance of fiscal discipline was enough to shake the market, even if the country's recent fiscal performance had not been nearly as bad as that seen in Greece, Ireland, Portugal, or Spain.

There were also more technical factors at play in eurozone bond markets. Global asset managers, including mutual funds in the United States and pension funds in Europe, had been trying to reduce their exposure to Greece, Ireland, and Portugal during 2010 and early 2011. Reducing their exposure to those peripheral markets, however, meant accumulating additional exposure elsewhere, and many had opted for increased allocations to Italy, which was then perceived as a liquid and safe alternative to the smaller peripheral markets.

The combination of political uncertainty and a poor technical position in the market led to sudden and dramatic pressure on Italian bond markets. The yield spread between Italian and German bonds, which had been trading well inside Spain's throughout the first two waves of the crisis, widened to well beyond Spain's as investors tried to offload very large positions in the Italian bond market. Importantly, the Italian economy was much larger than that of Greece, Ireland, or Portugal. Italy's economic output alone accounted for 16 percent of the eurozone's, and Italy's debt market ranked among Europe's biggest, similar in size to Germany's.[3]

By late summer 2011, weakness in Italy had dragged the Spanish bond market down with it. Tentative bond market intervention by the ECB, in line with the policy announced in May 2010, was insufficient to stop the rot. ECB bond market purchases were also ineffective because of increasing political calls for debt restructuring in Greece. Investors worried that in the future, they would be forced to take losses in other countries, too. Owning the bonds of peripheral eurozone countries was too risky a proposition.

To add a disturbing new twist, weakness was spreading even to core eurozone bond markets, including France, which had previously been viewed as a stable anchor.

The tension in the French bond market brought back memories from the last currency crisis Europe had experienced: the Exchange Rate Mechanism (ERM) crisis in the early 1990s, before the euro was created. During the most intense days of November 2011, investors around the world were starting to liquidate their French government bonds. France was vulnerable because the French banking system had extremely large exposure to weaker eurozone countries, for which the outlook looked increasingly dire.

The interconnectedness of government bond markets and banking systems was not fully appreciated at the time.[4] My research group had been focused on systemic risk in the eurozone banking system for some months, and our analysis consistently showed that the French banks had disproportionately large exposures to countries at the eurozone periphery, especially Italy. Against this background, it was no surprise to see the large French banks come under intense pressure as the tension spread to Italy and Spain.

During this period, my morning routine included checking the performance of various financial instruments relating to European banks, including the stock prices of the major French banks.

One morning, I was watching the stock prices of BNP Paribas and Société Générale: they were down almost 10 percent within the span of a few minutes. Such catastrophic declines in major bank stocks had not been seen since 2008, and I had to refresh my pricing sources several times to make sure the moves were real. These were not fringe institutions. They were among the largest banks in the world, and they were not supposed to trade like penny stocks. Based on the size of its balance sheet, BNP Paribas was indeed the largest bank in the world at the time, with assets of around €3 trillion, ahead of the largest U.S. bank, JPMorgan Chase.[5]

The rising tension was not without casualties. By October, the French-Belgian bank Dexia was teetering on the brink of failure. Dexia had total assets of $700 billion (a Lehman Brothers–size balance sheet). The Belgian and French governments were forced to orchestrate an emergency bailout to avoid a disorderly run on the institution.

The fall of Dexia only hastened the collapse of confidence in eurozone banking systems. Adding to the tension was the fact that the bank stress tests conducted by European bank supervisors had lost credibility after Dexia's near-failure. The European bank stress tests were modeled on those in the United States, which had been successful in achieving a swift recapitalization and stabilization of the U.S. banking system in 2009. However, the assumptions used in Europe proved to be too lenient. Just a few months earlier, the European Banking Authority's stress test had ranked Dexia as one of the best-capitalized banks in Europe. The supervisors' inability to foresee any of the problems that were building at Dexia rendered the stress-test process ineffective as a tool for bolstering market confidence.

As a result, banks started to refuse to lend to each other in the normally very liquid interbank markets. For banks, the money markets play a role similar to that of an overdraft facility on a personal checking account. Without access to borrowing from the money market, a small drain on the cash position of a bank can quickly turn into a fatal liquidity shortage. The natural reaction of banks was to hoard cash and stop lending.

European leaders scheduled another make-or-break summit for the end of October. In the run-up to the meeting, markets gyrated wildly as more or less credible stories hit inboxes and instant chats across trading floors in New York, London, and Singapore. Rumors circulated that the size of the bailout fund could be doubled or even quadrupled at the meeting, and the markets rallied in anticipation of such news.

A few weeks before the summit, U.S. Treasury secretary Tim Geithner had participated in a meeting for European finance ministers in Poland. This was an unprecedented step; Geithner had flown to Warsaw to try to persuade his European colleagues to follow the U.S. model for banking-sector stabilization from 2009. At that time, the United States had forced capital into all major banks, and this policy had been successful in stabilizing the banking system within a few quarters. But European leaders looked at advice from the United States with suspicion. Austrian finance minister Maria Fektor said, "Geithner should not be lecturing the eurozone on its problems," according to *International Business Times*.

In the end, the European summit was a major disappointment. Eurozone banks were required to hold more capital in relation to their assets. But contrary to Geithner's advice, European governments did not put any money on the table, and banks had little choice but to sell assets to try to satisfy the tougher new capital requirements.[6] An additional disappointment was European leaders' inability to agree on a meaningful enlargement of the bailout fund. In the end, there were plenty of words expressing support and good intentions. But despite the severe systemic tension at the very core of the eurozone financial system, European leaders had not committed one single additional euro to fight the crisis. Political disagreement had trumped economic logic, leaving the door open to full-blown financial panic.

Over the following weeks, markets sold off sharply. By November, markets were pricing in a high risk of imminent default for both various major banks and vulnerable countries. Investors frantically sold assets in other markets, too. In the period from June to November,

European bank stocks fell 40 percent and many of the largest U.S. bank stocks were down as much as 30 percent. Meanwhile, the euro gave back all its gains from earlier in the year, when the ECB was increasing interest rates.

The situation looked dire. But during November, important developments took place, both on the political front and within the ECB.

On the political front, Italian prime minister Berlusconi resigned, handing over responsibility to Mario Monti, a former Italian EU official and a respected technocrat. Tension between Berlusconi and other European leaders had been an obstacle to stepping up crisis-fighting efforts in the previous months. Germany saw the Berlusconi regime as an impediment to establishing long-term credibility for Italy and achieving financial market stabilization in the eurozone. The political uncertainty in Italy had also made the ECB reluctant to support the Italian bond market, and this contributed further to financial market instability.

With Monti in office, that dynamic changed. Both German chancellor Merkel and French president Sarkozy expressed full support for the new Italian leader and endorsed his plans for austerity and reform.

At the same moment, the ECB got a younger and more pragmatic new president. Mario Draghi replaced Jean-Claude Trichet at the helm of the ECB. Draghi used his very first meeting in November to announce a reduction in ECB interest rates from 1.50 percent to 1.25 percent. A second rate cut to 1.00 percent was announced at the next meeting. But this was a sideshow relative to the much more important liquidity support for banks. In December, the ECB announced unprecedented measures to support the banking system. Through an entirely new program, the ECB would single-handedly provide long-term funding for the entire banking system. Before the crisis, the ECB had provided only very short-term (two-week) funding for banks, and only in restricted quantities. Now banks could rely entirely on unlimited cheap financing directly from the ECB for a term of up to three years. The special bank-funding scheme added an impressive €1 trillion to the system over just a few months. This meant that banks had plenty of cash at hand and that fears about bank failures and bank runs could subside. After his first few weeks in office, it was clear that Draghi's presence at the ECB would mark the beginning of a new era.

The ECB's intervention to support eurozone banks was the core component of the third effort to stabilize the European financial system. The cash provided by the ECB not only reduced the risk of liquidity shortages and bank runs, but also gave the banks additional ammunition to buy sovereign bonds. Banks in Spain and Italy took advantage of the improved access to funding and accumulated significant additional exposure to government bonds in their own countries. For a period of time, improved funding conditions for banks translated into better funding conditions for European countries. It looked like a virtuous circle.

Adding to better sentiment, in March 2012 the Greek government managed to secure a debt restructuring deal with private-sector creditors. Ironically, the deal, in which private-sector investors took haircuts of up to 75 percent on their investments in Greek government bonds, was seen as a positive, as it avoided an even worse outcome: a disorderly default. The managed default helped reduce fears of a collapse in the Greek banking system and a possible exit of Greece from the currency union, and it made Greece's debt burden less unsustainable.

The impact on markets of these political and economic shifts was profound. Eurozone bond markets rallied sharply, with dramatic spillover effects on global equity and commodity markets. U.S. financial stocks rallied 20 percent within a few months, and the broader U.S. market also posted a quick double-digit gain. The euro also bounced off its lows, but it was a timid bounce. Recent policy steps had dumped a trillion additional euros into the market. This extra liquidity made the euro recovery more muted than those in the previous two recovery phases.

There was again hope that a final solution to the crisis had been found. Yet again the period of stability proved to be very short.

THE FOURTH WAVE: BREAKUP RISK
AT THE DINNER TABLE

The fourth wave of tension started in May 2012, and it had two main catalysts.

Greek issues again began to crop up. The country's two mainstream parties, PASOK and New Democracy, took a beating in the May 2012 election. Commentators had expected the deep recession and the tough austerity measures to cost votes for the old parties responsible for the current mess. But the extent of the political shift was more dramatic than anybody had expected. The election produced a polarized parliament with strong support for extreme parties on both the right and the left. In a surprise upset, the SYRIZA Party, a group of previously obscure communists on the extreme left, won more seats in parliament than the PASOK Party, which had been a major force in Greek politics for the previous 30 years.

The SYRIZA leader was Alexis Tsipras, a young, charismatic speaker with no experience holding public office. His main political objective was to renegotiate the conditions of the second Greek bailout, aiming to secure more favorable terms and reverse some of the unpopular austerity measures.

The complex second bailout deal had been reached just two months earlier. To avoid a disorderly default in Greece, European leaders had committed more bailout funds to Greece, and private-sector creditors had had to take losses as part of the debt restructuring.[7]

Greece had now exhausted all remaining political goodwill. Any demand for renegotiation from Greece was sure to be angrily received by leaders in capitals around Europe. Policy makers in Berlin and Paris quickly reversed their previous opinions and acknowledged that a Greek exit from the eurozone was now a possibility. German finance minister Wolfgang Schäuble told German broadcaster WDR: "We cannot force a country to stay in the euro."

The words were not aggressive on their face, but they marked a sea change from the previous stance of European officials. In the past, the possibility of breakup had been entirely dismissed. But the taboo had now been partially broken. Some politicians, typically those from creditor countries in northern Europe, went even further, suggesting that an exit might be desirable. Alexander Dobrindt, the general secretary of the governing Bavarian Christian Social Union, was one such aggressive voice. (He was subsequently reprimanded by Chancellor Merkel.)

This debate hit the mainstream media and was plastered all over the global press. A breakup of the eurozone had moved from being an esoteric theoretical idea to being a topic of dinner table conversation across Europe and around the world. In fact, discussion about a Greek exit was now so common that the term *Grexit* entered the financial press to describe the specific breakup scenario involving Greece leaving the eurozone. The level of press coverage is shown in Chart 4.2.

At the time, I wrote a series of three articles, called "Preparing for Greek Eurozone Exit," analyzing various elements of a possible exit. The analysis was widely read. Even investors who focused on U.S. equities and had never been significantly affected by events in a small European country in the past now wanted to become experts on Greece. It seemed that the risk of eurozone breakup was the only thing that really mattered for global investors in those weeks.

Since SYRIZA was the second-largest party in the Greek parliament, it had sufficient clout to block the formation of a

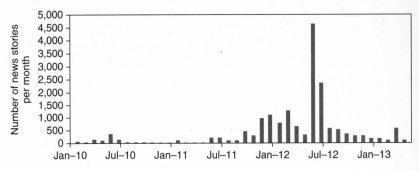

Chart 4.2   Press Coverage of Eurozone Breakup

Note: Shows number of stories with keywords "Leave", "Exit", and "Breakup" in the context of the euro that are available on Bloomberg and that come from over one hundred authoritative global sources.
Source: Nomura, Bloomberg

reform-friendly government. As a result, a breakdown in cooperation with Greece's European partners was a real risk. An increasingly
open debate about whether Greece should remain a member of the
eurozone started, and it had a notable negative impact on financial
market trends in the eurozone and globally.

The situation in Greece was a catalyst for a fundamental reassessment of the risks associated with investments across the eurozone. In my capacity as advisor to financial institutions on currency
issues, I hosted a global conference call on the topic of eurozone
breakup. The call volume was about ten times normal, and clients
I had never spoken to before were suddenly bombarding me with
questions about the specific consequences of a breakup. It was clear
that investors and risk managers all over the world were on high alert.
They were desperate to understand the new risks they were facing
in Europe and to adjust their positions and operations accordingly.

Meanwhile, a second and equally concerning problem was developing in Spain. In early 2012, the Spanish government had to
acknowledge that its fiscal deficit targets for the year were unrealis-
tic. At first, the impact was limited. Markets were in recovery mode.
Investors were optimistic about the impact of the ECB's injection
of liquidity into the banking system. But as bad news on budget
dynamics accumulated, market concerns about Spanish debt eventually led to a renewed rise in Spanish government bond yields.

Spain had dramatic budget shortfalls in the independent regions.
The Catalonia region in the northwest of Spain, with Barcelona as its
capital, was just one example of a region with significant budget problems. I remember speaking to the Spanish debt management office
in Madrid on a conference call in late 2011. At the time, the debt
management office was optimistic about the country's achieving its
budget targets. But the Spanish government had limited control over
the regions, and even the central debt management office seemed unaware of the extent of the budget problems in the regions. It seemed
implausible to me that the country could meet its targets given that
weakening growth would negatively affect revenue. But Madrid's
debt management team was biased by internal statistics for the federal

budget, which were holding up. Only a few months later, the regions revealed dramatic budget overruns, and the total national deficit rose to more than 8 percent of GDP, a third more than the target.[8]

To make things worse, Spain's economy was taking a nosedive. Spain found itself in a deepening recession. Adding to the difficulties, the declines in house prices, which had been surprisingly moderate early in the crisis, were accelerating and reached an annual pace of 15 percent in the summer of 2012. This, combined with asset sales by banks, was creating a toxic mix of declining asset values and increasing bankruptcies. As with the story in Ireland two years earlier, it was clear that the banks needed large amounts of fresh capital. The Spanish government would be on the hook, but everyone knew that its resources would fall short. The richer European countries would yet again be asked to bail someone out.

Markets were unsettled, to say the least. The situation in Greece had brought the discussion of a eurozone breakup out into the open. Meanwhile, the untenable situation in Spain was causing increasing speculation that Spain might leave the eurozone as a result of a chaotic sovereign default and a collapse in its banking system.

Investors' number one concern was that a Spanish exit from the eurozone would involve the conversion of Spanish financial instruments (such as deposits) into a new and weaker Spanish currency. In the presence of such risk, many institutions and corporations were concluding that maintaining deposits in Spanish banks was too risky. Even if the risk was perceived to be small, there was little upside associated with keeping deposits in Spanish banks.

The result was a quick drain of money out of Spain, similar to what is often observed in emerging markets ahead of currency devaluations. But in Spain, there was no dramatic currency movement. Spain remained a part of the eurozone, and capital flight was instead reflected in declining government bond prices and increasing tension in the banking system.[9]

The origin of the concern could be traced to the uncertainty about the ECB's ability and commitment to support government bond markets. The ECB's bond-buying program had been dormant during the entire fourth wave of crisis escalation in May and June, and this meant that market failure could no longer be ruled out. This had a major impact on market psychology, and it was a major departure from what had happened during the second wave of the crisis, for example. At that time, markets had clearly discounted the possibility of a disorderly default on sovereign debt based on the availability of backstop from the eurozone bailout fund (at the time called the European Financial Stability Facility, or EFSF) and the ECB. The destabilizing ineffectiveness of ECB bond market intervention was partially linked to statements from the German Bundesbank expressing its opposition to central bank bond buying.

The EFSF had worked relatively well when Ireland and Portugal needed support, but the numbers didn't add up for the much larger economies of Spain and Italy. The only way around this issue was for the ECB to provide the financing from its potentially unlimited balance sheet. However, the ECB appeared unwilling or unable to step in.

During this period, I went on a business trip to northern Europe to meet with institutional investors in Copenhagen, Amsterdam, and Frankfurt. In a typical meeting with investors, the focus is on the next three to six months. But this trip was different. Many investors seemed to have fundamentally lost confidence that policy makers would be able to resolve the crisis.

We debated the longer-term direction of Europe. Big questions were thrown around: Would Germany ever consider leaving the eurozone? Would the Netherlands contemplate its own exit? And was there any hope for Spain and Italy, given their failing and increasingly unpopular austerity programs, or would this be a full-blown breakup? It was a dramatic shift, especially for a part of the world where views are typically balanced and emotions are normally well controlled.

A fundamental doubt about the viability of the euro had been ignited, a doubt that in fact questioned the euro's survival.

The second Greek election did lead to some near-term relaxation in the markets. The SYRIZA Party's populist rhetoric was losing some of its appeal, and its popularity edged down. A reform-minded coalition government was eventually formed on June 20, led by Antonis Samaras from New Democracy. The new government committed to the existing bailout agreement, and this reduced concerns about an imminent and destabilizing Greek exit from the eurozone. But longer-term concerns about the euro's sustainability remained in place. Going into July, bond spreads in Spain were again widening and markets were getting increasingly disorderly. Despite the better news from Greece, the euro was heading sharply lower, driven by concerns about the basic fabric of the euro, and these concerns went much deeper than the specifics of Greece.

TOWARD STRUCTURAL CHANGE IN THE EUROZONE

The recovery from the fourth crisis wave was different from the recoveries from the previous three. After almost three years of repeated crisis waves, European policy makers were finally ready to change strategy.

At the European leaders' summit at the end of June 2012, there was a clear recognition that the underlying structures of the eurozone needed to change. Policy makers finally expressed a certain degree of humility, admitting that past tactical policy steps had been inadequate. In the face of severe market tension, they agreed that more European integration was needed to stabilize the currency union.

While this was a notable and historic shift, general political statements about the need for closer economic and political cooperation were not sufficient to immediately convince the market.

It took an unusually candid speech by ECB president Mario Draghi at an investment conference in London on July 26 to generate a turn in markets. Draghi passionately reiterated the ECB's dedication to the European currency:[10]

> Within our mandate, the ECB is ready to do whatever it takes to preserve the euro. And believe me, it will be enough.

In the next few months, the ECB spelled out its plan to restore order in eurozone markets. The essential new part of the strategy was a promise to buy unlimited quantities of government bonds in eurozone countries that were having funding difficulties. The new tool was named Outright Monetary Transactions (OMT), and its mere presence in the background as a new source of backstop gave the market more comfort, even if it was not being actively used.

The idea had clear parallels to Draghi's first policy innovation: the ECB's provision of unlimited long-term bank funding. This step—in which the ECB effectively assumed the function of lender of last resort—was a huge shift. It was sufficient to create a fourth wave of recovery.

MARKET STABILIZATION

Beginning in the summer of 2012, market conditions improved substantially, both across the eurozone and globally. In particular, bond market conditions in Spain and Italy improved notably, and global equity markets rallied strongly. The promise of money to finance bond purchases removed the risk of an imminent funding crisis for Spain and Italy, and it calmed markets more broadly.

Not only did market stabilization from the fourth crisis wave come about, but the measures taken would also change the dynamics involved in future waves of tension.

When the euro crisis reached Cyprus in March 2013, in the form of a chaotic bailout process involving shutdown of the entire banking system for more than a week, the spillover effects to the rest of the eurozone were much more moderate than they had been in the previous four waves. The ECB's more proactive new role had made the system much more resilient to shocks.

Similarly, when the Italian election in February 2013 produced the worst-case outcome, with no clear mandate for any of the major parties, the impact on markets was relatively mild compared to the previous crisis waves.

THE FALL OF THE ORIGINAL EURO

The crucial policy changes made in the summer of 2012 were a first step toward altering key institutional characteristics of the euro.

Crucially, the hard prohibition of central bank financing of governments, which had been an underpinning of the original euro,[11] had been softened. This prohibition had been a core German demand when the euro was conceived during the 1990s. But Berlin now had to compromise. The ECB had finally assumed a lender of last resort function, including for eurozone government finances.

Meanwhile, new elements were added to the institutional framework, including an ambitious plan to create a common banking union.

These alterations in the fabric of the euro were necessary to keep the eurozone together.

FUTURE CRISIS WAVES

The new policy direction started in 2012 has been important in averting an imminent market collapse. But the euro crisis is not over.

Let us not forget about the people in Spain who are struggling and those in Greece who are literally starving. The next eurozone crisis will not be like the four previous ones. Future crisis waves are likely to result from political conflict in some form, rather than from market breakdown.

Opinion polls on attitudes toward European institutions illustrate the political challenge ahead. The European Commission has its own annual survey that looks at sentiment toward Europe. One of the basic questions asked is: do you trust the European Union or not? In 2007, only 23 percent of Spaniards did not trust the EU. In 2012, the percentage had risen to 72 percent. This trend toward increasing mistrust of European institutions is visible across the entire eurozone, from Germany to Greece.

Such statistics cannot be ignored. Politicians and investors can patch up their ideas and portfolios all they like. But as long as the economy is depressed, the shop owner suffering in Madrid is not going to forget that he cannot clothe his children. This is the situation we are dealing with today—not just bank losses and low industrial production, but real pain for European citizens. Poverty is increasing, health conditions are deteriorating, and suicides are escalating in the weaker parts of the eurozone. Public frustration with the system that led to this unhappy state of affairs is coming to the fore. This disappointment could well become an insurmountable obstacle to significant further European integration.

The next crisis will be political, one that questions the common drive toward further integration and puts in jeopardy the needed strengthening of eurozone institutions.

European Integration: The Difficult Path

Why has the euro crisis been so drawn-out, and why have European policy makers allowed unemployment to sky-rocket? Because there is no political union binding the eurozone together. Decisions have to be made through compromises among 17 independent countries. This process is inefficient and slow.

The lack of political union is a severe constraint on the eurozone's ability to fight economic and financial crises effectively. This leaves crisis-hit countries in the monetary union stuck in a costly deflationary equilibrium. This type of adjustment is similar to that experienced decades ago when countries were on the gold standard. The economic pain fuels political tension that can sow the seeds for future crises.

Chapter 5, "The Big Choice: More or Less Integration?," puts Europe's choice in perspective. *More integration* would mean moving toward a mature currency union, similar to that of the United States. *Less integration* would involve a breakup of the currency.

Chapter 6, "The Revenge of Realpolitik: Europe's Dilemma," provides a snapshot of where the difficult integration process currently stands.

Chapter 7, "An Involuntary Gold Standard: The Economics of Inflexibility," describes how the monetary system that is currently in place in the eurozone resembles that under the gold standard almost 100 years ago.

Chapter 8, "Where's the Growth?: The Cost of Deflation," describes why the current setup is so negative for growth, especially in countries with high debt.

Chapter 9, "Europe's Political Fragility: The Seeds of the Next Crisis," outlines the main sources of political risk in the eurozone going forward.

CHAPTER
5

The Big Choice:
More or Less Integration?

When you form a bond, you often must give something up in order to gain something. And it is during a crisis that the true strength of a bond is tested. This holds for personal friendships as well as currency unions. Any crisis will expose weaknesses and imbalances that were not apparent during calmer times.

THE GIVE AND TAKE OF A CURRENCY UNION

The bond that is the foundation for a currency union should not be taken for granted. Members of a currency union have given up their ability to adjust their interest rates and to devalue their currencies, two of the most important mechanisms for macroeconomic adjustment. In a time of crisis, this leaves policy makers impotent, with few effective weapons for fighting economic weakness. It is a significant sacrifice. In return, its members should ideally benefit from support from the rest of the currency union when they are in need.

In a loosely integrated currency union without a sizable central budget, there is limited capacity to support members that are in difficulty. Such currency unions lack the fiscal flexibility to compensate for monetary inflexibility.

Those currency unions are living dangerous lives. They are much like a building with a weak foundation during an earthquake. If such unions are to survive in the long term, the foundation needs to be strengthened. Countries need to come together more closely. In the absence of closer cooperation, the structure is likely to crumble.

CURRENCY UNIONS COME AND GO

From a purely historical perspective, the odds are not in the euro-zone's favor. Over the last hundred years, at least 70 currency unions have broken up. The Scandinavian currency union dissolved in 1914. The currency union of the Austro-Hungarian Empire splintered in 1918. The Latin currency union ended in 1927. The ruble zone splintered around 1992. The Czechoslovak currency union came apart in 1993. There are many more obscure examples as well.

Many of these currency unions suffered from the same weakness: the lack of a unified political body and limited common fiscal capacity.

At the same time, currency unions that have been supported by strong central fiscal policy and a unified government have proved far more durable. Consider the United States and the Swiss Confederation. Both are examples of highly integrated currency unions. Though they have disparate states (called cantons in Switzerland), they have integrated banking systems, powerful central banks, and sizable federal budgets.

In both cases, the federal budget can be used to support suffering regions, and central banks can backstop banking institutions and government finance when crises arise. These currency unions have been so successful that we do not even think of them as currency unions any more.[1]

In order to put the current choice between more and less integration in perspective, policy makers may want to take a closer look at the evolution of two very powerful, but different, currency unions. One is the pinnacle of currency union success: the U.S. dollar. The other is the now-defunct currency union of the former Soviet Union: the rublezone.

LESSONS FROM THE UNITED STATES

The currency union of the United States began with the ratification of the Constitution in 1788. Today, the dollar is the currency of the United States of America. That is that. The fact that different states share the same currency is a nonissue.

The currency union of the United States had an advantage from the beginning: the common currency was established in conjunction with the political union among the different states. Even so, there were periods of significant regional divergence, both economically and politically, that tested the strength of the interstate bonds.

Early on, before strong economic structures had been put in place at the federal level, relationships between different regions could be tense. There were times when midwesterners wanted monetary expansion to support indebted farmers, whereas people in the northeast wanted monetary restraint to provide financial stability. Meanwhile, banking crises were regular occurrences in the nineteenth century and on occasion were also a source of conflict between the regions. However, the political bond was strong enough to keep the currency union intact, despite periods of severe economic hardship.

The exception was the irreconcilable political differences that developed between Northern and Southern states around slavery, which led to the Civil War. In 1861, 11 Southern states seceded from the United States, and the currency union broke apart.

In the East and the Midwest, the greenback was used. In the South, the Confederate dollar was the official legal tender. There was no longer just one U.S. dollar.[2]

Even after the war was over and the country was reunified, regional economic tensions had not been eliminated. The banking crises in 1893 and 1907 illustrated the difficulties associated with regional banking regulation and the absence of a proactive central bank.

The country needed a stronger monetary system, including a lender of last resort that would have the ability to backstop major banking institutions in times of crisis. Additionally, a larger federal budget could help to smooth out regional shocks.

In the twentieth century, structural changes were implemented that made the currency union more integrated and ultimately more resilient in the face of financial market tension and economic crises. In 1913, the Federal Reserve Act came into effect, creating a proper central bank with the capacity to provide emergency liquidity across the union. This reduced regional tensions caused by banking instability. In 1930, federal deposit insurance was introduced, further stabilizing the banking system.

In 1935, federal unemployment benefits were instituted as part of the Social Security Act. As a result of these programs, the size of the federal budget increased substantially. In the early 1930s, federal outlays were less than 4 percent of GDP. After 1935, outlays were closer to 10 percent of GDP. After World War II, federal outlays increased further, to 15 to 20 percent of GDP, according to the White House's historical budget tables.

The new federal structures worked as shock absorbers in times of crisis. The presence of the Federal Reserve served to reduce banking tensions. (At a minimum, banking crises became less frequent.) Meanwhile, the larger federal budget worked to counter the effect of regional shocks. When Hurricane Katrina hit Louisiana in 2005, federal support helped to limit the economic downturn. More generally, the United States's large federal budget means that significant permanent transfers from the richer to the poorer states also take place. For example, the state of Connecticut has an annual net contribution to other states of around 6 percent of its GDP. Meanwhile, Alabama is a net recipient of around 10 percent of its GDP from the rest of the United States.

Strengthened federal economic structures have reduced regional economic and political divergence. Importantly, the federal structures were backed by a strong political union, making them democratically legitimate.

The Great Depression created political support for more integration through powerful federal institutions. Strong federal leadership made rapid change possible,

Today, although states bicker with one another about their individual budgets, the federal government's control over the currency union is great enough to give everyone comfort, keeping real tensions confined to political rhetoric. By nearly all standards, the U.S. dollar is an example of a currency union success.

LESSON FROM THE USSR

The Union of Soviet Socialist Republics (USSR) came into existence as a political institution in 1922, following the Russian Revolution in 1917. Like the United States, the USSR was a union of independent states. And also like the United States, the soviet republics shared a common currency, the ruble.

The ruble was the legal tender in the entire USSR, and the central bank (Gosbank) was the only banking institution in the entire system. Gosbank extended credit to various entities in accordance with the government's five-year plans, which guided all economic activity. It was a crucial part of the centrally planned socialist economy.

The currency union lasted for nearly 70 years. If it is looked at in a vacuum, it was relatively successful. But political change swept across the entire Eastern bloc in the early 1990s. The reform process started by Soviet leader Mikhail Gorbachev led to the dissolution of the USSR in 1991.

Initially, the 15 independent former soviet republics all kept the ruble as their currency. However, it didn't take long for the independent states to have widely diverging economic trends and differing economic and political goals. What's more, their political systems were no longer unified. Deep-pocketed Russia was no longer politically obligated (by law) to support the less wealthy states, and one country didn't necessarily want to listen to another anyway.

Each country was left to its own devices. Ukraine resorted to large-scale monetary expansion, exceeding 20 percent of its GDP in some years. It started printing money (in the form of central bank credit) and used it to purchase goods from other republics, mainly Russia. In some cases, Ukrainian imports of Russian goods even led to goods shortages in Russia.

This issuance of additional rubles caused rising inflation across the entire currency area. In places where prices were fixed, goods shortages occurred. In the end, this was unacceptable to the Russian government. It instructed the Central Bank of Russia to start to differentiate between rubles created by other former USSR central banks and "its own" rubles. When that happened, the ruble zone splintered and independent currencies developed. The money created by the Central Bank of Ukraine was no longer accepted in Russia.

Eventually, all the former soviet republics with the exception of Tajikistan left the rublezone and returned to some form of national currency. This was not a stated political goal at any point, but it happened as a function of practical necessity.[3] The growing imbalances within the currency union and the lack of political unity meant that there was no alternative to currency separation.

The lesson is that uncontrolled policies, like Ukraine's monetary expansion, can quickly become politically unacceptable and can ultimately splinter a currency.

OPTIMAL CURRENCY AREAS

Further integration of the eurozone is not going to be easy. Politically, it will be very hard to overcome the inherent structural weaknesses in the original euro setup.

Canadian economist Robert Mundell received a Nobel Prize in Economics for his work on defining optimal currency areas. Mundell's work started a branch of economics that seeks to define when countries (or states) would benefit economically from adopting the same currency and forming a currency union.

The biggest advantage of a currency union is simple: it helps countries or states reduce transaction costs and facilitate trade. Buying and selling a Cartier watch or Italian biscotti is easier when the buyer and the seller use the same bills. Moreover, bigger and deeper common financial markets tend to be more efficient than small and illiquid markets. This was the main economic argument in favor of the euro when politicians were campaigning for its creation. Trading among different European countries would be as seamless as a transaction between a New Yorker and a Bostonian.

The drawback, however, is that when you enter a currency union, you give up control over some key economic policy instruments. When a specific country (or state) is affected by an adverse economic shock, there will be a cost associated with having fixed interest rates and fixed exchange rates if there is no other mechanism in place to deal with the problem. The economy cannot adapt as quickly as it could have done if it had had the independent ability to loosen policy.[4]

If it is looked at only through the lens of economic cost-benefit, a currency union is optimal if the benefits from lower transaction costs outweigh the costs associated with a reduced ability to adjust to shocks. But it is important to note that the costs and benefits are not necessarily static. They will evolve as the economy evolves and as institutional arrangements are amended. Specifically, an expanded federal budget could potentially compensate for the weaknesses associated with lack of monetary flexibility.

THE INEVITABLE BREAKUP?

The basic message from history is the following: successful currency unions have generally been closely integrated—economically, politically, and institutionally. When a currency union faces internal instability, it typically comes down to a choice between closer integration and a form of breakup. Importantly, whether more integration is feasible depends on the political situation. In the absence of a political union, significant integration may simply not be feasible.

Presidents Herbert Hoover and Franklin Delano Roosevelt completed the U.S. currency union within a relatively short period of time in the face of the Great Depression. Over a period of less than five years, from 1930 to 1935, the United States carried out dramatic additional economic integration, including federal deposit insurance and a significantly expanded federal budget.

The rublezone, on the other hand, splintered under chaotic circumstances. The common currency was torn to pieces in 1992 by irreconcilable differences among the newly independent republics of the former Soviet Union. The breakup of the rublezone illustrates how diverging political goals can ignite a crisis and cause a currency union to splinter. A currency union without a political union is inherently dangerous.

The eurozone has taken the initial steps to glue the currency union closer together. Importantly, the European Central Bank has assumed a more powerful position.

A larger federal budget that can carry out cross-border transfers within the currency union can help offset the costs associated with monetary inflexibility. More integration, in the form of a bigger federal budget, may optimize the currency union in a macroeconomic sense. But whether this is a workable arrangement depends on the individual countries' willingness to give up control in favor of this union. In Europe, there is limited support for more political integration. This is at the heart of the eurozone's current dilemma.

6

The Revenge of Realpolitik: Europe's Dilemma

D uring 2011 and 2012, it was undeniable that the eurozone was facing a severe crisis amid extreme market tension. The structure of the original euro—with limited coordination of economic policy and a defensive central bank—had proved unsustainable.

TOWARD MORE EUROPEAN INTEGRATION

A lack of centralized policy controls culminated in a public-sector debt explosion in Greece, necessitating a managed government default in early 2012. The absence of common banking supervision allowed banks in Ireland and Spain to become overly exposed to domestic real estate bubbles, leading to severe repercussions throughout the entire eurozone. Finally, the lack of a central bank that was willing to provide a lender of last resort backstop resulted in destabilizing volatility in some of the world's biggest government bond markets, and the shocks reverberated throughout the entire global financial system.

In June 2012, in the face of this dire new reality, the common currency's biggest supporters in Berlin, Paris, and Brussels took a leap of faith. Rather than risk the breakup of the euro—something that they could hardly fathom—they would attempt to unite Europe more closely. The policy makers would aim to put in place a structure that, in part, would resemble the United States of America.

Some of the most senior European officials produced a working paper containing a road map for bringing the eurozone closer together. It was called "Towards a Genuine Economic and Monetary Union." The title clearly admitted that the original version of the eurozone was an unfinished construct, a "nongenuine" partial step on the road to the real thing. The document was a step forward along a historical progression. But it was also a rare apparent example of open admission of failure from the European establishment.

The gravitas of the paper's authors signified its importance. Herman Van Rompuy, president of the European Council (the EU body in which heads of state gather) was the main author. His coauthors were Mario Draghi, president of the European Central Bank; José Manuel Barroso, president of the European Commission; and Jean-Claude Juncker, president of the Eurogroup (the body of Eurozone finance ministers).

The paper outlined an ambitious agenda for additional integration of the eurozone. In the authors' vision of the future, Europe would have a banking union, with central supervision of all eurozone banks and a common deposit insurance scheme inspired by the U.S. system. Europe would flourish under a fiscal union: a common eurozone budget with the capacity to support countries that were in difficulty. Eurozone countries would also be united through a strong economic union, which meant closer coordination of all economic policies and better ability to centrally control local spending decisions. Furthermore, the countries in the eurozone would move toward a form of political union, including directly elected eurozone officials—perhaps even an elected eurozone president. The details were not fully spelled out at the time, but this was the broad outline of the ambitious new vision.

The eurozone's political leaders signed up for this fundamental revamping of the common currency without much debate. You could even argue that they signed up for a new type of euro. After the original one had fallen, they knew that they had no choice. The easiest option, under the circumstances, was to continue with a process of gradual integration. The alternative was to oppose greater integration and face increasing market instability, disorderly government defaults, and a form of breakup of the currency union. The logic of realpolitik dictated this outcome.

THEORY VERSUS PRACTICE

Signing up for a basic concept is one thing. Delivering on specific objectives in a timely manner is an entirely different matter. This is particularly true in European politics, where 17 eurozone member countries and 28 European Union (EU) member countries have to agree before any major policy changes can be implemented.[1]

European leaders had endorsed in principle the blueprint for this new euro outlined by the quartet led by Van Rompuy. The conceptual shift was arguably historic, but the practical changes would turn out to be more piecemeal.

THE VISION OF A BANKING UNION

The eurozone banking union was a perfect example. The vision was to create a common banking system. It had three proposed pillars. First, it would include a mechanism for common banking supervision across the entire eurozone, harmonizing the existing system of potentially conflicting national regulations. Second, it would have a common rule-based framework for closing down insolvent banks, again to get around vested local interests. Third, all Eurozone banks would be supported by a common deposit insurance scheme, similar to the Federal Deposit Insurance Corporation (FDIC) in the United States. This pillar was meant to level the playing field for banks across the eurozone and protect retail depositors from losses, even in a situation of severe domestic tension.[2]

In theory, with these three components in place, weaker countries whose banks were in trouble could rely on support from the rest of the union. Just as the United States propped up the entire U.S. banking system across all 50 states after Lehman Brothers collapsed, it would be possible to both inject capital (equity) into and provide funding for banks in all eurozone countries to stabilize the system. This would ensure that credit would continue to flow, avoiding a disorderly deleveraging process akin to that observed during the infamous Great Depression.

In the final months of 2012, European leaders agreed on the details of a framework for common banking supervision. As of March 2014, the ECB in Frankfurt will take over the supervision of 200 eurozone banks (those with more than €30 billion in assets) that had previously been supervised at the national level.

Therefore, the first pillar of the banking union is on track to be implemented, with only a moderate delay compared to the original timetable. That was the easy part. The other and potentially more important pillars of the banking union have proven much more difficult to construct.

BANKING NATIONALISM

In the past, national interests typically made it impossible to close unstable banks.

In the countries that could afford it, the end result had been expensive government bailouts. This had been the story since 2008 in Germany, the Netherlands, Spain, Italy, and Ireland (although it remains debatable whether Ireland will ultimately be able to afford its bank bailout).

In the countries without enough funds to foot the bill, however, efforts to save the local banks took a different form. Cyprus was the most extreme example of how far local politicians were willing to go protect major banks at home.

Cyprus had an oversized banking system relative to the small size of the country, and bank balance sheets were partly inflated by large expatriate deposits from Russia and the United Kingdom. The banks had been overexposed to Greek government bonds, and some of the largest banks had taken a huge hit during the Greek debt restructuring in February 2012.

By March 2013, the European Central Bank (ECB) was getting uneasy about continuing to provide liquidity to these banks, which were deemed insolvent. The scale of the losses was such that the Cypriot government did not have sufficient capacity to recapitalize the banks. Cyprus's European partners recommended closing the two largest banks and letting the investors take losses. However, the Cypriot government wanted to protect the industry, viewing it as being important to the overall economy (which was built around financial services and other professional services).

On one Saturday morning in March, I woke up early. On weekend mornings, markets are closed, but I still cannot keep myself from checking the news as one of the first things I do. That morning, I almost could not believe what I saw. I had to check at least three different sources to confirm the story.

The Cypriots had reached a bailout agreement with their European partners, according to which all depositors would face a one-off tax on their entire deposit. The "tax" (a type of wealth confiscation) would be levied at 6.75 percent for deposits of up to €100,000 and 9.9 percent for larger deposits. This was how far politicians were ready to go to avoid winding down their prized banks. They were willing to randomly confiscate the deposits of large parts of the population, including those that were supposed to be protected by the local deposit insurance scheme.

The news was shocking. Never before during the euro crisis had depositors been asked to foot part of the bill for a bank bailout. The news had the potential to destabilize not only Cypriot banks, but also weaker banks in the rest of the eurozone.

For an entire week, the banks in Cyprus were closed while policy makers made up their minds. There was no good solution. It was a matter of picking the poison. In the end, the idea of a deposit tax was rejected by the Cypriot parliament.

This, in turn, forced the government to dramatically restructure the two largest banks, including closing down the second-largest one. While small depositors were protected, those with larger deposits in Cyprus's two biggest banks would take large losses—estimated at between 30 and 80 percent.

The Cyprus story illustrates how far local politicians are willing to go to protect their main banks. Cyprus's politicians failed because their negotiating position was so weak. But in almost all other cases, winding down banks that were in trouble had proved essentially impossible.

THE REALPOLITIK OF THE BANKING UNION

European leaders had realized the importance of separating these national considerations from the process of bank supervision and regulation. There was agreement in theory on the necessity to adopt common rules. But the details will take years to hammer out. At the time of writing, we don't even have a firm timetable in place for setting common rules for unwinding banks.

As a result, the process for dealing with troubled banks remains chaotic, with politics still being the driving force on a case-by-case basis.

The Spanish bank bailout during 2012 was a clear example of the gap between vision and reality. Tensions in the Spanish banking system had been one of the key catalysts for creating a banking union in the first place.

European leaders agreed that the European bailout fund (initially the European Financial Stability Facility [EFSF], now the European Stability Mechanism [ESM]) should have the ability to inject capital directly into troubled banks, as the Troubled Asset Relief Program (TARP) in the United States had done. This was a shift toward socializing banking recapitalization costs in the eurozone. Since Spain's banks and Spanish government debt were under tremendous market pressure during the summer of 2012, this collaboration was important from a financial stability perspective. Direct capital injections from the European bailout fund had a major advantage: such injections into Spanish banks would not affect the debt level of the Spanish government. The bailout fund could stabilize banks without destabilizing the Spanish sovereign bond market (as had happened in Ireland).

The news about this breakthrough in the negotiations among European countries was announced at a late-night press conference hosted by Herman Von Rompuy in June 2012. A deal had been made allowing for direct bank recapitalization. This was the interpretation of Von Rompuy and the Spanish government.

But over the following weeks, it became clear that the Germans had a different interpretation. Germany agreed that the ultimate goal was a banking union that would allow such direct bank recapitalizations using the European bailout fund. However, the Germans did not agree that this logic could be applied to the legacy losses that were currently affecting Spain's banking system. They argued that the more flexible system could be used only in the future, after common banking supervision had been put into effect.

In a statement to Reuters in October 2012, Chancellor Angela Merkel made her stance absolutely clear:

> There will not be any back-dated direct recapitalisation [from the rescue fund]. . . . If direct recapitalisation is possible, it will be possible for the future.

A banking recapitalization package for Spain was agreed upon, but under the rules of the "old system." This meant that the Spanish government was on the hook for the funds. The European bailout fund disbursed about €40 billion in bank recapitalization funds, which the Spanish government was able to distribute to banks that were in need. But the link between banks and countries had not been broken. As a result of the transaction, Spain's public debt-to-GDP ratio jumped about 4 percentage points, adding to the upward pressure on the debt ratio from both fiscal deficits and declining GDP.

Whereas the United States quickly injected federal money into the nation's banks in 2009 using TARP, without regard for which state those banks were located in, the Europeans have yet to implement a system whereby cross-border transfers can be implemented without burdening national governments' balance sheets.

After a few months of uncertainty immediately following the "theoretical agreement," it was clear that the second pillar of the banking union, the common mechanism for bank resolution, would be discussed in earnest only after common bank supervision had been put in place. Hence, the second pillar of the banking union is currently a vision for the future. It will be debated in 2014 and beyond. But it is not yet a reality.

With regard to common deposit insurance (the third pillar of the banking union), there is simply no tangible progress. At this juncture, plans for a common deposit insurance scheme, inspired by the FDIC in the United States, have been postponed indefinitely (or at least until a new German government is willing to take a clear stand). The Germans are refusing to sign up for implicit transfers to other countries through such a scheme. They have their own well-funded schemes domestically and are not ready to share the candy.

For example, the German association of savings banks has been campaigning aggressively to slow the development of a banking union, with the specific aim of ensuring that local deposit insurance funds will not be used for any cross-border purposes. In an unprecedented step, the association bought advertisements in various German newspapers and printed an open letter to Angela Merkel, calling for the banking union to be put on hold to protect German savers.

The bottom line, at this point, is that the banking union is a one-legged stool. The only completed leg is common supervision. There is nothing else to prop it up.

SUGARPLUM DREAMS OF A FISCAL UNION

Another key component of reforming the basic structure of the eurozone is the vision of a fiscal union. Most academic economists will tell you that a fiscal union is a key element in ensuring the long-term stability of a currency.

But what is a fiscal union? When the International Monetary Fund and European Council president Van Rompuy talk about a fiscal union, they have a common budget for the eurozone in mind—a budget that can facilitate cross-border transfers between different eurozone countries, ideally from strong to weak, to enhance the stability of the overall system. In the German understanding, however, a fiscal union means a system of controls so that excessive deficits in other eurozone countries can be avoided. The German interpretation of the fiscal union seeks to minimize expenditures in the individual countries rather than adding any extra central spending power.

The German desire for more budgetary control was reflected in the agreement to create a so-called Fiscal Compact. European leaders agreed on the concept in late 2011 during the third crisis wave.[3] The Fiscal Compact essentially puts in place a set of strict restrictions on budget deficits in individual countries, beyond those already embedded in the Stability and Growth Pact.[4]

A real fiscal union that involves actual transfers among countries is taboo in Germany, however. Illustrating the divide in opinion between the different countries, German policy makers and the German press frequently use the concept of a "transfer union" as a derogatory term to describe what Germany is actively seeking to avoid. German taxpayers have no appetite for paying for pensions in Greece or unemployment insurance in Italy. German politicians have explicitly ruled out a transfer union, and changing this position will be a hard political hurdle to overcome.

The result is that plans to build a real fiscal union that would be able to send money back and forth among different countries have largely been put on hold. The idea of a "federal eurozone budget" is a nonstarter in most European capitals. It does not matter that most economists would agree that a common eurozone budget would be a key element for avoiding destabilizing weak growth outcomes in certain regions of a currency union during a downturn. There is just no political appetite for taking a step in this direction.

The recent debate about the broader European Union budget is a further illustration of the inherent tension between the long-term goal of further integration and the lack of political commitment to giving European institutions greater influence and resources.

The European Union works with a seven-year budget for all of its 28 member countries, and negotiations on the 2014–2020 budget started in late 2012. The European Commission had asked for a big budget increase, whereas the United Kingdom and other less "integrationist" countries called for a significantly reduced budget.[5] After the usual late-night negotiations, a historic budget deal was reached in February 2013. But it was historic in a way that seems inconsistent with the vision of greater European integration. The budget deal was the first in more than 50 years of European cooperation to dictate declining resources for the community's budget.

The EU budget is set to remain at around 1 percent of the EU countries' GDP per year in the period to 2020. Meanwhile, the funds available for proactive growth stimulation, including the cohesion funds used to support weaker regions, will stay essentially constant at just below 0.5 percent of EU GDP. Finally, most of the cross-border transfers will be funneled to the poorest EU member countries in Eastern Europe, rather than to the eurozone countries that have been hit with deep recessions, like Greece and Spain.

The very small EU budget and the even smaller fiscal capacity to address pockets of weak growth within the eurozone, illustrates the gap between the vision for the future eurozone and the policy steps that are actually being taken.[6] Europe is talking the talk, but sadly, it is not really walking the walk.

THE UTOPIA OF POLITICAL UNION

Finally, political union (the fourth element in Van Rompuy's plan) remains largely a fantasy. The basic idea does not have widespread public support. In fact, many citizens of Germany, Spain, Greece, and France are calling for something different—less integration.

It seems even less likely that such support will emerge as economic strains increase and support for European institutions collapses. At this point, most people would regard a proposal for an elected eurozone president as nothing more than a bad joke.

The goal of creating a political union in the eurozone remains highly elusive, an almost utopian concept.

THE ROLE OF THE EUROPEAN CENTRAL BANK

The various steps toward additional integration that have been outlined here have played a role in that they have signaled a certain will to pursue greater European integration. But the steps toward a banking union that are actually being taken are happening slowly, and tangible progress on building the elements of a fiscal and political union is even harder to spot.

Political promises about future additional integration were not sufficient to stabilize markets. The euro crisis has shown very clearly that intervention by the ECB has been the deciding factor in stabilizing the system in times of extreme stress. This was the case in late 2011, when eurozone banking systems were facing a "Lehman moment" and the ECB offered unlimited three-year liquidity for banks. It was the case again in the summer of 2012 when sovereign bond markets were unstable and the ECB committed to providing unlimited support.

The evolution of the ECB's role into that of a more powerful lender of last resort is consistent with what you would expect in a mature monetary union. The United States went through a similar evolution around 100 years ago. More important, realpolitik rendered ECB intervention the only politically feasible option. There was no political capacity to intervene forcefully enough through other means.

UNLIMITED MONEY—BUT WITH CONDITIONS

There have also been significant obstacles to giving the ECB more power. Attaching conditionality to the ECB's support for sovereign bond markets was the quickest and easiest way to make the dish politically edible in Germany.

There is a historical dimension to the stance taken by those who oppose giving the ECB more power. Germany's experience with hyperinflation in the 1930s, driven by out-of-control money

printing to finance the government's budget needs, has had a profound impact on German attitudes toward appropriate central bank
policies. German hyperinflation destroyed the financial system,
wiped out the savings of the middle class, and took down large parts
of the real economy. This experience has been important in shaping
Bundesbank policy for five decades, and it was important in guiding
German demands when the underlying framework for the original
euro was negotiated in the 1990s.

The history meant that the Germans and other northern Europeans
wanted to ingrain a ban on monetary financing of fiscal deficits in the legal foundations of the ECB (currently the Treaty on the Functioning of
the European Union). This has been a nonnegotiable German demand
since the euro was created. In the German view, a situation in which uncontrolled government spending leads to uncontrolled monetary expansion (and uncontrolled inflation) should be avoided at all costs.

Against this background, the ECB's promise to provide potentially unlimited support for sovereign bond markets was a sea change.
To ensure the effectiveness of the policy, the ECB had to commit to
making the funding unlimited. But to make the policy politically
acceptable, it had to attach conditions. To get around the legal and
ideological constraints of the policy and bring German policy makers on board, it was necessary to attach certain conditions, especially
in relation to fiscal performance, to the program.

POLITICS DICTATES GRADUALISM

A single-step jump from a hard currency backed by a conservative
central bank (as the Germans had envisaged when the original euro
was constructed) to a currency with much softer characteristics and
backed by a liberal central bank was not feasible. A degree of transition was necessary.

For these political reasons, the central bank–funded backstop for
sovereign bond markets was available only to countries that were

willing to agree to a program of reform and austerity (in line with the template from Greece, Ireland, and Portugal). While this condition made the program legitimate to countries like Germany, it also created uncertainty in the markets. The "insurance policy" provided for sovereign bond markets through the ECB did not provide coverage for all contingencies.

Given the conditionality, there continue to be sizable sovereign spreads in Italy, Spain, and elsewhere. Spain has so far avoided applying for ECB support (out of fear of onerous austerity requirements and the domestic political consequences of giving in to such demands).

The outcome is an incomplete backstop, one that averts an outright funding crisis, but that achieves only partial spread compression. It is a vulnerable equilibrium because it rests on continued political cooperation (more on this in Chapters 14 and 15). The price of conditionality has been insufficient easing of financial conditions in the periphery and further deterioration in debt sustainability.

The ECB had to reinvent itself to assume a greater role as a lender of last resort and to provide an explicit and implicit backstop for both banks and eurozone government bond markets. Limited additional integration, including initial steps toward a banking union and an elusive fiscal union, were not sufficient to calm the markets. Meanwhile, other forms of backstop, such as a dramatically bigger European bailout fund, were politically difficult and potentially impossible. They required the explicit approval of eurozone parliaments and governments, and the political dynamics in Germany, Holland, and Finland were not supportive of such a step. The ECB's action, on the other hand, did not require any direct political approval. The implicit transfers involved in expanding the ECB's balance sheet were less transparent to the public and therefore politically less problematic (although you can argue that from a democratic perspective, they were highly problematic). For this reason, a backstop provided by the ECB was the solution with the fewest political obstacles.

REINVENTING THE EUROZONE THE HARD WAY

In 2012, under pressure from severe market turmoil, European policy makers took important steps to reinvent the eurozone and the euro. But the various steps toward greater economic and institutional integration are part of a slow political process.

These steps were taken not because a more integrated eurozone has strong public support or because there is a strong consensus within the economics profession that keeping the eurozone intact is the most favorable outcome on economic grounds. As has generally been the case in European decision making since World War II, it has been a process guided by politics—driven by the establishment's desire to keep Europe together along with fear of the unknown (what would happen in a situation of disintegration and splintering of the currency).

In some ways, the European policy response in 2012 exceeded expectations. Open political conflict between countries and within key institutions (such as the ECB) has mostly been avoided. Despite extremely adverse economic conditions, a degree of solidarity has generally prevailed, and outright political crisis has been averted. Meanwhile, the ECB has reinvented itself. Its more proactive stance, including the promise of a backstop for government bond markets, has calmed the markets. So far, forceful commitment has been sufficient. At the time of this writing, the ECB has not spent a single euro on actually buying government bonds. The signaling effect was itself sufficient to generate a market turnaround.

The problem is that expectations were so low in the first place, calibrated to the severe legal and political constraints within which the eurozone must operate. The eurozone beat expectations because the bar was so low.

The political reality in the eurozone continues to be that it will be impossible to achieve fast-paced integration. A complete currency union, including a fiscal and political union, is not a feasible near-term objective.

Today, the euro crisis is about to enter its fifth year, and common eurozone deposit insurance remains unlikely within this decade. We may have put sufficient mechanisms in place to avoid disorderly government defaults driven by market pressures by committing the ECB balance sheet (as long as the politics remain stable). Thus, the risk of a self-fulfilling liquidity crisis has been substantially reduced. But we have not put in place a system of proactive transfers between eurozone countries through a common budget or any other mechanism, such as direct bank recapitalizations. Hence, the growth problem in the periphery remains unresolved. Moreover, there is no momentum whatsoever, in terms of establishing a more formal political union, that could help overcome the other obstacles.

Therefore, the current system may achieve only a minimum degree of stabilization. It may cut off the worst tail risk in financial markets, but it will hardly provide a basis for quick economic recovery, and it has not removed solvency concerns from financial markets. The current path of limited integration implies that the cost associated with an incomplete currency union remains high. The adjustment process remains inefficient and slow, and this will translate into real economic pain for millions of European citizens in the years to come, potentially leading to severe political instability.

CHAPTER

7

An Involuntary Gold Standard: The Economics of Inflexibility

The European countries abandoned the gold standard about 80 years ago in an effort to increase economic flexibility and escape deflation. Today, Europe has no official link to gold. However, the way economic adjustment inside the eurozone works resembles what happens under the gold standard. This was not what European countries signed up for when they joined the euro, but in many respects it is what they have: a de facto gold standard.

At the European Central Bank (ECB) press conference in June 2013, there was one emotional question from a Spanish journalist that captured the essence of the problem at hand. As Bloomberg reported,

> I'm afraid I will be a little bit dramatic, because I'm from a country that has an unemployment rate of 27 percent—that is a number of a great depression—and fiscal policy that is contractionary. And the monetary policy in Spain and also in other countries are also contractionary, because new credit is not available for little- and medium-sized companies. Are you telling Spaniards or Portuguese or Irish people, or even Italian people, that the ECB can't do anything else with—with inflation nicely lower than 2 percent?

As always, I was watching the event live on my computer screen, and Mr. Draghi did not really have a great answer. How could he have? The ECB cannot respond to the specific situation in Spain. This inflexibility is part of the system. That is the problem.

It is ironic that the monetary system that European countries uniformly abandoned generations ago, and that John Maynard Keynes called a "barbarous relic," is now stealthily sneaking up on Europe once again.[1]

THE MECHANICS OF THE GOLD STANDARD

In a gold standard, the price of a currency is fixed in relation to a certain quantity of gold. For example, from 1834 to 1933, the United States adhered to a gold standard in which $20.67 were convertible into an ounce of gold. If you wanted to, you could go to your local bank and convert paper money or deposits into gold coins. Unlike bills, which can be printed, gold cannot be created by the central bank. Because the money supply is outside the direct control of the central bank in a gold standard, the ability to tinker with policy to stimulate an economy is limited.

THE GOLDEN AGE OF THE CLASSICAL GOLD STANDARD

Before World War I, the world's major industrial economies operated on a gold standard. Each country had fixed the value of its currency relative to gold.

Because all major industrial economies operated on the gold standard, exchange rates between them were essentially fixed. Moreover, as a general rule, most economies at the time were fiscally conservative. This left little room for active macroeconomic policy, almost regardless of a country's economic circumstances. Setting of interest rates was dictated by the need to ensure a stable exchange rate relative to gold, and government spending decision were not used to actively manage the economy, since the dominant philosophy of the time was fiscal conservatism.

Instead, the central economic adjustment mechanism operated through prices and wages. Prices automatically adjusted downward in times of economic weakness and adjusted upward in times of economic strength.

When a negative shock hit an economy and money flowed out, the central bank responded by raising interest rates. The goal was to reverse the capital movement and avoid losing gold reserves. Higher interest rates also served to depress domestic economic activity, which then set price declines in motion. Over time, declining prices and wages would lead to increased competitiveness relative to the country's trading partners. Exports would become stronger, trade flows would improve, and foreign currency earnings that could be converted into gold would increase. In downturns, the main economic adjustment mechanism was deflation.

The gold standard had its golden age, so to speak, from 1870 to 1913. Economists and historians often call this period the *classical gold standard*. Unchecked capitalism, including largely unregulated labor markets, was a hallmark of this period. The absence of regulation and the weakness of unions, if they existed at all, meant that wages were quite flexible. Business owners were able to cut wages more or less at will in response to changing market conditions.

The working class had little influence on the political processes or on wage setting. The right to vote was often limited to property owners. During this period, poll taxes were a common way to restrict the voting rights of the poor. Meanwhile, strikes or other labor initiatives to fight wage declines were generally either illegal or blocked by ad hoc government intervention. This was certainly the case in the United States.[2]

During this period, the gold standard operated relatively successfully. Although recessions were quite frequent, the overall system was not questioned. Recessions were allowed to run their course until prices had fallen sufficiently to allow an economy to regain its competitiveness. Importantly, because wages were relatively flexible, it was possible to regain competitiveness within a reasonable period of time and mostly without dramatic increases in unemployment.

Obviously, an evaluation of the success of the gold standard may have been somewhat dependent on whom you asked. A business owner who could reduce wages freely would be more supportive of the overall system than an unskilled worker who had been forced to take a large pay cut during an economic downturn. Nevertheless, in terms of the behavior of aggregate economic output, the system's performance was respectable.[3]

THE PROBLEM WITH GOLD

The gold standard was temporarily suspended during World War I, when war spending took precedence over fiscal discipline. After the war, policy makers attempted to revive the old system, but the world was not quite the same. Structural changes had taken place, making the system different from what had existed before World War I. Union influence was stronger, making labor markets less flexible. In addition, the political situation was different. The working-class population had gained voting rights.

In this new world, the process of adjustment through prices and wages was slower. More prolonged spells of depressed output and elevated unemployment occurred.[4] Spikes in unemployment and output losses were bigger than before. Thus, recessions were more prolonged and more painful than had been the case previously. These changes made it more difficult to stick to a rigid gold standard. Policy makers might lose an election if they decided to support this painful strategy. Deflationary policies became unsustainable.

The United Kingdom's experience during the interwar period illustrates the shortcomings of the gold standard. During the war, when the gold standard was suspended, prices in the United Kingdom had risen fast, and British exports had become relatively uncompetitive.

After the war ended in 1918, policies, including interest rate increases by the Bank of England, were put in place to bring down the price level. In 1925, then Chancellor of the Exchequer, Winston

Churchill, restored the pound sterling to the gold standard at its pre-war exchange rate.

But prices fell relatively slowly in response to the policy tightening, and international competitiveness remained a problem. In the early 1920s, unemployment was stubbornly high at 10 to15 percent as the economy suffered from tight monetary and fiscal policy. Towards the end of the decade, unemployment spiked further to above 20 percent when domestic problems were compounded by the global shock from the Great Depression. In the five years prior to 1931, the U.K. unemployment rate spiked more than 10 percentage points to above 21 percent.

The United Kingdom's attempt to reinstate the gold standard had failed in spectacular fashion. The arrangement was too costly in term of rising unemployment in a world of representative democracy and limited wage flexibility. The Labour-led government eventually was forced to abandon gold.

Many academic papers have been written about the failure of the interwar attempt to revive the gold standard. This research has shown that the countries that left the gold standard the earliest had the strongest economic performance. Sweden, for example, enjoyed a faster recovery as a result of a combination of a more competitive currency and increased monetary flexibility.

The lesson was that the rigid adjustment mechanism imposed by the gold standard had become too costly. Allowing adjustment through exchange-rate fluctuations, which could happen much more quickly, led to less loss of output and more tolerable unemployment scenarios.[5]

More important, countries learned that giving up monetary flexibility is economically dangerous. This lesson applies both to the gold standard, where the price of currency is fixed relative to gold, and to a fixed-exchange-rate regime, where the price of the domestic currency is fixed relative to a foreign currency. Hence, most major countries are fiercely protecting their monetary independence: their ability to set interest rates, control the money supply, and allow the exchange rate to respond to changing conditions.

Of the 20 most powerful economies in the world (the members of the Group of 20, or G20), nearly all have opted for a policy framework of independent monetary policy and flexible exchange rates. The only exceptions are the eurozone member countries and Saudi Arabia, which relies almost exclusively on oil exports and has an exchange rate that is fixed relative to the dollar.[6]

EUROPE'S INVOLUNTARY GOLD STANDARD

While the large majority of the leading economies around the world have aimed for flexible monetary regimes that are capable of dealing with unexpected economic shocks, the eurozone countries have gone the other way. They have locked themselves into a rigid system of fixed exchange rates and severely constrained macroeconomic policy freedom.

Active monetary and exchange-rate policies within a specific country are precluded by design. Interest-rate determination (and other aspects of monetary policy) has been outsourced to the ECB, which sets one interest rate for the entire region based on aggregate economic performance. Monetary policy cannot be a source of stimulus for an individual country.

Exchange rates between all eurozone countries are irrevocably fixed. In addition, the ability to use active fiscal policy is severely restricted through a combination of self-created institutional constraints. Originally, the Stability and Growth Pact, put in place at the creation of the euro, was used for this purpose. The key stipulation in the pact was that nominal fiscal deficits should stay below 3 percent of GDP. Later, during the euro crisis, a stricter set of rules embedded in the so-called Fiscal Compact, was agreed upon.

Since these institutional constraints are supposed to be binding, the inability to use fiscal policy actively for stimulus purposes during a crisis is similar to the framework that was in place under the gold standard.

Today, fiscal policy in the eurozone also tends to be procyclical, especially in the most troubled countries: fiscal policy is tightened in a weak economy as a result of the various fiscal rules, such as those in the Growth and Stability Pact (and potentially loosened in a stronger economy). For example, France has been battling a recession since late 2012. Nevertheless, in 2013, the country is pursuing fiscal austerity, which will add to its growth problems, in part because of pressure from European institutions.

Moreover, there is no meaningful common eurozone budget to fund cross-border transfers, and there is no realistic plan to create such budget capacity. The EU budget to support growth in regions that are in need is tiny—around 0.5 percent of EU GDP.

The inability to transfer money between countries within the eurozone means that local tensions in specific eurozone countries can escalate almost ad infinitum. The U.S. state of Louisiana received large-scale federal support in the wake of the devastating Hurricane Katrina in 2005. In the eurozone, there is no federal circuit breaker to stop the rot, whether it arises from natural disasters or home-grown macro problems.

Adding to the asymmetry in the policy response, there has been no attempt by stronger countries, such as Germany, to offset the effect of deflationary policies in the poorer countries by pursuing expansionary fiscal policies. Not only is there no common budget that can automatically counter the effects of inflexible monetary policy, but there is also no serious attempt to coordinate policies to ensure a balanced approach to growth.[7]

All told, troubled eurozone economies have no effective policy tool to support growth in the short to medium term. Adjustment happens the old-fashioned way: through deflation of wages and prices (potentially complemented by long-term structural reform). Over time, this process, which is often described as *internal devaluation*, is supposed to boost external competitiveness. But this is a very slow process. It will take at least several years and potentially as long as a decade. In the meantime, there are no tools to put out the fire. Economic policy makers in each country are like firefighters without water.

NOT WHAT THE LABEL SAID

The underlying workings of the current gold standard–like system are not obvious to everybody, and the European establishment is doing its best not to be too transparent about the huge sacrifices required by the current system. Nevertheless, the costs associated with the inflexible framework are very visible—just look at high unemployment rates and persistent recessions.

The sad part about the current economic hardship is that much of this weakness should have been fairly predictable. Both economic historians and optimal currency area theorists warned well ahead of time that economic adjustment within the euro could turn out to be very costly in a crisis.

The eurozone is now stuck in a rigid economic policy regime. Countries that are suffering from weak growth have little ability to stimulate activity because monetary policy is outsourced to the ECB and because fiscal policy is constrained by strict rules that remain binding in the current crisis situation. Moreover, the option of currency devaluation is not available within the currency union.

In the business cycles since World War II, recessions generally lasted a few quarters and were followed by quick recoveries. Before the euro, policy makers could fight weak growth through monetary easing, fiscal stimulus, and occasional currency devaluations. These were the tools that helped economies recover.

This is not how it works in the current regime, and swift recovery should not be taken for granted. In the gold standard–like world, the main roads to recovery are price-level adjustment and structural reform, and both take time.

European countries did not think of the mechanics of the eurozone as being similar to those of a gold standard when they joined around 1999. Nevertheless, the eurozone economies are now locked in a system similar to that produced by the gold standard 100 years ago, in which deflation is the main source of adjustment.

The various efforts to pursue limited additional integration of the eurozone will not materially alter the constraints on policy flexibility and asymmetry, at least not in the next few years. As a result, eurozone countries with weak growth are likely to remain stuck with an adjustment process similar to that under a gold standard for some time. The economic consequences of these severe constraints have been devastating already, and there is little reason to expect that we are close to a turning point.

This is not what countries signed up for when they applied for euro membership in the 1990s. Today, several European countries are in the middle of an adjustment process the likes of which has not been seen for decades. Unfortunately, economic performance may remain historically weak for years to come.

Where's the Growth?: The Cost of Deflation

The costs associated with rigid macroeconomic policies are very real. Significant economic and psychological pain is being felt on the streets of Madrid, Rome, Athens, and beyond. People are suffering from a lack of jobs, lower pensions, lower living standards, and worsening health conditions. Recently, a woman who was heavily indebted and about to be evicted from her home walked into a bank in Valencia, poured gasoline all over her body, and set herself on fire. An older couple in Seville, profiled in the *New York Times*, have been sleeping in the lobby of their apartment building with their two grown and jobless children after being thrown out of their property.

POLICY CONSTRAINTS AND ERRORS

In its current form, the European common currency requires slow and painful economic adjustment. Local policy makers in countries with high unemployment have few effective tools at their disposal to revive growth and generate jobs. On the ground, the persistent slump is causing a loss of faith in the future. An entire generation of recently educated young men and women in the peripheral countries has little prospect of getting a decent job.[1] This is a high price to pay.

The policy makers in the eurozone who designed crisis responses did not think through all the consequences of their decisions. They did not properly account for the policy constraints that were embedded in the currency union. They did not adequately incorporate the effects from deleveraging in the financial system.[2]

These miscalculations led to an unbalanced policy framework with a recessionary bias. The result has been severe economic contractions in many eurozone economies and declining living standards for millions of European citizens.

The official forecasts have been wide of the mark for several years. They always seem to assume economic recovery within a few quarters, as if the business cycle still behaved the way it did in the "good old days" before the financial crisis hit. But the actual recovery remains elusive. Huge forecast errors, broken political promises, and continued economic suffering are multiplicative.

The weaker eurozone economies can be compared to a person with a weakened immune system. A cold turns into pneumonia, which can eventually threaten death. The inflexible policy regime within the currency union makes it hard to fight off an otherwise manageable economic cold. This is the structural growth challenge that is at hand.

INADEQUATE PESSIMISM

In late 2009, just before the euro crisis began, the International Monetary Fund (IMF) was projecting a gradual economic recovery in Greece. According to its forecast, real growth in Greece would be marginally negative in 2010, followed by a moderate recovery during 2011 and 2012 and a more respectable level of expansion of GDP (around 2 percent) in 2013.

Of course, the actual path has been dramatically worse. GDP dropped 3.5 percent in 2010, then tanked by more than 6 percent in 2011 and again in 2012. Real GDP is now projected to decline by another 4 percent in 2013, based on the IMF's World Economic Outlook from April.

The forecast errors have been enormous. Adding up the numbers, Greece's GDP was originally projected to expand by a cumulative

3 percent from 2010 to 2013. However, the actual outcome will be a cumulative shrinkage in GDP of 20 percent. A forecast of gradual recovery has morphed into a deep depression.

The forecast errors for Greece have been extreme, but they are not unique to that country. Official sector forecasters have continued to revise down growth expectations year after year in places like Portugal, Spain, and Italy.

The latest example of overoptimism—or rather, inadequate pessimism—is the European Commission's forecast for Cyprus from February 2013. That projection called for a decline in GDP of 3.5 percent in 2013, followed by a more moderate decline of 1.3 percent in 2014. A more realistic forecast at this point, given that the local banking system has been decimated through deposit confiscations and capital controls, would be for a cumulative drop in GDP of 15 to 25 percent in the next few years.

Cyprus is a tiny part of the overall eurozone economy, and from a purely mathematical perspective, it hardly matters in terms of the overall eurozone GDP. But it is another illustration of the broader tendency toward miscalculation of risk and overly optimistic economic projections, especially for the most troubled parts of the eurozone.

THE COST OF DEFLATIONARY POLICY

Standard monetary policy has run out of power in the eurozone, as interest rates are already near zero[3]. Exchange rates within the eurozone are locked. Fiscal policy is no longer a stimulus option because self-imposed deficit limits restrict flexibility. In addition, there are drags on growth from global deleveraging and more homegrown tensions in the eurozone banking system.

Beyond the policy inflexibility and the banking tension, there is something even more fundamental going on. The often-overlooked cost of deflation is hitting the eurozone as well. The irony is that the current strategy is designed to encourage this deflation. Because the currency is fixed, a drop in the price level relative to the price levels of other countries (real depreciation) can happen only through actual declines in price levels.[4] Economists call this *internal devaluation*. As was the case many decades ago, when the gold standard was in place, lower wages and prices are meant to boost competitiveness. But in today's world of high leverage, the *medicine is the poison*.

Because the mechanism through which deflation has a negative impact on growth is a bit technical, I will give it a simple name that better describes what it is about.

I will call it the *hit 'em while they're down effect*. It works like this: you borrow $200,000 to buy a house. That amount is fixed, and it is determined in relation to your current wage of $50,000 a year. Say the annual mortgage payment is $20,000, and you have enough slack in your budget to afford it. But what happens if wages in your sector or in the entire economy are heading lower? Your salary falls 20 percent. Now you have to make a $20,000 mortgage payment out of a $40,000 salary. If your wages continue to fall, it may eventually become impossible for you to service the debt.

Wage deflation makes it harder for this borrower to service debt, and declining revenue will have a similar impact on corporations. Consider this on a huge scale, including households, small businesses, and large corporations with billions in borrowing in a country such as Spain.

I call it the hit 'em while they're down effect because deflation hurts the weakest balance sheets in the economy: the households and corporations with fixed nominal debts and declining nominal income and revenue. The side effect is a higher frequency of bankruptcies, which have their own costs.

Essentially, deflation tends to make borrowers poorer and lenders wealthier (other things being equal). There is a perverse redistribution of real wealth from debtors to creditors. This redistribution will tend to generate suboptimally high savings in the aggregate as a result of precautionary behavior and credit constraints.

Under the classical gold standard in the United States, farmers in the Midwest, who had borrowed to grow their crops, complained about the effects of persistent deflation. In the 1896 presidential election, they demanded an exit from the gold standard and a more flexible money supply system. This just illustrates how deflation hurts the constituencies with debt in the economy. This follows from basic economic principles.

WHEN DEFLATION HURTS THE MOST

This is the basic idea. But the pain associated with deflation will vary over time depending on the structure of the economy and the health of the financial system. Deflation is likely to be particularly costly in two special circumstances.

The cost of deflation is likely to be higher when the banking system is already under stress. This is because credit constraints for weaker borrowers are likely to be more severe and problematic when the banking system is weak.

The cost of deflation is also likely to be larger when debt levels are elevated. If there is little debt in the economy, the effect of deflation should be small. However, when debt levels are high, this effect is large and can have an important negative impact on the overall economy.

Unfortunately, a number of eurozone countries have exactly this combination of weak banks, high debt levels, and deflationary dynamics.

A number of prominent economists have analyzed the basic cost associated with deflation, although often in very general and conceptual terms.[5] Meanwhile, to my knowledge no detailed studies have been done to measure how costly the deflationary adjustment will be given the extremely high household and corporate debt levels in the eurozone. Some analysis has been done in the context of Japan, which has seen two decades of deflation. But the eurozone has not been the focus of any studies of the effect of deflationary policy. Since deflationary adjustments are inherent in the current crisis-management strategy, this is a remarkable gap.

Moreover, European economies have very little experience with deflation. It has been a very long time—way back in the gold standard days—since Europe has seen persistent deflation.

And obviously there is a crucial difference between now and then. Debt levels were much lower then than they are today. A hundred years ago, most households did not have a bank account and most corporations had only limited financial leverage. The overall ratio of bank credit to GDP was in the 20 to 40 percent range in advanced economies. Today the ratio is closer to 100 percent.[6]

This makes the deflationary adjustment far riskier now. High debt levels and deflation combine to create a toxic mix, as we are witnessing in Spain. It is no surprise, therefore, to see bankruptcies and nonperforming loans continuing to rise several years into the crisis. In 2012, no fewer than 9,066 Spanish companies went bankrupt, compared to a long-term average of less than 1,500 per year, according to data from the National Statistics Institute.

While bankruptcies in the United States peaked several years ago, they are still increasing in Spain and other peripheral eurozone economies. In early 2013, this disturbing trend has continued. It is impossible to say for sure what is the exact cause of this deterioration. Some may argue that the spike is due to weak growth rather than deflation. But the fact is that many borrowers are taking it on the chin, and that deflation is exacerbating this issue.

The cost of the deflationary adjustment and broad-based deleveraging in certain banking systems is imposing a very significant burden on eurozone countries. However, it is not being discussed very explicitly. This may be an analytical oversight, or it could be partly for political reasons. Regardless, it is a fact, with very negative implications for eurozone countries that are facing an already very difficult adjustment.

Maybe the eurozone should look at the situation in Japan, the one advanced country with a long recent experience of deflation. In 2013, Japan has embarked on the most aggressive monetary expansion of any country in the entire postcrisis period. Why? It wants to use brute force to escape the deflation trap. Deflation is not a fun place to be. Most countries do their very best to avoid it.

FALSE HOPES ON EXPORTS

It is hard to find pieces of good news in the eurozone growth story, but European officials are putting a lot of faith in an export-driven recovery. The European crisis-fighting strategy is based on structural reforms (in addition to fiscal austerity). Over time, these reforms are supposed to increase competitiveness and growth. The internal devaluation that is at the heart of the gold standard–like adjustment should, in theory, support improved export performance over time.[7]

The German experience with its Agenda 2010 reforms in the early 2000s has helped shape the current policy's focus on competitiveness. As discussed in Chapter 2, in the early 2000s, Germany embarked on a radical reform program that helped reduce wage growth and improve productivity. The German labor market reforms and the subsequent German export boom in 2004 to 2008 are seen today as a template for generating strong growth in the eurozone more broadly. This is the rare example of how structural reforms supported growth, albeit with a lag of some years, despite the constraints of the currency union.

In the summer of 2012, I attended a meeting with a senior member of the ruling German Christian Democratic Union (CDU). It was very clear from the presentation that there was a strong belief that the German template could be replicated in the rest of the eurozone. A key phrase from the meeting was, "We took the pain; others will have to take it too." The German belief that there is no solution other than to improve competitiveness through wage restraint and reform is strong.

The basic reasoning is not necessarily wrong. But it would be naïve to think that the German export model can simply be replicated across the eurozone.

WHY THE GERMAN EXPORT BOOM CANNOT BE REPLICATED

There are a number of reasons why expectations of an export-led recovery have to be tempered. The basic fallacy is that the German model of export-driven growth can somehow be replicated within a reasonable time frame.

First, Germany did not face any credit constraints when it undertook its reforms 10 years ago. However, countries like Greece, Ireland, Portugal, Spain, and Italy are facing high funding costs and economic and political uncertainty. As a result, people are holding back on large-scale investments. To expand exports on a significant scale, investment is likely to be needed. But investment remains depressed, and it will take time for companies to get comfortable with new regulations and laws, even when the country is moving in the right direction.

Second, the German export boom in the mid-2000s was partly the result of strong global demand. Global demand growth was on a strong trajectory in those years, around 5 percent. Now the momentum is meaningfully lower: below 4 percent. Moreover, the eurozone countries whose trade is focused on moribund eurozone markets are currently facing external demand that is even further below the trend from 10 years ago. Since the European economies are very closely integrated via trade links, it is virtually impossible for everybody in the region to enjoy strong export-driven growth at the same time.

Third, Germany is a very open economy. Its export output makes up more than 50 percent of GDP. In Greece, exports are less than 25 percent of GDP, and in Spain, exports account for only around 30 percent of the economy. This creates a basic arithmetic constraint on how much growth you can squeeze out of exports in these countries. In Germany, a 5 percent increase in exports will boost growth by 2.5 percent, everything else being equal. In Greece, however, a 5 percent increase in exports will lead to only around 1 percent extra growth. Many of the eurozone countries that are dealing with competitiveness problems are trying to grow exports from a very low base. This means that the impact on growth will be fairly moderate. This is just a mathematical fact.

From this perspective, the German export model is hardly one that can be easily replicated. Stronger exports in the eurozone can help at the margin, but they will not restart growth on a broader basis. As always in Europe, it depends a lot on which specific country you are looking at. Ireland and Portugal are among the more open economies, and they could see a sizable impact on growth from stronger exports (assuming that strong exports can be achieved). Greece, France, and Italy are at the other end of the spectrum, with relatively small export sectors, even if you include exports of services.

Finally, the euro has remained quite strong relative to other major currencies, despite the various crisis waves and the increasingly obvious growth underperformance. Some people are celebrating the euro's resilience as evidence of the currency's success. In reality, the relative strength of the euro is a mixed blessing.

In the first half of 2013, the euro remained in the middle of its historical range on a trade-weighted basis (averaging out the various exchange rates with its main trading partners). That level of the euro is not supportive of growth in the region. In order to meaningfully support exports and overall growth, the euro needs to be at the weak end of its historical range. We are far away from those levels now, and even if we were to get there during 2013, it would support growth in the eurozone only with a lag of one to two years, based on the historical relationship between the currency and export performance.

THE EUROZONE GROWTH CRISIS

Regardless of how you look at the numbers, the conclusion is the same: growth in the eurozone is historically weak. The eurozone has been in recession for three out of the last five years. The unemployment rate in the eurozone is the highest in its history (around 12 percent). Weakness is permeating, with France being potentially the latest country about to enter a prolonged recession. The severe economic weakness in Italy and Spain is shown in Chart 8.1.

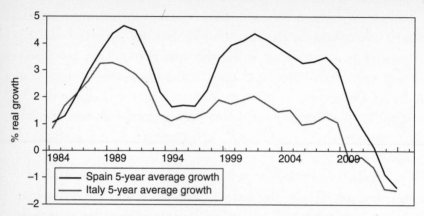

Chart 8.1   Historically Weak Growth in Italy and Spain

Source: IMF WEO

These negative trends may sound academic when they are expressed in sterile economic language. However, the pain is very real indeed. More than half of the recently educated generation in Greece and Spain cannot get a job. The most extreme indicator of the crisis is perhaps the increasing suicide rates in troubled eurozone economies. Greece used to have a stable and low suicide rate, but that is no longer the case. From 2009 to 2011, the suicide rate jumped 37 percent, and that does not even capture the recent period when the economy was the most depressed.

In the face of this persistent growth crisis, it is remarkable that there is no aggressive growth strategy in place or in the works. Fiscal tightening in the eurozone is set to continue during 2013, although the tone from the IMF and the European Commission concerning the pace of fiscal consolidation in 2014 and 2015 is shifting towards less tightening. Nevertheless, the best case seems to be one in which the drag on growth from the fiscal side goes toward zero. There is no prospect for any outright support for growth, although the politics surrounding this issue could change in the aftermath of the German election.

CONVERGENCE TURNS TO DIVERGENCE

In addition to the disturbing trends in terms of aggregate growth performance, there is an alarming pattern of economic divergence within the eurozone. This directly goes against the promises of those who implemented the euro. The common currency was meant to make the poorer countries more prosperous. This process of convergence was at the core of the set of European values that underpinned the early integration process, before the creation of the original euro. Instead, the prolonged recessions have clawed back the riches, and then some.

The convergence trends that were celebrated during the honeymoon years in the early 2000s are being reversed. One particularly stark example of the divergence is the record low unemployment in Germany and the record high unemployment in Spain—well above 25 percent. There are reports of labor shortages in certain parts of Germany, whereas it is almost impossible for a generation of young labor market entrants in Greece and Spain to find decent jobs at home.

This divergence is not confined to the most troubled countries on the periphery. Even within the core of Europe, the divergence is escalating. The unemployment rate in France (near 11 percent in early 2013) is more than twice that in Germany (just above 5 percent in early 2013). This is the largest gap in labor market conditions in the two countries since modern labor statistics began. Since no change in the policy framework that could engineer a reconvergence of growth dynamics in short order is in sight, we should expect continued divergence.

The greater divergence between countries' macro performance implies that country-specific factors matter much more for eurozone investments than they did in the past. Just look at the returns of Spanish and German equity markets in 2012. The German DAX index was up 30 percent, while the Spanish IBEX index was down 5 percent. This divergence is a reflection of the extreme differences in growth between the two countries as well as in differences in required risk premia. During the euro's honeymoon years, such a divergence would have been deemed impossible.[8]

Politically, the divergence is problematic. It was one thing to see all the eurozone economies suffering in tandem during the global financial crisis in 2008 and 2009 in the face of a large external shock (and with various scapegoats outside the eurozone available).

However, the current economic weakness is uneven, and it is not possible to project anger toward rating agencies, investment banks or other external forces. The issue is homegrown: a function of European institutional limitations and the policy mix decided on at home.

MISSING CREDIBILITY

Eurozone growth has been weak since 2008. Meanwhile, officials continue to assert that growth is just around the corner. The forecasting errors have been enormous, and the broken promises put the entire strategy in doubt.

Public support becomes harder to obtain when there are these credibility issues. Why hand over sovereignty to policy makers in Brussels when they cannot deliver on their own objectives?

An example of this occurred when François Hollande was elected president of France in the spring of 2012. He tried to push for a revised European agenda with a stronger focus on growth and less emphasis on austerity.

Infrastructure investment was one idea that was being kicked around. It was one of the few elements of his growth plan that did get some backing. The idea of so-called Project Bonds was one specific initiative: a special financing instrument for infrastructure investment, with a sweetener in the form of equity from the EU budget.

The Project Bond Initiative was launched in 2013. But guess how much money the EU committed? €230 million. This is equivalent to just 2 percent of the loan amount of €10 billion given to tiny Cyprus in 2013. So much for boosting infrastructure investment in the eurozone! This shows you how little support there is for a comprehensive eurozone growth strategy if it costs anything.[9]

Very recently, European policy makers have finally acknowledged that progress has been insufficient in terms of job creation, especially for a generation of young workers in the periphery. Acknowledging the problem is a first step, even if it is very late in the game. But it is hardly a solution in itself.

During the summer of 2013, German policy makers have been touring European capitals in an effort to set up bilateral programs to support job creation for younger generations in Portugal, Spain, Italy, and even France. The basic idea is a good one. But given the poor track record of previous grand policy plans in Europe, it is hard to have confidence that quick results will be achieved. This is especially true when you look at where the money for the programs is going to come from. German finance minister Wolfgang Schäuble provided a hint in a speech in May: "We are working to use the existing funds more efficiently," he said, according to the *New York Times* (D'oh!).

In reality, these new job creation initiatives may kick off in earnest only during 2014, and the results are likely to be clearly visible only years later. It would be naïve to expect a quick fix to an unemployment problem of the current magnitude.

FADING FAITH IN THE EUROPEAN PROJECT

Citizens may accept a period of pain if they don't know its permanence. When hope fades, the social psychology is altered and radical changes can happen.

In 1999, the European electorate was sold a product (the euro) that promised low transaction costs and higher growth. Instead, they entered a time machine that transported them back to the gold standard, where adjustment was done the hard way: through deflation.

Making things worse, the crisis-fighting strategy itself has failed in terms of delivering the promised growth and jobs, causing tremendous damage to its credibility. This process is a fragile one. The political risk should not be underestimated. It is unclear whether it will be possible to maintain political stability and preserve support for the European integration effort in the face of such dismal economic conditions.

CHAPTER

9

Europe's Political Fragility: The Seeds of the Next Crisis

Greece moved away from authoritarian rule in 1974. For almost 40 years, political power was divided between two parties. On the right, the New Democracy Party supported conservative views. On the left, the PASOK Party provided a socialist alternative. During Greece's 40 years of democratic rule, PASOK and New Democracy were each in government for roughly half the time. Neither party was too far from the center, and it was essentially a two-party system.

EXTREME POLARIZATION

On the surface, the political situation in Greece remains broadly unchanged. At present, New Democracy has formed a coalition government with PASOK, and it has a slight majority in the Greek parliament. The two old parties seemingly remain in control.

But if you dig down deeper, the political situation looks dangerously fragile. It took two separate elections within a few weeks in the spring of 2012 to form the current government. Support for the two centrist parties has plummeted, and previously obscure movements on both the extreme left and the extreme right have gained tremendous ground. It was only because of the technicalities of the Greek election system, which gives the largest party 50 bonus seats in parliament (regardless of its specific share of the vote), that the old centrist parties could obtain a majority.[1]

Recent opinion polls show how fragile the Greek political situation is. A further shift away from the two traditional mainstream parties has taken place since the election. Polls from early 2013 show that PASOK has been nearly demolished. It is down to around 8 percent of the vote, and New Democracy has not been able to pick up the slack. Instead, disgruntled voters are opting for extreme alternatives. On the left, the SYRIZA Party, an amalgamation of communist factions, has around 29 percent of the vote. SYRIZA is currently the most popular party in Greece. On the right, the neo-nazi Golden Dawn Party has more than 10 percent of the vote. Golden Dawn currently ranks as the third most popular party. An extreme right movement that derives its support partly from anti-immigrant propaganda is set to beat PASOK in future polls.[2]

Importantly, the SYRIZA Party continues to call for a renegotiation of the bailout agreement with international lenders, and such a renegotiation would call into question Greece's future membership in the eurozone.

This illustrates how unstable the political picture has become. The euro crisis and the economic pain associated with it have led to an extreme form of political polarization: a situation in which politics are unprecedentedly fragile.

Early elections in Greece could be explosive. They could put a government in place that is on a clear collision course with European institutions and the International Monetary Fund. Though new elections are not scheduled until 2016, the tenuous economic situation (or something else altogether) could trigger an early election.

GROWING EUROSCEPTIC MINORITIES

Greece is an extreme example of how the euro crisis has polarized the political landscape and created a highly uncertain backdrop. While its situation is extreme, Greece isn't alone. Opposition to European integration is showing up in different ways across the continent. Within the official political sphere, as evidenced by actual voting, we have seen increased support for various eurosceptic parties in a number of countries, including France, Finland, Holland, and Italy.

In France, Marine Le Pen from the National Front campaigned on a nationalist platform during the 2012 presidential election. Her views about the euro are clear: she wants to return to the French franc in order to pursue independent economic policies to bring down the French unemployment rate. According to Le Pen, the euro has "asphyxiated our economies, killed our industries and choked our jobs."[3] Ms. Le Pen did relatively well in the first round of the presidential elections in 2012, gaining 18 percent of the vote (although not enough to make it to the final round). It was the National Front's best election result since her father founded the party in the 1970s.

In Finland, the eurosceptic True Finns party got 19 percent of the vote in the 2011 parliamentary election. It is now the third-largest party in the country, and the biggest opposition party.[4] The party's leader, Timo Soini, has been particularly vocal in his opposition to eurozone bailouts: "The bail-out system is hugely immoral and cannot work," he told Fox News. The party's stance had an influence on Finland's negotiating position with regard to the Greek and Spanish bailouts during 2011 and 2012. Finland controversially demanded segregated collateral in return for its portion of loan guarantees for the European bailout fund (initially the European Financial Stability Facility [EFSF] and later on the European Stability Mechanism [ESM]).

In Holland, Geert Wilders's Party for Freedom received 16 percent of the vote in the 2010 election, making it the third-largest party in the Dutch parliament. Wilders has said: "The euro is not in the interest of the Dutch people," according to the *Telegraph*. But support for the Party for Freedom dropped to 10 percent in the latest election, in September 2012, as the mainstream parties made a strong comeback.

In Italy, Beppe Grillo's Five Star Movement (M5S) got about 26 percent of the vote in the February 2013 elections.[5] Grillo's personal blog is the single most followed in Italy, and the main political goal of the movement is to bring down the establishment. Its 54 members of the senate were sufficient to block the formation of a majority government for several months after the election.

Together, these examples show the trend toward greater support for anti-European protest movements.

Nevertheless, the eurosceptic forces have so far been unable to gain much direct political influence.

ANGER ON THE STREETS

The public anger is more visible on the streets than in parliaments. The opposition to the current policy path of painful austerity and increased European influence on national policies has shown up outside the formal political system. More people are striking, and there are more frequent public protests.

Spain has seen three general strikes since the beginning of the crisis, with two of them being in 2012. Portugal has had four general strikes during the euro crisis, and Greece has had more than 20. Such strikes were very rare before the euro crisis.

Meanwhile, protests against austerity measures and other painful reforms have frequently been able to gather large crowds.

Portugal, which is normally a peaceful country with relatively few public protests, had more demonstrations in 2012 than in any of the previous 20 years. The protests escalated particularly in September 2012, when the government was planning to increase workers' social security contributions. This year, thousands of people protested austerity measures. In Lisbon, a crowd chanted: "Get out IMF! Screw the troika!" according to an article in the *Wall Street Journal*.

In Greece, demonstrations and strikes have been commonplace since 2010, especially in connection with major budget votes in the Greek parliament. The largest demonstration happened early in the crisis. On May 5, 2010, there were more than 100,000 protesters in the streets of Athens, and the protests turned violent (bank offices were attacked and two people died). Fires have been burning in the streets of Athens on several occasions since then.

Meanwhile, in Spain, tens of thousands of people protested recently in Madrid, Barcelona, Seville, and Zaragoza. At one time, thousands of young unemployed citizens set up a camp in the

Puerta del Sol square in Madrid, with tents, mattresses, and even a pharmacy, according to Reuters.

DECLINING TRUST IN EUROPEAN INSTITUTIONS

Some political changes are observable. Other political changes are much less visible. But under the surface, there has been an important shift in attitudes toward European institutions.

Every year since 1970, the European Commission has done a survey of public sentiment on European issues, called Eurobarometer. It tells you how sentiment has evolved under the surface. The public support for European institutions has declined in a very pronounced and very broad-based fashion over the last six or seven years.

In the latest survey, 60 percent of respondents said that they do not trust the European Union, up dramatically from just 16 percent in 2006. Interestingly, the decline in trust (and the parallel increase in mistrust) is very broad-based. Public support for the European Union is declining in both the north and the south (see Chart 9.1).

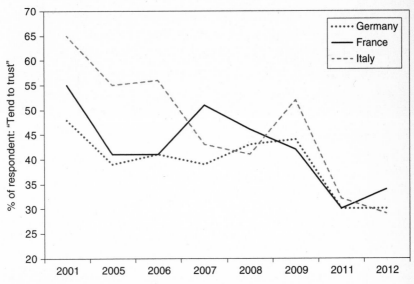

Chart 9.1   Declining Support for the European Union

Source: Eurobarometer.

Meanwhile, interestingly, distrust in the European Central Bank (ECB) is also accelerating both in the core and in the periphery. The ECB is not trusted in Spain (75 percent), Greece (81 percent), or Germany (52 percent), to name some examples.

The Eurobarometer survey also has a question about support for the common currency. Opposition to the euro has been growing in the hardest-hit countries. However, the opponents of the euro are still in the minority in Greece (31 percent), Spain (30 percent), and Portugal (37 percent).[6]

This shows a conflict between a lack of trust in European institutions and a lack of willingness to abandon the euro. Fear of the unknown, fueled by scaremongering by the establishment concerning the consequences of exit, is at play here. At some point, however, the pain associated with the current policy path may be so severe that these fears will be pushed into the background.

One thing is crystal clear, however: there is almost no public support for pursuing a European fiscal or political union. The Eurobarometer survey has a very telling question about the preference for outsourcing tax policy to European institutions. The large majority of EU citizens are in favor of keeping tax policy as a national decision (68 percent). Just 28 percent are in favor of coordinating tax policy with the EU.[7]

This clearly illustrates the political limitations of further integration. While direct opposition to the euro and even the ECB may be manageable in most countries, there is no appetite for giving up sovereignty where it really matters. Creating a real fiscal and political union goes directly against current public opinion. Policy makers are well aware of this. It explains why the integration process has limited momentum. It is a fine balancing act.

CENTRIST SUPREMACY

Eurosceptic sentiment may have indirectly slowed the integration process. In Germany, for example, pressure from the right wing of the Christian Democratic Union (CDU) has probably pushed

Chancellor Angela Merkel to adopt a more conservative approach to dealing with the euro crisis. But there have been few examples of these movements gaining any direct influence.

Why is this? The answer is that even if the protest movements have gained support, they have not really been able to bite into the core centrist voters and wrestle majorities away from the mainstream parties.

Many of the parties that were in power during the global financial crisis and the early phases of the euro crisis have seen their support drop dramatically. In most cases, however, voters have generally shifted toward other centrist forces rather than toward the extremes. As a result, governments in the eurozone periphery continue to be led by centrist mainstream parties (albeit different ones from a few years ago).

In Ireland, the Fianna Fail party, which has been part of most modern Irish governments, fell dramatically from grace in the face of the economic crisis and an embarrassing international bailout. Fianna Fail got only 10 percent of the vote in the February 2011 election. However, the new government was formed under the leadership of another centrist party, Fine Gael. Together with the Labour Party, a coalition with a large majority was created. In reality, a historic shift in the vote had little influence on the overall policy direction.

Something similar happened in elections in Portugal and Spain during 2011. There was a big change in the vote, but centrist forces remained in control, and there was little impact on policies.[8]

In Italy, the situation is more complex. Three-time prime minister Silvio Berlusconi had to step down in the face of international and domestic pressure in the autumn of 2011. This led to a temporary technocrat government, led by Mario Monti, from then until February 2013. After the February 2013 election, there were a few months of political deadlock. Nevertheless, the center left eventually formed a government with the support of Berlusconi's party.

In each of these cases, the new government has generally been advocating another variation of the same centrist ideology. There has been no decisive break away from essentially pro-European thinking. Even in Greece, both PASOK and New Democracy are strongly pro-euro, and they continue to comply with demands from their European partners as part of the bailout agreement.

Discontent is there, but there is no evidence that a revolution (even a small one) is just around the corner.

MAINTAINING THE STATUS QUO

Early in the euro crisis, it was commonly thought that a deep recession in the eurozone periphery would lead to widespread social unrest and strong political opposition to the austerity demands.

Many political and economic analysts predicted that the backlash against austerity would quickly cause reforms to stop, triggering sovereign defaults and departures from the eurozone. Many of these analysts used the template from Argentina, where austerity became politically untenable after a few years, leading to a dramatic currency devaluation and a disorderly government default in 2001.

A key element in the surprising stability has been that centrist mainstream parties, both center left social democratic parties and center right conservative parties, have almost uniformly supported the vision of gradual further European integration.

In the peripheral countries, austerity and reform have never been seriously questioned. The centrist parties have all backed the basic strategy prescribed by the core countries.

In the core, the centrist forces have been able to rally around a strategy of controlled financial support for countries in need. In Germany, for example, both of the main parties (the center right CDU and the Social Democratic Party) are strongly supportive of the euro and in favor of "more Europe." Within Merkel's CDU, the chancellor has silenced voices of internal rebellion, such as those calling for a Greek exit from the eurozone. Meanwhile, the Social Democratic Party is calling for more European integration, not less.

Importantly, most governments in the eurozone have had out-right majorities in parliaments, helping to create a degree of policy continuity. This has meant that key budget votes, for example, have typically not been major cliff-hangers. The centrist consensus has been able to progress with basic reforms and maintain the status quo to some degree.

Broadly speaking, the local centrist establishments have not questioned the European establishment. No major party within the eurozone, whether left or right of center, has overtly opposed the general strategy outlined from the European core. No personality from the mainstream parties has been suggesting a fundamental re-thinking of the euro project.

Multiple factors contribute to this attachment to the status quo.

First, despite the economic mess, many people (especially the older generations) still believe that the European project is a catalyst for stability and peace. Peace triumphs over economics, so to speak.

Second, there has been a depolarization around the political cen-ter in European politics as the difference between blue-collar and white-collar workers has become more blurred.[9] Increased support for far right and far left parties means a polarization at the extremes. But within the center itself, the difference between center right and center left has become more marginal, a reflection of the centrist consensus.

Third, many people have a real anxiety concerning the unknown. Taking radical steps to change the current economic regime and break away from the euro would be a complicated matter with un-known consequences. A lack of detailed analysis of the consequences of breakup perpetuates this fear. Even some of the smartest people in the world do not fully understand what might happen and cannot predict the outcome. Why wouldn't the general population be a little anxious? Pro-euro governments feed this anxiety. Many people are affected by two decades of pro-euro campaigning, and it is hard for the die-hard euro fans to suddenly change their opinion, even if the facts have changed dramatically.[10]

THE WEAKNESS OF THE ANTI-ESTABLISHMENT

Still, how come the protest movements have not gained broader support?

One reason is that they have been unable to articulate a good alternative to the current path. When no clear alternative (to limited integration) is spelled out, why question the status quo? The protests have been anti-intellectual, and their nonanalytical approach has not been that appealing to the informed voters at the middle of the political spectrum.

Another reason has to do with the narrative told by the centrist forces, which focuses on the cataclysmic consequences of exit from the euro, while downplaying the rather large economic cost associated with the current trajectory.

To maintain this narrative, policy makers have been keen to avoid any suggestion that exit from the euro could work. This is a narrative constructed around political goals, rather than an objective analytical foundation (an economic cost-benefit analysis). But it has been working, at least up to now.

The success of the political center has played a great role in deterring any real opposition that could become a threat to the centrist establishment (although Italy may be the new wild card in this respect). The outsiders have not been able to present a credible alternative, and the insiders have had no desire to do so.

FRAGILE THINGS CAN BREAK

Maintaining pro-European policies is essential for keeping alive the hope that a more integrated eurozone will emerge in the future. This is itself a key factor in maintaining financial market stability in the eurozone, because it is the hope of future integration that is underpinning markets. Moreover, political stability is what makes cross-border funding arrangements feasible in the shorter term. Since this is crucial to stabilizing the peripheral bond markets, this is another important element of financial stability.

This is why thinking about risks to the current political status quo is crucial when evaluating the overall stability of the system, both financially and economically (the two cannot be separated). Since the eurozone is made up of countries with diverse political histories, it is difficult to generalize about it. The nature of political risk varies from country to country. Nevertheless, the political risks that the eurozone is facing can be grouped into four broad categories. Let us go through them one by one.

RISK FROM BROADENING PROTEST MOVEMENTS

Up to January 2013, the various protest movements around the eurozone have had difficulty appealing to the broader electorate. But they are gaining some momentum, and this is the first type of political risk to watch. Though these parties have received less than 20 percent of the vote in key elections, this is quite a bit more than they received in previous years. Moreover, the Italian election has shown that increased economic hardship and dissatisfaction with the political establishment have the potential to generate larger support for protest movements. The Five Star Movement got 26 percent of the vote and is now the biggest single party in Italy, although it is obviously far from having a majority on its own.[11]

Increased support for protest movements may come organically when citizens become more disgruntled and current governments are unable to deliver on their promises. This effect of this process is cumulative over time. Meanwhile, entirely new protest movements, such as youth movements protesting against unprecedented unemployment, may mushroom. The rise of social media means that public sentiment is harder to predict. The Arab Spring and the Italian election have clearly demonstrated that.

The emergence of a more coherent alternative may also embolden the various protest movements. For example, the status quo can be questioned more forcefully with analytical arguments than simply with populism; this could also make a difference. Over time, a more credible and analytically based alternative has the potential to create the broader appeal that is needed if these movements are to gain real influence.

Something of this nature is already starting to happen in Germany. In April 2013, an entirely new German political party called Alternative für Deutschland (AfD), came forward. This group, which is supported by a long list of academics, wants to dismantle the euro and return Germany to the deutsche mark.[12] It is not a protest party in the normal sense, but rather an intellectual alternative to the current policy framework. The party chairman is an economics professor and a former member of Merkel's CDU. The party is seeking to appeal to basic German principles, such as respect for law and order, and it is pointing to the objective failure of the current crisis resolution strategy. Within just a few weeks of its launch, the party had more than 10,000 members, and it may be able to get representation in the German parliament (by getting more than 5 percent of the vote). While it seems unlikely that a party such as AfD will gain much direct political influence, it may serve to harden the CDU's Europe policy. Such indirect effects could be important.

RISK OF REVOLT WITHIN THE POLITICAL CENTER

Opposition from outsiders is one avenue for political change. Opposition from within the establishment is another possibility, and a second key political risk. The centrist consensus has been a source of political stability. This is a fact, regardless of whether or not you agree with the basic philosophy. If this consensus were to be questioned from within, it would be a major shock to the current political structure.

After the chaotic bailout of Cyprus in March 2013, some cracks in the centrist consensus began to appear. This may have been the first time that a senior official close to the political establishment expressed serious doubt about the very survival of the European project. After the Cyprus bailout was agreed upon in March, Athanasios

Orphanides, the respected former governor of the Central Bank of Cyprus (and former ECB Governing Council member), made the following blunt statement to the *Financial Times*:

> The European project is crashing to earth. This is a fundamental change in the dynamics of Europe towards disintegration and I don't see how this can be reversed.

While recessions have affected Greece and Spain since 2010, it is only more recently that they have spread to Italy and France. As the economic recession hits the broader eurozone and the recovery remains elusive, parts of the establishment may eventually have second thoughts.

One key question pertains to France's willingness to implement deflationary reforms along the lines of what we have seen in southern Europe. We could face a revolt from the political center if France's Socialists are unwilling to implement the reforms demanded by the EU. This is an issue that will be coming to the fore in coming years, as France's budget deficit is set to remain above the EU limit of 3 percent of GDP.

At the moment, many of the governments may seem to be in a relatively safe position, given the current composition of parliaments, and given that new elections are a few years away. But political dynamics can change quickly. Spanish politics have been shaken in 2013 by a corruption scandal at the heart of the ruling conservative party. Italian politics have been affected by a controversial bank bailout in early 2013.[13] Unforeseen events, including personal scandals, have the potential to quickly shake political structures in unpredictable ways.

RISK FROM BACKLASH AGAINST BAILOUTS

A third type of political risk relates to aversion to serial bailouts. In the core, bailout fatigue might set in. Bailouts have never been popular. Nevertheless, we have been on a serial bailout path for a number of years. It started with domestic bank bailouts in 2008 and 2009, and it morphed into bailouts of specific eurozone countries, starting with the bailout of Greece in early 2010, followed by those of Ireland in late 2010, Portugal in 2011, Spain in 2012, and Cyprus in 2013. Moreover, it may not end there. Slovenia could be next and Portugal may need a second bailout, for example.

The German Bundestag has approved large commitments every time it has been asked, and with a convincing majority, and other parliaments have paid up too, although there have been hiccups along the way (in Finland and Slovakia, for example).

Meanwhile, the ECB has also done its part, with emergency support for eurozone banks and sovereigns. The backstops provided by the ECB have generally met less opposition, since this happens outside the normal political process. But certain voices in Germany have balked.

Looking ahead, a backlash against further government bailouts and the increasingly liberal ECB policy remains a risk. The northern European countries may eventually form an alliance within the European Central Bank opposing the aggressive use of liquidity support for the periphery. The idea of a eurobond is a nonstarter, and this shows that the capacity for pooling of debt among the eurozone countries is limited.

The Finnish public, for example, has been promised that Finland will never take a loss on its contributions to different incarnations of the European bailout fund. The Finns' demand for special collateral is a function of these concerns and was needed to get political support for the bailouts at home. If this promise is violated by a haircut on official sector loans to Greece or Portugal, it could have major implications for sentiment in Finland. At the same time, this dynamic is enormously unfair to other countries that have loaned money alongside Finland. It could create resentment elsewhere if Finland were protected while others took losses.

Similarly, runaway ECB liquidity support for eurozone governments could create explosive political tensions within the ECB.[14] What would happen if Italy needed large-scale monetary financing of its deficit? What would happen if France needed support from the European Central Bank and continued to run excessive deficits?[15]

This is how the fabric of European solidarity and political cooperation could be tested. If political tension rises within the ECB's governing council, this could ultimately put the integrity of the euro itself in question, leading to a rising risk of breakup.

The risk of the splintering of the eurozone from its core, as happened about 20 years ago when the rublezone broke apart, is linked to whether Germany and other large countries can maintain sufficient control of policy in the periphery. This in turn, depends on political and social trends in the periphery.

In this sense, the risk of a backlash against the pooling of debt in the eurozone will rise along with opposition to austerity in the periphery. The two risks reinforce each other, creating a potentially unstable political equilibrium with dramatic economic and financial market implications (more on this in Chapter 15).

RISK FROM A CONSTITUTIONAL CRISIS

The final source of political fragility stems from a looming constitutional crisis in the eurozone and in the EU. The political process for constitutional changes is different from the normal political process. Typically, change is enacted through an indirect democracy. We elect representatives to parliaments, and they act on our behalf. In many countries, constitutional issues are handled through referenda. Constitutional changes are different in that they are subject to direct democracy.

Changes to European treaties that are significant enough to affect national constitutions may call for referenda. This is the one situation in which the political establishment cannot filter the demands of the public. As a result, public referenda entail elevated risk for the current policy path and the establishment's vision.

This is important because there is a huge gap between public opinion (which is negative toward EU institutions) and the stance of the political establishment (which supports the current integration path). Referenda pose a real danger to the centrist consensus and have the potential to trigger significant political discontinuity by breaking the status quo.

This risk is not just hypothetical. There is a long history of failed referenda on European treaties. Denmark rejected the Maastricht Treaty in 1992, and Danish entry into the euro was rejected in another referendum in 2000. Sweden rejected adoption of the euro in a referendum in 2003. Holland and France rejected the European Constitution in 2005. Ireland rejected the Lisbon Treaty in 2008.

Given that public sentiment is becoming more eurosceptic, it will not be easy to approve new treaties aimed at handing more authority to European institutions. At the same time, such referenda will be hard to avoid. The European integration process is entering a critical phase, as some of the most sacred pieces of national sovereignty are at stake (control over tax policy, control over social systems, and the ability to supervise major local financial institutions). Linked to this, calls for referenda are already emerging.

In Italy, Mr. Grillo has called for an online referendum on Italy's euro membership. In the Netherlands, a citizens' petition in March 2013 has already created a debate about a need for a public referendum on future EU treaty changes.[16] Even in Germany, which has never before had a referendum on EU treaties, powerful voices, including that of Finance Minister Wolfgang Schäuble, have called for a German referendum on a new EU treaty.[17]

This would be a historic development, but the risk would not be the German referendum as such. Rather, the risk would be the spillover effects in other countries. If Germany has a referendum, the Netherlands and Ireland will surely have one, and Spain, Italy, and France may have a very hard time avoiding one. Denying the citizens a vote on key issues such as giving up fundamental elements of their sovereignty would be too overtly undemocratic.

France has a particularly troubled history with European referenda. The European Constitution referendum failed in 2005, and the French vote on the Maastricht Treaty on euro membership in 1992 very nearly failed (just 51 percent were in favor). Current opinion polls point to increased euroskepticism in France.[18] If there is a referendum in France, the risk of a "no" is high, especially if French unemployment continues to rise into the campaign.

Adding to this issue, Europe might see an epidemic of referenda in coming years. As it happens, we are also facing separatist referenda in Scotland and in Spain's Catalonia region. Meanwhile, the United Kingdom is heading for its own EU membership referendum.[19] This is likely to add to calls for more direct democracy in the eurozone more broadly.

The most likely scenario is one in which key referenda on a new treaty for the EU (and possibly for the eurozone) will happen during 2015 or 2016. Most likely, economic growth in the eurozone will remain weak for the next few years, and as a result of this, public support for European institutions may have deteriorated further by that time.

A failed referendum on the new EU treaty in a core eurozone country or a few peripheral countries would lead to a constitutional crisis. This would amount to a historic setback for the integration process, and it would pose a major challenge to financial markets.

POLITICAL UTOPIA

Fifteen years ago, then German chancellor Gerhard Schröder called the euro "a sickly premature baby." He worried about creating a European currency without a political union to back it. The risks he worried about have materialized. The eurozone (in its original weak form) was not equipped to handle a serious crisis. Today, Mr. Schröder's recommendation is to go ahead and create a proper political union in Europe, finishing the job that was started in 1999.[20]

This is where the rubber meets the road. The goal of a political union remains elusive. It is still a desire of the elite, but it is not a goal that is currently within reach. In fact, it has moved further out of reach since the creation of the euro because public sentiment toward European institutions has deteriorated dramatically in the last few years. Indeed, even within the establishment in the core the eurozone the merit of ever closer integration is starting to be questioned. In June 2013, the dutch coalition government made an official statement saying: "The Netherlands is convinced that the time of an 'ever closer union' in every possible area is behind us"[21].

The economic need for further European integration is colliding with public sentiment, and this is creating political fragility along multiple dimensions.

Policy makers have stepped onto a difficult path of further European integration, and the recent relative financial market stability rests on increased cross-border cooperation. But political risk will continue to accumulate as long as growth remains missing. Political risk tends to materialize in unpredictable ways and could eventually evolve into a full-blown crisis. Political stability could be in jeopardy just when the economy and the markets need it the most.

The Mechanics
and Implications of Breakup

The alternative to further integration is some form of breakup of the euro. If the member countries cannot agree on a common path, the logical alternative is to return to independent economic policies, including independent currencies.

The topic of breakup is complex and not well understood. There are plenty of myths to dispel.

I start with the basics. In Chapter 10, "When a Currency Splinters," I describe the mechanics of currency breakup. When exactly has one currency become two? As it happens, we came very close to this in Cyprus in early 2013.

In Chapter 11, "The Devil's Guide to a Eurozone Breakup," I try to debunk some of the common myths about how breakup works and whether it is feasible. A key point is that there are many different types of breakup, each with its own special considerations.

Chapter 12, "What's the Worst-Case Scenario?" analyzes the special case of full-blown breakup, in which the euro would cease to exist altogether. This is the worst-case scenario, involving immense legal complexity and potentially a total freeze of the global financial system.

Chapter 13, "Who Should Stay and Who Should Go? The Economics of Exit," goes through the implications of a single country's exit from the eurozone. This chapter highlights how the exit of strong countries (ignoring political considerations) arguably would be a preferable form of breakup from a purely economic perspective.

CHAPTER
10

When a Currency Splinters

Does it matter whether your dollars are in California or in Florida? It should not. In a common currency area, the currency is supposed to have uniform value. There is no difference between a dollar in San Francisco and a dollar in Miami. The notes and the coins are the same, and bank deposits have the same purchasing power throughout the entire currency area. In the United States, all dollars are created equal.

Occasionally, however, a currency does splinter. On February 8, 1993, for example, the currency of the former Czechoslovakia broke into two pieces: one currency for the Czech Republic and another currency for Slovakia. Currency in Bratislava was suddenly no longer the same as currency in Prague. In fact, during the American Civil War, the dollar splintered, albeit temporarily.

When a currency area breaks up, currency in different jurisdictions is suddenly no longer equivalent. If Greece were to leave the eurozone, the value of currency in Greece would decline sharply. The international purchasing power of the Greek currency would deteriorate. The morning after the breakup, a Greek citizen would no longer be able to buy the German-made BMW that he had been about to purchase the day before with the money he had saved. The Greek currency would be a currency on its own, with a weaker exchange rate relative to the euro and to other currencies around the world.

But how would this really work? What would be the underlying mechanics of a breakup of the euro? Since the topic remains taboo in European policy circles, there is a shortage of information from official sources. However, if you look back far enough, history provides key pieces of the puzzle concerning the meaning of currency splintering.

WHEN MONEY IN THE BANK IS NOT "MONEY IN THE BANK"

During the nineteenth and early twentieth centuries, the U.S. banking system was fragmented and crisis-prone. Major banking panics occurred in 1873, 1893, and 1907.

The last of these banking panics, in 1907, started with a run on the now-infamous Knickerbocker Trust in New York. The panic quickly spread and affected the sector more broadly. The trust industry had grown tremendously in size over a short period of time, but confidence in it had been shaken as excessive speculation by certain institutions was revealed. This was the catalyst for a wave of distrust, and depositors became uneasy, withdrawing large sums of money from the institutions they deemed the most vulnerable.

Since the Federal Reserve System had yet to be created, there was no common central bank.[1] Clearing of checks, for example, was the responsibility of the private sector. The New York Clearing House, a self-regulated consortium of major commercial banks, took on this role in New York State.

The banking trusts, however, operated outside the regular banking system and they did not have direct access to clearing through the Clearing House. Hence, when Knickerbocker Trust faced a run and was running out of cash, there was no central bank to provide emergency liquidity. Instead, the New York Clearing House suspended clearing. Checks written on balances at Knickerbocker Trust could no longer be cleared, and cash could no longer be withdrawn from the institution.

Various attempts were made to halt the run on the sector, including the provision of credit by the New York Clearing House and cash deposits in New York banks by the U.S. Treasury in Washington. But on October 26, 1907, the New York Clearing House decided to suspend the convertibility of all deposits in New York banks as a last resort to avoid further liquidity drains on the banks.

Normally, a dollar in the bank is always convertible into a dollar of cash. These days, there is even the expression "like money in the bank," meaning something that is totally safe or guaranteed. But with convertibility suspended, a dollar in the bank was in reality no longer equal to a dollar in the wallet. A depositor who wanted to draw on his savings in the final months of 1907 could no longer convert his deposits into cash (and goods) at par.

For some months, the lack of convertibility meant that currency in the form of physical cash traded at a premium to bank deposits. Quickly, an active broker market for deposits developed, in which you could sell deposits to investors at a discount based on supply and demand. The conversion rates were listed in New York papers on a daily basis, similar to the daily quotes for company stocks. The bottom line, however, was that money in the bank was not "money in the bank" during this period. The discount of deposits versus cash reached 4 percent during the final months of 1907, which marked the height of the crisis. That is, to get $100 in physical cash, a depositor would need to sell $104 worth of deposits.

The suspension of convertibility of deposits did not mean that the currency union of the United States had broken down. The U.S. dollar (the greenback) remained the legal tender across the various states, and there was no differentiation between physical dollars in New York and those located elsewhere during this crisis (as opposed to during the Civil War). However, the crisis of 1907 provides a clear illustration of how the concept of continuous central clearing and convertibility underpins the value of different types of cash instruments. Suspension of convertibility means that different types of cash are no longer equivalent; a type of exchange rate will develop between them.

The U.S. financial system has obviously matured since 1907. As we discussed in Chapter 5, the Federal Reserve System was created in the years following the 1907 panic, and the Federal Deposit Insurance Corporation (FDIC) was created in 1933, during the Great Depression. Since then, deposits in U.S. banks have always been convertible into physical cash at par. It is from this perceived security that the expression "like money in the bank" has developed.

This irrevocable convertibility has become an ingrained part of the understanding of what a U.S. dollar is and how the U.S. financial system operates. The word *cash* is now used interchangeably to refer to both physical cash (notes and coins in your wallet) and liquid deposits (checking deposits) in your bank account.

But more than 100 years later, the situation in the eurozone still has some elements in common with the banking panic of 1907 in the United States. In March 2013, a banking crisis in Cyprus, one of the smallest member countries in the eurozone, forced the Cypriot authorities to close all the country's banks entirely for a week. When the banks were reopened, severe restrictions on capital movements were imposed. Certain deposits were simply confiscated by the state[2]; others were subject to severe limitations on withdrawals and transfers. The Central Bank of Cyprus even put a restriction of €300 on the amount of money a Cypriot could withdraw from his bank account in a day.

In Cyprus, a euro in the bank was no longer equivalent to a euro in the wallet. There was no official listing of the "price of deposits" in the daily newspapers, but there were stories about dodgy offers to unlock frozen deposits for a fee. The full convertibility of deposits had been broken in Cyprus.

CONVERTIBILITY AS CURRENCY GLUE

The concept of convertibility can be used to describe the ability to always convert bank deposits into cash at par (one to one). But it can also be used to describe the ability to convert cash across borders without any restrictions.

A defining feature of a currency union is uninterrupted ability to conduct currency conversion at par between all areas within that union. The convertibility is the glue that keeps the currency together, regardless of the state or country in which the cash (physical or electronic) is located. If you never have to worry about whether a dollar in Dallas is the same as a dollar in Los Angeles or a dollar in New York, then you have a currency union with full confidence.

If convertibility at par between cash in two different jurisdictions is suspended, an exchange rate will develop between the currencies in different jurisdictions. The exchange rate will then be a function of the supply of and demand for the local currency relative to foreign currencies, and the exchange rate may be visible in official markets or in black markets, depending on whether or not capital controls allow free market currency transactions.

For example, when the Central Bank of Russia suspended the convertibility of ruble balances originating in Ukraine during 1992, the Ukrainian currency (called karbovanets at the time) immediately started to trade at a discount because of lack of confidence in the unit. In fact, it did not take long before the Ukrainian currency was trading at a discount that exceeded 50 percent relative to Russian rubles.

Once convertibility is jeopardized, the currency union will in effect have splintered. The next question is how to guarantee the convertibility.

Back in the pre-Federal Reserve days, the convertibility between dollar deposits in New York banks and physical dollars relied on continuous clearing by the New York Clearing House. When such clearing services were no longer available, as was the case in late 1907, this meant that deposit balances could no longer be used for regular payments (deposit transfers, clearing of checks, and so on). As a result, a wedge developed between the price of deposits and that of physical cash. These "inconvertible deposits" would trade at a discount to cash in the broker market.

Similarly, today the convertibility of currency between different jurisdictions within a currency union depends on a system whereby a central bank ensures that bank balances automatically clear across borders, and in which physical cash is allowed to move unhindered from state to state (or from nation to nation in the case of the eurozone).[3]

The *convertibility is broken when unlimited clearing is suspended.* From a practical perspective, this marks the point of breakup of the currency union. The breakdown in cross-border convertibility of bank balances is likely to be the first step toward the splintering of a currency. For example, this was what happened when the rublezone broke up. The trigger point came when the Central Bank of Russia refused to accept bank credits created by Ukraine. From this point, convertibility at par was suspended, and an exchange rate between the two types of currency developed. Separation of physical rubles (notes and coins) happened only at a later stage.[4]

CYPRUS'S NEAR-BREAKUP EXPERIENCE

During the crisis in Cyprus in early 2013, there was also an element of breakdown in the cross-border convertibility of currency in Cyprus relative to that of currency in the rest of the eurozone. When the banks opened on March 28, 2013, after a weeklong forced bank holiday, restrictions on cross-border currency movements were put in place. Cross-border wire transfers were prohibited, except in special circumstances, and export of physical currency was initially restricted to €1,000 per trip per person.

Convertibility was limited to a certain amount for physical cash and to bank transfers for certain transactions. Otherwise, convertibility was suspended.

Hence, currency in Cyprus was no longer fully convertible into euros elsewhere. You could argue that a form of breakup has already taken place. De facto currency separation happens when a currency is no longer fully convertible at par. In Cyprus's case, we entered a gray area. Not all currency located in Cyprus is fully convertible in unlimited amounts across borders. Convertibility remains in place for certain transactions (although it potentially requires preapproval by the authorities). Whether you call this a breakup or not depends on your temperament.

A total breakdown in convertibility like that seen when the rublezone splintered in the early 1990s has so far been avoided, albeit just barely. During the last week of chaotic negotiations on the bailout of Cyprus in March 2013, the European Central Bank (ECB) explicitly threatened to suspend liquidity provision to Cyprus, according to the *Wall Street Journal*:

> Emergency Liquidity Assistance could only be considered if an European Union/International Monetary Fund program is in place that would ensure the solvency of the concerned banks."

Failure to reach a bailout agreement would have forced the ECB to suspend the provision of liquidity for the majority of the banking system in Cyprus. This would have jeopardized the cross-border convertibility of Cypriot euros in a more dramatic fashion. This is how close we were to an outright currency splintering.

UNINTENDED BREAKUPS

The concept of convertibility is never mentioned when times are good. Nobody ever talked about the convertibility of euro cash and deposits before the financial crisis erupted, just as nobody is discussing it in the United States, where the durability of the currency union is unquestioned.[5]

However, when market tensions reached a climax in the summer of 2012, the word was suddenly rediscovered. Mario Draghi, the ECB president, talked about the need to eliminate convertibility premiums in government bond markets. What he meant was that fears of a eurozone breakup and related currency splintering had started to show up in asset pricing around the eurozone. Rising government bond yields reflected not only risk of default, but also a premium for potential currency depreciation in the event of a breakup of the euro. Draghi wanted to confront that trend, and for good reason. When convertibility is in question, a currency union is on truly shaky ground.

Convertibility is particularly in the limelight when it is in being acutely threatened. This was the problem in Greece and Spain in the summer of 2012, and it was the problem again in Cyprus in early 2013.

In principle, breakup can happen by choice or by accident. The debate about the euro crisis and the possible breakup of the euro has often revolved around whether staying in the eurozone would be the best decision for Greece (and for other potential exit candidates). Over the last few years, there have been dozens of op-eds in the *Financial Times* arguing back and forth over whether Greece should opt to leave the common currency or not.

The debate implicitly assumes that political leaders will make an active decision about whether to stay inside the euro. But as we have illustrated earlier, the key trigger of currency splintering is the breakdown of cross-border convertibility. In the absence of convertibility, there is no common money.

In principle, the suspension of currency convertibility can happen either by the choice of the exiting country or by a decision of the core. Hence, the suspension of convertibility can happen without an explicit political decision in the exiting country.

In the case of the rublezone, it was Russia's decision, at the center of the currency union, to suspend currency convertibility. Ukraine got its own currency not by its own choice, but because Russia would no longer tolerate sharing the same money.

The euro could also splinter this way. The ECB is supposed to provide liquidity only to solvent banking institutions. If a banking system is insolvent, and there is no prospect of recapitalization, suspension of cross-border convertibility should happen semiautomatically. This would have been the case in a disorderly default in Greece (that is, one without recapitalization of the banks), and it would have been the case in Cyprus had the major banks not been restructured.[6]

It is up to the ECB to make these choices, although it would probably consult key European political leaders in some way before making such crucial decisions. But ultimately, the ECB is in control of the functioning of the currency union, and it has the power to cut the flow of liquidity and suspend convertibility when it deems this appropriate.

Hence, currency separation can happen as fallout from a political crisis that makes it impossible for the ECB to continue to provide liquidity. In those instances, as was the case when the ruble-zone splintered, the breakup would be formalized politically only at a later stage.

In reality, the mechanism behind currency breakup is relatively simple. If physical cash and deposits balances are not freely convertible at par across borders, the currency has effectively splintered. What are much more complex are the political dynamics that trigger the suspension of convertibility and the subsequent economic and financial market implications of the breakup.

The Devil's Guide
to a Eurozone Breakup

In the spring of 2012, I met with a senior official from the European Central Bank (ECB) at its headquarters in Frankfurt. Our plan was business as usual: we were discussing the financial markets and the outlook for the economy.

I had brought along a study on the economic and financial market consequences of a euro breakup that I had been working on for several months. It was a heavy 150-page document analyzing the consequences that were relevant to a breakup scenario. When I handed over my paper, the official accepted it only reluctantly and said:

"A person at the ECB reading this would be like a priest reading the devil's bible."

Was he serious or was he joking? I still don't know. But his comment reflected the prevailing sentiment. Policy makers abhorred even contemplating a euro breakup in any form.

ABSURD FANTASY

During the euro crisis, the possibility of euro breakup had repeatedly been dismissed by officials at the ECB as well as by officials in Brussels and in other important European capitals (although less so in London than in Paris or Berlin).

Jean-Claude Trichet, the ECB president from 2003 to 2011, had perhaps the most extreme example of this attitude. In 2010 and 2011, his standard response to reporters was that the idea of a breakup was "an absurd fantasy" that was not worthy of any additional comment.

FANTASY MEETS REALITY

Soon the evolving euro crisis necessitated a change in the rhetoric.

It happened for the first time in November 2011. Greek prime minister George Papandreou, in an act of desperation aimed at saving his government's future, proposed a national referendum in Greece on the bailout package that had been negotiated with Greece's European partners. Facing the risk of a referendum that would clearly reveal the public's opposition to austerity and make cross-border cooperation almost impossible, European leaders changed their tactics. They suddenly acknowledged that Greece's membership in the eurozone should not be taken for granted.

French president Nicolas Sarkozy broke the taboo with the following quote, as reported by the *Financial Times*: "The question is whether Greece remains in the eurozone, that is what we want. But it is up to the Greek people to answer that question."

It was just six months later, in May 2012, when a breakup was suggested again. The Greek election initially gave the extreme left-wing SYRIZA Party the ability to block the formation of a reform-friendly government. In the face of this reality, European policy makers again admitted that a form of eurozone breakup was possible.

Belgian central bank governor and ECB Governing Council member Luc Coene expressed the changed sentiment in an interview with the *Financial Times*:

> The ideal would be if all member states stayed in the club—that would be the best for everyone, even the Greeks. But, of course, if one member decides it no longer has a shared interest in being a member, you must allow them to get out—that is part of a democratic system.

Finally, when there was doubt about whether Cyprus would agree to the terms of the bailout offered by its European partners in

March 2013, it was clear that Cyprus's eurozone membership was also in question.

Eurozone officials acknowledged the possibility of breakup only under extreme pressure and out of political necessity. Meanwhile, there was never any attempt to evaluate the merits of breakup analytically.

As usual in the history of European policy making, politics dominated economics.

THE MYTH OF THE IMPOSSIBLE BREAKUP

Throughout most of the crisis, until the Greek situation forced the issue, European officials have been trying to stick to their guns. The standard narrative has been that any form of breakup would be devastating and therefore clearly undesirable. Conveniently, they have some academics backing their position.

For example, Barry Eichengreen, who is a respected economic historian and a professor at the University of California, Berkeley, has argued in a series of academic papers and on voxeu.org that:

> [Exit from the eurozone] would be the mother of all financial crises.

Mr. Eichengreen's viewpoint is widely quoted and referred to by other academics and policy makers. For example, his post on the topic on the widely followed European economics blog voxeu.org has been viewed by 140,000 readers.

He argues that any speculation about a possible exit from the eurozone would cause huge bank runs in weaker countries. For this reason, it has been ruled out a priori.

If you want to preserve the euro at all costs, it is convenient to argue that abandoning the euro is the worst thing that can happen in the world. But that does not make it true.

It may well be that a full-blown breakup, with all eurozone countries moving back to their legacy currencies, would be cataclysmic.

Having a major reserve currency such as the euro cease to exist would certainly be completely unprecedented in history and would surely be extremely costly (more on this in Chapter 12). But this conclusion does not apply to all breakup scenarios.

The impact of a breakup of the eurozone will depend crucially on a number of parameters, including who is exiting, how the process is planned,[1] whether the exit coincides with a government default, and the nature of the postexit policy response. For example, the implications of an Italian exit would be on a totally different scale from those of a Greek exit.

Making a blanket statement that all forms of eurozone breakup would be cataclysmic is just too simplistic. The effect of a breakup depends on the circumstances, and the circumstances change over time.

A BEAUTIFUL BREAKUP FROM HISTORY

The breakup of Czechoslovakia in the early 1990s illustrates that orderly currency separation is feasible.

The Czechoslovak currency union was dissolved in 1993. The transition from one Czechoslovak currency to separate currencies (the Czech koruna and the Slovak koruna) took place with minimal direct disruption of the Slovak and Czech economies.

It required careful planning to overcome the logistical challenges. The political decision was taken in a single session of parliament, after which the currency separation was implemented immediately.[2]

The central bank had all the logistics set up even before the parliament made the political decision. For example, the stamps used to distinguish Czech and Slovak notes after the currency split had been printed secretly in a remote location in Latin America months before they were actually needed.

During the transition, banks and post offices were closed, borders were sealed, and mail service was temporarily suspended. There could be no movement of money during the transition. Thousands of government employees, police, and members of the military worked around the clock to ensure that all aspects of the operation proceeded smoothly and fairly.

The new currencies were introduced within a few days. There was no financial crisis, and the effects on the real economy were minimal. The operation was so successful that the International Monetary Fund (IMF) has since used it as a template for guiding other currency separations around the world. The example from Czechoslovakia shows that the orderly breakup of a currency union is indeed possible.

THE MYTH OF UNCONTROLLABLE DEPOSIT FLIGHT

Those who argue that breakup is impossible often say that any hint of a potential breakup would immediately trigger devastating capital flight, including crippling runs on deposits.

This is a risk that would have to be managed carefully. A poorly planned exit could well be devastating for the banking system. Ideally, the decision to exit would need to be made quickly and secretly, and with banks and borders closed immediately after the decision was taken (as was done in Czechoslovakia).

One factor that may be crucial in reducing capital flight problems is that retail deposits are typically quite sticky.[3] The behavior of depositors in Greece in 2012 illustrates this.

In Greece, we had several weeks of extreme uncertainty, both in the run-up to the debt restructuring in February 2012 and again around the election in May 2012. During those months, there was a lively debate in the local and international press about a possible "Grexit." Nevertheless, most of the Greek deposits stayed in the system. During the first half of 2012, 87 percent of domestic deposits stayed in the Greek banking system. The worst month was May 2012, when domestic deposits dropped by 5 percent. It was a notable decline, but it was not in itself devastating or outright destabilizing.

It is also worth noting that issues concerning capital flight are fundamentally different in a situation in which a strong country is exiting the euro. A German saver would probably still feel safe with money in a German bank, regardless of whether Germany was a part of the eurozone or not (although reverse capital flight into Germany would have to be addressed in that case). A similar argument would apply to an exit by another strong country, such as Holland or Finland.

This illustrates why it is nonsensical to make blanket statements about the implications of a country's leaving the eurozone. Breakup in the form of the departure of a strong country, such as Germany, would fundamentally alter the dynamics of capital flows and make them quite different from a situation in which a weak country leaves (and it may raise different issues of political stability in the region more broadly).

Runs on the banks stem from a breakdown in confidence. But a carefully planned and communicated exit strategy, including actions to protect depositors and limit capital outflows (or inflows) during the transition phase, could help minimize the risk of destabilizing deposit movements.

The Cyprus template is obviously not one to follow. The various policy blunders surrounding the bailout negotiations, including the lack of a clearly articulated strategy from the outset, worked to undermine confidence.[4] Nevertheless, developments in Cyprus have shown that cross-border capital controls are a tool that could be used by eurozone countries during a transition period.

Smart policy and effective communication are the key to maintaining confidence. Without them, problematic capital flight is a high risk. The path out of the euro would not be an easy one. But there is a path.

THE POLICY RESPONSE MATTERS

Early in the crisis, investors and politicians were intensely concerned about the contagion effects resulting from a breakup. How would a Greek exit from the euro affect the rest of Europe and the world?

These concerns were closely tied to the risk of uncontrolled deterioration in government bond markets across the region. At times, it seemed as if the various eurozone government bond markets could fall like dominoes.

In response to these worries, policy makers have established a comprehensive backstop infrastructure, including additional support from the ECB, which has assumed a lender of last resort role for sovereign bond markets. The relative calm in European markets in the face of the Cyprus crisis in March 2013 illustrates the effectiveness of these backstops. Less than a year earlier, bond markets in Spain and Italy were in virtual free fall in response to fears about a Greek exit from the eurozone.

This shows that the increased capacity to support banks and sovereigns makes a crucial difference. The risk of markets spiraling out of control as a result of runaway contagion is substantially smaller today (assuming that cross-border political cooperation is maintained). This matters in relation to exit scenarios, too. If the European bailout fund and the ECB have more powerful tools at their disposal, the risk of severe contagion effects from exits is also reduced.

Given this, some prominent eurozone policy makers have in fact now admitted that certain types of breakup would be manageable. "I think that for many experts, for the FDP, for me too, a Greek exit from the Eurozone has long since lost its horror," German economy minister Philipp Rösler said in July 2012, according to the *Telegraph*.

A month later, Luxembourg's prime minister, Jean-Claude Juncker, said, according to the *Telegraph*: "From today's perspective, it would be manageable but that does not mean it is desirable."

German chancellor Angela Merkel has not endorsed such comments. The myth of the impossibility of breakup remains a convenient tool to bind the eurozone together. The narrative is more a function of its political usefulness than of its truthfulness, however.

THE HOUSE ON FIRE ANALOGY

We have moved from a situation in which any talk of breakup was seen as "an absurd fantasy" to a situation in which policy makers admit that certain types of breakup cannot be ruled out and can be managed.

But we have not come to a point where various exit scenarios are analyzed in detail. There is still a shortage of sound analysis of what the costs and benefits of exit would be. Moreover, the economic consequences of exit are never put in the context of the alternative: continuing on the current path.

The irony is that the current path of gradual but limited further integration of the entire eurozone has itself proved to be rather devastating. The unemployment rate currently exceeds 25 percent in both Greece and Spain, and eurozone growth is set to be negative again in 2013. The current downturn in the European economy is arguably the worst since the end of World War II.

It is far from obvious that the "horrors of breakup" are actually worse than the horrors of sticking with the euro. The cost of exit may be more concentrated around the transition phase, while the cost of sticking with the euro accumulates gradually over time. The high up-front cost may explain why policy makers do not dare to consider the possibility of breakup.

It is bizarre that some of the most important economic decisions of our time—that is, whether to stay in the currency union or not—are being taken without a comprehensive cost-benefit analysis. The lack of detailed analysis of the consequences of a breakup is reminiscent of the inadequate scope of the analysis conducted ahead of the euro's creation. The official stance of European policy makers remains that "the euro is irrevocable," and the majority of economists also argue that the cost of breakup is so large that this should not be considered as a policy option. But where is the working paper that documents this? No official studies that actually spell out the consequences of various breakup scenarios have been done. For political reasons, such analysis is deemed inappropriate.

Meanwhile, in countries such as Greece, Ireland, Portugal, Spain, Italy, and Cyprus, the cost of staying in the eurozone is getting more and more unbearable. In 2013, hopes for economic recovery have again been dashed.

In April 2013, the former prime minister of Portugal, Mario Soares, suggested in an interview with the national Antena 1 Radio that default was the only solution for Portugal:

> Portugal will never be able to pay its debts, however much it impoverishes itself. If you can't pay, the only solution is not to pay. When Argentina was in crisis it didn't pay.

This quote shows that even personalities who were once considered part of the establishment—Mr. Soares personally negotiated Portugal's entry into the European Economic Community in 1986—are starting to consider radical policy changes.[5]

While this is politically extremely controversial, it is time to think objectively about the costs and benefits of exit.

A brief story may illustrate. In March 2013, a hotel in San Diego caught fire. Three hotel guests were trapped on the second floor. Heavy smoke rose through the building, and the temperature was rapidly rising. As the flames got closer to the victims, it was clear that the only way for them to survive was to jump from the building. And they did. The three victims jumped from the second floor onto the street. One broke a leg; another broke an ankle. It was painful, but they survived. When it was clear that the cost of staying would have been devastation, they were all willing to take the risk of jumping and suffer the pain involved.

Using this analogy, eurozone policy makers are always focusing on the pain associated with breaking a leg from the jump. But they are ignoring the cost of the fire itself, which could be deadly over time.

There are those who will continue to argue, either for political reasons or because of a misguided use of economic theory, that any form of breakup would be infinitely costly. They may be right that a full-blown euro breakup, which require a number of special considerations, would be extremely costly. But each case of breakup is very different. A single country's exit from the euro, if it is planned and managed properly, can be done without intolerable pain.

The greater obstacle to exiting from the euro is the political capital invested in the project and politicians' inherent aversion to radical change.

12

What's the Worst-Case Scenario?

A full-blown breakup would be a special and extreme form of breakup in which all the eurozone countries go back to their own currencies and the euro ceases to exist altogether. There is no historical precedent for the disappearance of a global reserve currency such as the euro. This extreme case of currency splintering raises complex legal and even philosophical issues. It is not a scenario for the faint-hearted or for those who appreciate a degree of predictability.

Take a deep breath and change the setting for a minute. A different perspective may help illustrate the very special issues involved.

LEGAL WARFARE

In July 2012, the U.S. Marshals Service seized Argentine state assets worth $23 million in the form of deposits and shares held by a little-known New York–based financial agent, BH Option Trust. A few months later, an Argentine Navy ship was held in the main port of Ghana in West Africa. The incidents in New York and Ghana are both related to an ongoing legal battle over Argentina's legacy debts. More than 10 years after Argentina's sovereign default in 2001, the fight over unsettled financial claims against the Argentine government still goes on.

Around $5 billion worth of Argentine sovereign bonds have never been restructured or paid out. These bonds are at the center of a seemingly never-ending legal dispute. The bonds remain in the hands of a few hedge funds and a group of Italian retail investors, but the Argentine government refuses to acknowledge its obligation. The owners continue to fight, taking aggressive legal action to get their money back. Courts around the world—from New York to the United Kingdom and Belgium—have repeatedly made rulings in their favor. The creditors have been given the right to seize Argentine state assets abroad as a means of receiving payment.

This shows how unresolved international legal disputes can drag on for years. Such fights entail significant legal costs. But more important, the indirect costs can be enormous. The legal proceedings can disrupt the normal course of business for corporations, for governments, and for entire countries. The legal infighting concerning Argentina's legacy debt is focused on a relatively isolated issue. It illustrates the consequences of open conflict between a single-minded sovereign and the international legal system. In addition, it has been very costly, both to the creditors and to Argentina.

The eurozone should keep this in mind. Think about the consequences of a legal dispute involving hundreds of different financial instruments, many trillion euros worth of assets, and thousands of counterparties spread around the entire world. It would be a legal nightmare. A full-blown breakup of the euro would be exactly such a disaster.

The legal underpinnings of the euro include no provisions for a breakup, and a full-blown breakup would leave financial markets devastated by ruthless legal warfare. Legal issues would have to be dealt with in an ad hoc fashion, case by case. Courts would have to make thousands of decisions, contract by contract, regarding which currency to use and at which exchange rate. The legal uncertainty would be immense, and processing the decisions could take years.

THE END OF THE EURO

In the autumn of 2011, markets in the eurozone were deteriorating fast. The Spanish and Italian bond markets had come under intense pressure, and policy makers had no credible backstop in place to support the markets.[1]

The markets were in a state of panic. Because there was no obvious credible solution, an imminent funding crisis for important eurozone sovereigns was a real risk. But could the eurozone survive if a founding country, such as Italy, were to default under disorderly circumstances and leave the euro? It was a troubling question. After a meeting in Rome in the autumn of 2011 with Angela Merkel and Nicolas Sarkozy, the Italian prime minister, Mario Monti volunteered an answer[2]:

> [Sarkozy and Merkel] confirmed their support for Italy, saying
> that they are aware that the collapse of Italy would inevitably lead
> to the end of the euro.

The rising risk of a potentially full-blown eurozone breakup triggered by a funding crisis in Italy was a cause for new thinking. It raised philosophical issues: What would the end of the euro actually mean? What would happen to bank notes, deposits, bonds, and equities denominated in a currency that no longer existed? Would a euro note (or euro coin) be any different from Monopoly money if the currency itself had died? This last question was unfathomable.

GETTING AWAY FROM THE NOISE

It can be difficult to think clearly about long-term issues when you're on a trading floor. The noise level tends to follow the minute-to-minute price action in the market. You get a good sense of what is moving the market in the short term, but the noise distracts you from longer-term issues. Inevitably, you try to make sense of the short-term news flow and the related market wiggles.

In the middle of the panic in the autumn of 2011, I decided to work from home for a week to get away from the noise. Our short-term strategy had already been clearly spelled out. We were very bearish on eurozone peripheral bonds and on the euro, given the deteriorating market dynamics and the lack of a credible policy response at the time. It was time to think about the long-term scenario that nobody wanted to contemplate: the full-blown breakup of the euro.

It was mind-boggling. What would happen to all the financial assets and liabilities denominated in euros, amounting to trillions, if the euro ceased to exist? Would they all be worthless? Would the old euros change into new currencies?

Almost no research had been done on the topic, so I took a different approach. A few colleagues and I reached out to experts in the field of contract law and the process of sovereign default. In addition, we had detailed discussions with internal experts from the legal departments of Nomura Securities in London and New York.

At the same time, we frantically studied historical examples of currency union breakups and previous instances of currency redenomination. We studied the legal details of the redenomination process that took place when the euro was introduced in 1999. At the time, the euro replaced both the previous national currencies and assets and liabilities that were denominated in ECU (the precursor currency to the euro, used by some institutional investors). We also studied historical examples of currency union breakups, including the breakup of the Czechoslovak currency union, the breakup of the ruble zone, and even the breakup of the Austro-Hungarian Empire almost 100 years earlier.

The conference calls we engaged in involved seasoned experts in financial contract law with experience from past debt restructurings and knowledge of obscure examples of case law throughout history. We learned about concepts that we had never heard about before: *lex monetae*, frustration of contract, and the peculiar specifics of English law. And we became very familiar with the concept of *redenomination* (the term used by lawyers to describe a change in the means of payment on a contract). It was like going back to school, except that the teachers spoke with a more distinct version of Oxford English than I had ever heard before.

The more we learned about the legal aspects of shifting from one currency to another, the more convinced we became that the legal constraints involved in a full-blown eurozone breakup could turn out to be far more important than the basic economics.

We also came to the conclusion that many of the economists who expressed strong opinions in the media about the preferred policies for the eurozone seemed to be unaware of many of the binding legal aspects involved in the process of breakup. Not everybody was thinking before he or she spoke.

WHAT GOVERNMENTS CAN AND CANNOT CONTROL

One basic lesson from our research was that governments have the ability to alter financial contracts governed by their own laws, including the currency used in those contracts. Within law, there are two relevant terms here.

The first term is *governing law*. This essentially specifies which body of law governs a certain financial contract, whether it be English law, German law, or New York law, to name a few examples.

The other term is the *legal jurisdiction*. This term refers to which courts will deal with a dispute. Each financial contract will specify, sometimes in very small print, which courts—Italian courts, Japanese courts, or French courts, again just to name a few examples—will make any needed rulings.

Often, but not always, the two terms overlap. If both the governing law and the jurisdiction are English, it means that English courts will have to make a ruling using English law. But sometimes the situation is more complex, and the governing law and the legal jurisdiction of a financial contract are not the same.

By studying history, we could find plenty of examples of governments changing their country's currency. In general, this was done through so-called currency or legal tender laws, which were typically approved by parliaments as part of the transition process from one currency to another.

In the full-blown breakup scenario, in which all eurozone member countries would go back to their own national currencies, governments would be able to redenominate many financial assets (such as bank deposits) into the new local currency. It was clear from our legal analysis and the historical examples we had encountered that governments were in control of their own laws and would be able to redenominate financial assets and liabilities governed by their own laws. This was the easy part.

THE PROBLEM WITH INTERNATIONAL LAW

While governments could control their own laws, there was a basic problem with international laws. Such laws were outside their reach. Redenomination of contracts using foreign law, such as euro bonds issued under New York law or large syndicated loans to companies issued under English law, would not be possible. The crux of the problem was a mismatch between the areas of legal control and the countries that needed to control their currency. So even if Spain would like to redenominate a Spanish government bond issued under English governing law, it would not be able to do so.

This creates a paradox: what would happen to financial assets and liabilities that were outside the jurisdiction of the eurozone countries if the euro ceased to exist? For example, if the euro ceased to exist as a function of a full-blown breakup, what would happen to a loan made in euros by a U.S. investment bank to a big industrial company in Poland? Would the loan now be in U.S. dollars? Would it now be in Polish zloty? Or would something else happen? The lender might have one preference and the borrower another. There would be a potential dispute of this nature for every single financial contract, but ultimately a judge would decide. These disputes would be the catalyst for widespread legal warfare.

A TASTE OF LEGAL WARFARE
IN THE EUROZONE

Europeans got a taste of legal warfare during the Greek debt restructuring in early 2012. At the time, the Greek government was trying to force private-sector bond owners into a deal that could cut its debt by at least half. To make the deal happen and impose these huge "haircuts" on investors, the Greek parliament voted to change the legislation underlying government bonds issued under Greek law.[3] Many investors had not realized that this was possible when they initially bought the bonds (in some cases many years earlier). But given its control of local legislation, the Greek parliament could change the terms of the bonds retroactively. The changes were effective in ensuring that more than 95 percent of private investors participated in the restructuring deal, despite taking punishing losses of more than 50 percent of their investments. The parliament did not change the currency of the government bonds at the time, but it could have done so if the plan had been to exit the euro. This could make for some angry investors.

TRILLIONS OF ZOMBIE EUROS

In a full-blown breakup scenario, the implications would be dramatic on an entirely different scale. There would be trillions worth of assets and liabilities denominated in "zombie euros" and outside the reach of eurozone governments. There was no precedent for how redenomination of such assets would be handled. There was no example of this in history.

Importantly, the legal experts agreed that these contracts would remain valid. In their terminology, contracts would not be *frustrated* just because the euro had died. Instead, courts would have to come up with a suitable alternative currency for payment. It would be a legal nightmare, but the various financial contracts that underpin the financial system would not be null and void.

Never before had the world experienced a full-blown breakup of a major international reserve currency. The euro was the basis for thousands of different financial instruments around the world, many of them governed by the law of countries (and states) outside the eurozone itself, such as New York law. For example, the large majority of financial derivatives globally, many of which are denominated in euros, are governed by either English law or the law of the State of New York.

Exit of certain countries from the euro would be economically complex, but it would avoid many of the extreme uncertainties associated with a full-blown breakup, in which the euro would essentially cease to exist as a currency.

REDENOMINATION ANGST

This uncertainty about the present and future euro added to concerns that created a state of panic in late 2011. Investors and banks suddenly had to deal with a risk they had never thought about before.

The unsettledness reached a crescendo when we published our findings in a research report. The paper, written with coauthors Nick Firoozye and Charles St-Arnaud, was called "Currency Risk in a Eurozone Break-up—Legal Aspects." It sounded pretty boring. But the paper attracted unprecedented attention. Its key findings of the paper were quoted immediately by the *Wall Street Journal*, the *Financial Times*, and all the major financial markets blogs. The *Business Insider* blog even labeled it "one of the hottest weekend reads in Finance." You know there is a problem when financial contract law is suddenly hot!

Redenomination risk also became a part of the standard vocabulary within Treasuries and risk management functions around the world, in line with mainstream terms such as *credit risk*, *interest-rate risk*, and *currency risk*.

Those weeks were a bit of a blur. Each day, I had dozens of conference calls with risk managers, treasurers, and portfolio managers around the world. They were all learning a new language, with words such as *redenomination risk* and *frustration of contract* becoming part of their vocabulary. They needed to understand what would happen to their assets and liabilities in various breakup scenarios and adjust their exposures accordingly. They were facing a risk that they had not thought about before, and they needed to reposition their portfolios. The conference calls involved corporations, banks, and investment firms. That was to be expected. But even market participants from the official sector were lining up for advice. While central banks and supranational bodies are close to policy making, they still need to protect themselves financially. They too were drawing up contingency plans and taking precautionary action for various horror scenarios.

Perhaps most noteworthy, just two weeks after the publication of our paper, the Financial Services Authority in the United Kingdom asked all risk managers of major U.K.-based financial institutions to submit detailed assessments of the risks associated with the potential redenomination of assets and liabilities on their balance sheets. Redenomination risk was now also part of the official sector's monitoring of the financial sector.

It was all rather unnerving. I had to be careful to do more yoga than normal so as not to have my head spinning from seeing eurozone financial markets collapsing and thinking about what could happen if a disorderly breakup of the eurozone materialized.

The most troubling aspect of our analysis was the size of the problematic exposures. Local law contracts appeared to be manageable and had historical precedents, but estimating the size of foreign law exposures was another story.

The numbers were frightening. I summarized the size of the exposures in a paper written for the Wolfson Economics Prize (a large one-off prize for the best proposal on how to plan for an orderly exit from the euro):

Euro-denominated exposure in foreign law contracts is very large. In addition to the relatively well-defined exposure in bond markets (in the region [of] EUR1.9 trillion), there may be around

EUR3.8 trillion of exposure in the form of cross-border EUR-denominated loans. In addition, FX related derivatives may involve outstanding notional amounts in the region EUR15–25 trillion (depending on the foreign exchange rate used). Finally, there are extremely large indirect exposures through interest rate derivatives, in the region of at least EUR150 trillion.

All these instruments were governed by foreign law and would create major redenomination issues in a full-blown breakup scenario. Nobody had previously attempted to quantify the amount of eurozone assets governed by foreign laws. Nobody knew how much these positions amounted to. As it happened, our research in this field landed us among the finalists in the Wolfson Economics Prize competition in 2012. More important, the numbers were so big that a full-blown breakup scenario seemed to be guaranteed to create an enormous legal and economic catastrophe.

THE FALLOUT FROM GLOBAL LEGAL WARFARE

The legal deadlock associated with a full-blown breakup would have major implications for financial markets and the real economy. In fact, the legal aspects of the process could well dominate all other considerations.

Think about a situation in which the euro has splintered into shreds. Thousands of counterparties to trillions of euro-denominated assets and liabilities governed by foreign law are trying to determine their future exposures and their day-to-day cash flows.

It is hard to imagine exactly how disruptive this scenario would be. There would be millions of missed payments, enormous and arbitrary valuation losses within the financial system, and a host of related bankruptcies. Meanwhile, deadlock within the legal and financial systems would ensue.

The legal system would have to make thousands of rulings, contract by contract, about zombie euros. There would be no logical easy answer. The legal system would be overwhelmed, and a huge backlog of cases would pile up. It would take years, if not decades, to sort out.

The scale of the eurozone problem is obvious when you compared it with the legal mini-nightmare of Argentina. Argentina defaulted on its foreign law bonds in 2001 and has ignored the decisions of international courts on the remaining government legacy debt. For a period of more than 10 years, Argentina has essentially been unable to have any form of property or financial assets outside Argentina (except within embassies enjoying special sovereign immunity). The financial instruments that are at the center of the Argentine dispute are worth around $5 billion. In the case of the full-blown breakup of the eurozone, however, the legally contentious exposures would easily be worth $5 trillion, or even as much as $200 trillion if you count derivatives exposures.

Adding to the complexity, there would be thousands of counterparties in hundreds of different countries and dozens of legal jurisdictions battling over payments, compared with Argentina's single problematic counterparty.

MITIGATING THE WORST REDENOMINATION NIGHTMARE

I have proposed putting in place a standardized mechanism for redenomination of contracts in this scenario to avoid complete legal deadlock and a total freeze of the global financial system. Such a solution would require a directive at the European Union level and follow-through at the highest level in other legal jurisdictions around the world.

The best solution would be to determine that international euro-denominated contracts should be settled using a new basket currency, which I call the ECU-2, the value of which would be derived from the values of the new eurozone currencies versus the dollar (using weights based on European Central Bank [ECB] equity shares).

This would provide a standard way to settle claims, easing the burden on the legal system and providing a uniform and relatively fair way to settle claims in economic terms. This would not eliminate the cost of the full-blown breakup, but it would probably be the "least disorderly" way of handling the process.[4]

THE WORST TYPE OF EURO BREAKUP

Still, there is little doubt that the death of a major reserve currency such as the euro would create an all-out war within global legal systems. And the lack of continuous settlement of the most basic instruments would freeze the global financial system for some time. Even in normal circumstances, it can take years for the courts to make complex legal decisions. In a full-blown euro breakup, the various legal systems, particularly those in London and New York, would be overwhelmed. The lack of settlement (payment of interest and principal) on trillions worth of standard financial instruments would trigger something resembling financial market anarchy, not only in Europe, but also globally.

The full-blown breakup would be the worst-case scenario, the type of breakup with the most devastating consequences for financial markets and the global economy.

13

Who Should Stay
and Who Should Go?:
The Economics of Exit

W hat if the leaders of each eurozone country took a break from their day-to-day policy making and thought about the currency issue from scratch: should I stay or should I go? What would be the key parameters to consider when thinking about the cost and benefits of leaving the eurozone?

The implications for the country that is going and for those that are staying differ fundamentally depending on who is leaving: a small country or a large one, a weak country or a strong one. In addition, the pre- and postexit policies will determine the overall impact on the economy and the financial markets.

If a very small country leaves, the impact may be limited to the impact on the country itself. The departure of Cyprus, assuming that financial stability in the eurozone is not affected, would hardly have a noticeable economic impact on the rest of the region. The departure of Germany, on the other hand, would have a large spillover effect on the remaining eurozone, since the value of the "remaining euro" would decline as a function of Germany's departure.

Each type of breakup is different. The full-blown breakup is an extreme special case. If a single country were to leave the eurozone, the remaining 16 countries would continue to use the euro. The enormous legal complexity involved in the euro's ceasing to exist altogether (as would be the case in the worst-case, full-blown breakup scenario) would be avoided. For the 16 or so countries staying behind after the exit of a single country, the structure of the eurozone would in principle be the same: to a certain extent, the status quo would be maintained.

Part of the analytical challenge in thinking about breakup (even the simpler forms) is that there are so many different effects in play at the same time. Beyond the short-term issues associated with the actual transition from the euro to an independent currency, there are two main longer-term economic effects involved.

The first is the impact on trade in goods and services with other countries. The second is the impact on the country's ability to service its debt to lenders in other countries. The second effect is an under-appreciated aspect of potential eurozone exit.

These effects need to be considered simultaneously when evaluating the merits of exit holistically. To get to the bottom of the issue, you need to understand the structure of debt, including some exotic legal parameters that economists rarely pay attention to.

HAVE THEY DONE THE ANALYSIS?

It is impossible to know for sure what type of analysis of the cost and benefits of breakup has actually been going on behind closed doors in governments and central banks around the eurozone (unless you were among the very few who were actually doing the analysis).

For good reasons, such analysis has been kept secret in an effort to maintain the façade that the breakup option was never up for consideration.

The *Economist* speculated in August 2012 that Angela Merkel might be reading an internal classified memo about a breakup of the euro. The cover title was, "Tempted, Angela?" This was just speculation, though.

Nevertheless, even within the establishment, some analysis is likely to have been done. Reuters reported in May 2012 that staff members within the Eurogroup (the body of eurozone finance ministers) had agreed to prepare country-by-country contingency plans for the aftermath of a Greek exit. Meanwhile, one day during one of the most intense waves of the crisis, I got a direct hint of what type of analysis was being done.

Out of the blue, I was contacted by e-mail by the office of the prime minister of a eurozone country (it would not be right to reveal which specific country). The question was, "Can you discreetly provide a breakdown of our debt between foreign and local law?" It was a bizarre situation—like Tiger Woods calling you and asking you which clubs were in his own golf bag.

The explanation was that very few people were familiar with the breakdown, and those in the prime minister's office wanted to avoid drawing attention to the analysis they were doing, including among those in the government itself. In any case, this type of analysis was relevant only if you were analyzing the effects of exit from the eurozone or a type of debt restructuring. Plan B–type options have indeed been considered, but always in secret.

THE TRADE EFFECT AFTER EXIT

If a country experiences currency depreciation following its exit from the eurozone, you would generally expect exports to increase and imports to moderate. Everything else being equal, the net effect should be to help boost the country's overall growth.[1]

There is little doubt that if Greece or Portugal exited the eurozone, its home currency would depreciate dramatically. I have estimated that the decline could easily be as large as 40 to 50 percent. For a country such as Italy or Spain, the fall could be in the region of 20 to 35 percent.[2] The actual currency moves following breakup would depend on the specific policy steps being taken and on broader economic trends. In any case, these estimates give a sense of the possible magnitudes. Specific estimates of currency moves in a eurozone breakup are shown in Chart 13.1, with changes calculated relative to a starting exchange rate of 1.30 to the dollar (roughly the average in the first half of 2013).

Arguably, the trade benefit from currency depreciation following exit would be greater when the country is initially uncompetitive

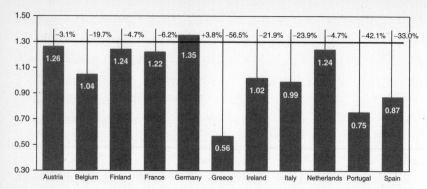

Chart 13.1 Valuing National Eurozone Currencies After Exit

Source: Authors calculations

and its currency is overvalued. In this situation, currency depreciation would allow the country to regain competitiveness and to recapture market share in global export markets. In addition, having a weaker currency would make imports more expensive, encouraging the substitution of domestically produced goods.

An economy's established trade habits also determine the effect on growth, as I mentioned in Chapter 8. An economy with larger exports relative to GDP would see a greater benefit. For example, Portugal would benefit more from currency depreciation than Greece, because its exports of goods and services account for a larger proportion of the economy.

The trade effect is the least controversial part of the analysis, and plenty of research has been done in this area over decades of economic research. In general, you would expect the trade effect to be positive for countries that experience depreciation following exit. Meanwhile, the effect would be the opposite for countries that experience appreciation following exit.

THE EFFECT FROM DEBT OVERHANG

If trade were the only area affected, the analysis would be relatively simple. However, trade is only one part of the picture. Currency devaluation can dramatically affect the real value of a country's debts to other countries—and ultimately its ability to pay them.

The overhang of existing foreign debt will be harder to repay with a weaker currency. The economic fallout through this mechanism is called the *balance sheet effect*.

It works like this. If an economy has large debts in foreign currency, those debts increase, in relative terms, as the domestic currency depreciates. Thus, those debts become harder to repay, especially for entities that have a domestic focus and revenue that is mainly in the domestic currency. Because lenders become more cautious as solvency comes into question, this could cause a credit crunch. Lack of credit will tend to lower investment and may even entirely starve certain companies and sectors of funds, ultimately forcing bankruptcy. Governments can also be hit. In some extreme cases, the balance sheet effect could cause governments to default.

Looking at previous currency crises, this aspect of currency depreciation can be the nail in the coffin for the weaker countries. Conversely, a strong exiting country could be relatively unaffected (the negative balance sheet effect materializes only when a currency depreciates).

LESSONS FROM THE ASIAN CRISIS

To understand what the balance sheet effect could be, it is helpful to look at what economists and investors learned from the Asian crisis.

The Asian crisis ravaged countries such as South Korea, Indonesia, and Thailand in 1997 and 1998. Despite large currency depreciations during this crisis, there was no immediate pickup in growth in these countries. In fact, these countries had both large currency depreciations and large drops in GDP. This was perplexing to many, including to the International Monetary Fund, which during the crisis was advising governments in the region to allow orderly currency depreciation (and to tighten fiscal policy).

Actual economic trends went against the traditional relationship between currency moves and real GDP that is stipulated in simple macroeconomic models.[3] In Thailand, the currency depreciated around 60 percent in the second half of 1997, but the positive effect on growth was entirely absent; in fact, the economy contracted 1.3 percent in 1997, and GDP dropped a further 10.5 percent in 1998. In Indonesia, the numbers were even more extreme, with a currency depreciation of more than 80 percent in late 1997, but a contraction of GDP by 13.1 percent in 1998.

The answer proved to be this balance sheet effect. Corporations, banks, and governments had borrowed in foreign currencies, mainly U.S. dollars. When their own currencies weakened, it became harder for them to service their external debts. Construction companies in Thailand, shipbuilders in Korea, and banks in Indonesia had fixed amounts of foreign currency debt. As their own currencies weakened, they needed more of the local currency to pay back the foreign lenders in the United States, Europe, and Japan. Their domestic currency revenue was not worth as much in foreign currency any more. On top of the immediate effects, there was a negative confidence shock that caused international lenders to become cautious, even where relatively healthy borrowers were concerned.

The crippling nature of the credit squeeze surprised many. Before the crisis, few investors were aware of the size of foreign currency debts. The lack of knowledge about the size and impact of the debt overhang caused miscalculations about the impact of currency depreciation.

In the debate about a eurozone breakup, investors and policy makers initially focused on trade effects resulting from exit. But as the Asian crisis has shown, balance sheet effects can dominate.

BALANCE SHEET EFFECTS ON STEROIDS

Within eurozone countries, borrowing generally happens in euros.[4] Governments issue bonds in euros to finance fiscal deficits. Companies borrow euros from banks and in capital markets to invest and expand. Households borrow euros from banks and mortgage lenders to finance consumption and to buy property. There are always exceptions, but the large majority of debt in the eurozone is in euros.

The question is whether these debts will stay in euros following breakup, or whether they can be converted into the new local currencies. The answer depends on the nature of new legislation implemented by governments at the time of a eurozone exit and on the underlying legal parameters of financial assets and liabilities, including deposits, loans, and bonds.

While there are no official statistics on the breakdown of debts between local and international law, it is possible to construct an estimate of the size of the debts that would stay in euros after exit from the eurozone (for reference, I have included proprietary estimates of the breakdown in the data appendix to this book).

What's interesting is that the countries that are under the most pressure, with the exception of Italy, have the most problematic debt structure.

In Greece, for example, all the remaining government debt was swapped into foreign law bonds as part of the debt restructuring in early 2012, and it is now "outside the reach" of Greek policy makers. This means that these bonds would stay in euros regardless of what funky laws they pass in Athens.

Following exit and a switch to local currencies, Ireland, Portugal, and Greece would have foreign currency debts well in excess of 100 percent of GDP. Spain is not far behind, with foreign currency exposure of around 80 percent of GDP following exit from the eurozone.

For comparison, Thailand and Indonesia, which felt considerable pain from the balance sheet effect in the Asian crisis in the late 1990s, had foreign currency exposures of just 30 to 60 percent of GDP going into their respective crises.

If the countries with problematic debt structures left the eurozone, the burden of their foreign currency debts would balloon as their domestic currencies dropped in value. In Greece's case, if you assume a 50 percent drop in the currency value, foreign currency debt would suddenly jump from around 100 percent of GDP to more than 200 percent of GDP (assuming all else equal).

The amount and structure of debt currently would almost certainly lead to widespread bankruptcies in the corporate sector in countries such as Spain and Portugal in the face of large-scale currency depreciation. The foreign currency exposures that would result from exit are so large that it would be a balance sheet effect on steroids.

Linked to this, the risk of sovereign debt default would also be elevated for countries with large debts to foreign creditors. Greece is the most obvious example of this, even after the debt restructuring in 2012 reduced debt levels to some degree.

From this perspective, the negative influence associated with balance sheet effects could easily outweigh the positive impact from trade for a sustained period of time. In reality, exit without some form of debt default seems impossible, with all the additional uncertainties that would entail, including a total breakdown of European cooperation and potential exit from the European Union (in addition to the exit from the eurozone).

ITALY AND FRANCE ARE DIFFERENT

A detailed look at the structure of liabilities for Italy and France reveals a somewhat different picture from the composition of debt in Portugal, Ireland, Greece, and Spain.

While both these countries have high levels of government debt, private-sector external debts are smaller, and the structure of overall debt is different. Since the large majority of both Italian and French debt is issued under local law, it would be possible to convert (redenominate) these debts into the new local currency in conjunction with an exit from the eurozone.[5] Foreign investors who owned this paper might not be very happy, as they would take a loss when the bonds were converted into a weaker Italian currency. But that is the point. For the country that is exiting, the real debt burden can be reduced by redenomination into a weaker local currency. Countries with debts issued under local laws have this advantage: an option to escape part of the balance sheet effect.

So exit without government default is potentially possible for Italy and France—an often-overlooked but very important detail. Most economists and investors simply look at the high debt levels and the fact that its debts are in euros now, and conclude that Italy cannot stand on its own outside the eurozone. But if you look at the specific structure of the country's debt, including the breakdown between local law and foreign law, you get a more nuanced conclusion. Not all euro debts are created equal, and Italy specifically would be able to convert a big chunk of its public and private debt into the new local currency. The same applies to France.[6]

This creates an interesting scenario. France and Italy could possibly have a positive trade effect from exit without a devastatingly negative balance sheet effect. Certain countries might start to use this argument in their favor, although it would probably require a dramatic escalation in political tension between the core and the periphery before the cold cost-benefit analysis would start to figure more prominently in the discussion.[7]

CIRCUMVENTING THE BADNESS

What if a strong country left? Germany and Holland, for example, are generally viewed as being competitive as things stand. This means that exit would lead to currency appreciation relative to the "remaining euro." In this scenario, there would be no negative balance sheet effect. This is the scenario that the people who argue that any form of breakup is impossible seem to have entirely forgotten about.

Relative to the problems with the exit of a weak country, the *exit of the strong* has two important positive side effects. First, Germany would still be able to repay its euro-denominated debts (in fact, perhaps even more easily than before). Second, because the 'remaining' euro would be weaker as a result of a strong country leaving, countries like Portugal would have stronger growth (because of the trade effect) and would actually have an easier time servicing their debts in the future.

George Soros, one of the most successful financiers of our time, has made this point forcefully in a number of op-ed pieces. In a piece on *Project Syndicate* from September 2012, he put it this way:

> Since all of the accumulated debt is denominated in euros, it makes all the difference who remains in charge of the monetary union. If Germany left, the euro would depreciate. Debtor countries would regain their competitiveness; their debt would diminish in real terms; and, with the ECB under their control, the threat of default would disappear and their borrowing costs would fall to levels comparable to that in the United Kingdom.

There is no free lunch, however. Exit of the strong would also mean that the trade effect would work in reverse for the stronger countries. Moreover, there might be an issue of financial stability in the remaining eurozone, depending on the policies implemented following Germany's departure.[8] Finally, banks and financial institutions in Germany would incur losses on foreign assets as a function of domestic currency appreciation (depreciation of foreign currencies). Even so, it would be easier for Germany and Holland to cope with these adverse shocks than for countries such as Greece and Portugal to cope with another economic blow that could even jeopardize their fundamental political and social stability.

From this perspective, it would be a shift in the burden sharing. The strong economies would shoulder more of the burden, but to the benefit of the region overall. In many respects, particularly looking at how the euro would depreciate after an exit by Germany, the eurozone as a whole might be better off if Germany left (strictly from a financial perspective).

For a researcher evaluating a euro breakup on a purely economic basis, this seems to be the least bad scenario. Whether it is also preferable to the current path depends on whether further eurozone integration to overcome the current deficiencies of the currency union is achievable. If it is not, the least costly breakup may be economically the most desirable option.

MARKET IMPLICATIONS

The various types of breakup differ fundamentally in their implications for regional and global markets. Here are a few lessons for investors.

In an exit by a weaker economy (such as Portugal or Greece), you would want to short the government bonds. Given the negative balance sheet effect, there would be a high risk of default. In addition, a short position in the local banks would probably pay off, as the banks have large foreign debts of their own and would face the fallout from severe tension in the corporate sector as well as the risk of government default. The implications for global markets depend crucially on the size of the country exiting. An exit by a very small country, such as Cyprus, is unlikely to cause major regional or global spillover effects. On the other hand, an exit by a much larger country, such as Spain, involving severe bond market tension and potential default would be a major shock to the global banking system and to global markets more generally.

In a French exit, the dynamics would be different. Balance sheet effects would be less dominant, and government default could presumably be avoided. French stocks might actually rally (probably after dramatic short-term volatility), based on the assumption that balance sheet problems would be manageable and that the trade effect can work its way through the system over time as competitiveness improves. However, the new French currency would depreciate relative to the remaining euro, and potentially substantially in the short term (even if the longer-term equilibrium is only moderately weaker relative to the remaining euro). Hence, foreign investors should take a loss on the currency into account.[9] This would affect both stock and bond holdings, and other investments as well. For the bonds, given the low current yields on French government bonds (around 2 percent on a 10-year bond), this would create a potentially large net loss from the combination of currency losses and duration losses, even if default was not a possibility.

In a German exit, investors would want to own German government bonds, as they would have a gain from currency appreciation and probably have additional gains from extremely low expected future interest rates, as well as a safety premium relative to other markets. German banks, on the other hand, could be in bad shape, as they would face a currency valuation loss on their foreign assets in euros (and liabilities, such as deposits, would be redenominated into a new and stronger German currency). Outright bank failures might not happen. Germany has backstopped banks in the past when this was needed, and would be likely to do so again. But bank equity holders could take major losses. Looking at the region, sovereign defaults in the rest of the eurozone could probably be avoided, and there would be no detrimental negative balance sheet effects overall. In fact, growth in the eurozone in the aggregate should be able to recover as a function of healthy rebalancing, potentially supporting markets over time (especially if a breakup of the EU can be avoided). Although the transition would be uncertain, the final outcome could actually be bullish for European equities overall. The remaining euro (without Germany) would be substantially weaker relative to other major currencies, but the growth outlook in the region could be meaningfully improved.

Because markets are forward looking, it is always crucial—at any given point in time—to assess the degree to which a certain scenario has already been reflected in prices. For example, in the summer of 2012, when sovereign spreads were very wide, you could agree that a degree of exit risk was already embedded in market prices. At the current juncture, however, with spreads being substantially narrower, there is neither a large default risk nor meaningful exit risk priced into key sovereign bond markets[10].

THE DIFFERENCE BETWEEN "SHOULD" AND "WILL"

Free democratic countries can choose their own destiny. Greece, Cyprus, or even Germany can decide to leave the eurozone, if that is the country's desire and if it has the political will. While there is no legal provision for exit in the EU treaties, policy makers have already admitted (albeit under pressure) that democratic countries can make such choices.

If decisions about European currency issues were based only on economics, policy makers would be busy tallying up the costs and benefits of exit, and comparing them to the costs and benefits of staying in the eurozone. Within such a framework, the deepening current recessions in the periphery would be viewed as potentially tilting the balance in favor of the breakup option (for some countries, in connection with a decision to default on their government debt).

Similarly, an analysis based purely on economic and financial market effects would lead to the conclusion that an exit by strong countries is likely to be the least costly form of breakup and would circumvent many of the issues associated with negative balance sheet effects and financial market instability. It may indeed be the optimal economic solution altogether, if further integration of the eurozone cannot be achieved fast enough.

But there is a difference between what *should* happen if economic considerations dominate and what *will* happen, given political and historical realities.

If Germany chose to opt for exit, there would be a huge backlash, and potentially even a total breakdown in European cooperation, including a disintegration of the European Union and the common market.

The reason is history. While World War II ended almost 70 years ago, there is still a sense that Germany has a special responsibility for Europe. This is the sense domestically in Germany as well as in Europe more broadly. This creates a huge political dilemma: the solution that is least painful economically may well be politically impossible.

Historical changes in currency regimes have generally happened out of necessity, not because of a forward-looking proactive choice. Milton Friedman, the Nobel Prize–winning economist, once put it this way:

> Only a crisis—actual or perceived—produces real change.

When President Nixon unilaterally decided to break the dollar's link to gold in 1971, it was a necessity resulting from an escalating crisis. Gold reserves were declining, and speculation against the dollar was accelerating. Increasing economic and market pressure forced the decision.

When Russia decided to break away from the rublezone in 1992 it did so because of intolerable policies in Ukraine and other former Soviet republics that were causing inflation and goods shortages in the entire currency union.

When Argentina defaulted and devalued the peso in 2001, it did so because it had exhausted all other policies. It was the last resort, after all other feasible options had been attempted.

Even when Germany signed up for the euro about 20 years ago, it also did so out of necessity (as discussed in Chapter 2). It was the condition required by its international partners—particularly France—in exchange for allowing German reunification to take place.

The bottom line is that the analysis of the costs and benefits of exit will become truly relevant only when countries are pushed into a corner, faced with intolerable pain, and forced to make a radical choice. This could happen in a number of countries, but Germany would seem to be the last eurozone country that is likely to be facing that situation.

Hence, unless the political dynamics in Europe fundamentally change, the types of breakup that are the most relevant for investors and eurozone citizens are the ones that will happen as a function of escalating economic hardship that ignites irreconcilable political differences. These specific scenarios involve the exit of weaker countries, among which France may eventually be in the future if there is no acceleration in reforms. In sum, the tail risk to really worry about is the one that emanates from political crisis: confrontation between strong and weak countries within the eurozone, leading to radical policy change and a form of exit from the eurozone.

The Future Euro:
Investment Implications

The original euro has fallen, and a new version of the euro is under construction. European officials like to call it EMU 2.0. But it is not finished yet, and it is too early to tell for sure what form it will ultimately take.

One thing is certain, however. Developments in Europe have had an unprecedented importance in recent years. News from the eurozone has dominated global financial markets in a way that was unthinkable just a few years ago.

Chapter 14, "Europe at the Center: Europe's Effect on Global Financial Markets," describes how trends in eurozone markets have been a dominant driver of global markets. Going forward, what I call *political risk premiums* will remain a key driving factor for eurozone asset prices and a source of unusual global market volatility.

Chapter 15, "A Road Map for the Future Euro," spells out the leading possible paths ahead for the euro. The interplay between politics in the periphery and in the core will determine whether we end up with a hard euro, a soft euro, or a form of breakup. Investors and savers need to think about entirely new parameters when they ponder which path forward is the most likely one and how it will affect asset markets.

14

Europe at the Center: Europe's Effect on Global Financial Markets

MF Global was a brokerage firm specializing in futures and options, with headquarters in New York. Its franchise spanned the world, and thousands of different clients in the United States, the United Kingdom, and elsewhere relied on its services for hedging and investment purposes. It was a powerhouse, especially in commodity futures, and it was one of the world's largest derivative brokers overall.

In the autumn of 2011, investors began to hear whispers that MF Global had taken new and significant positions in the euro-zone's peripheral bond markets, especially Italian government bonds. These positions, combined with unprecedented volatility in these previously stable markets, quickly became toxic.

A few weeks of intense escalation of the euro crisis in late 2011 catapulted MF Global into distress. Speculation about its position sizes turned into grave concern after MF Global incurred significant losses on its bond portfolio.

Investors and clients of MF Global quickly lost confidence in the institution—investors refused to extend more credit to it, and clients desperately attempted to extract their money. The institution quickly collapsed. The resulting bankruptcy ranked as the eighth largest in U.S. history based on the firm's $40 billion in assets.

This type of bankruptcy—a major U.S. institution taken down by volatility in European markets—was unheard of just a few years ago. But MF Global's demise is just one example of the decisive influence that European economic and financial developments have had on institutions all over the world over the last few years.

GLOBAL FINANCIAL MARKETS ARE SPINNING AROUND EUROPE

Movements in European asset markets, especially government debt markets, have become a dominant driver of global asset markets. Global bank stocks have been pushed around relentlessly, and global government bond markets have started to mimic the European pulse.[1] Currencies have been rocked, too. The Swiss franc, for example, saw dramatic appreciation in August 2011 as eurozone investors looked for protection against uncertainty and poured money into the tiny mountain state.

Even the mighty American stock market, usually driven by U.S. news only, has become a victim of the eurozone's problems. Between 2010 and 2012, the S&P 500 Index managed to rally 28 percent. But when you look closely, this respectable three-year return masked huge month-to-month swings. In the months when eurozone sovereign spreads were declining (that is, improving), the S&P delivered a cumulative return of 47 percent. In the months in which eurozone sovereign spreads were increasing (that is, worsening), the S&P delivered a negative cumulative return of 19 percent. Predicting eurozone dynamics has been absolutely crucial for timing the U.S. equity market for the last few years.

The dominance of European issues has also been crystal clear from my interactions with investors, especially during the most intense crisis waves, when market correlations were extreme. It was no surprise to see global macro hedge funds do comprehensive analyses of European economic and political issues. But it was unheard of to see investors and traders who normally focused exclusively on U.S.

assets suddenly have a keen interest in everything to do with the eurozone. I got calls from regional banks around the United States, corporate treasurers in the Midwest, and mutual fund managers around the world. These investment professionals normally would not spend much energy on developments in a small European country. Now it was all they cared about, and they wanted the inside scoop on the latest developments in Greece, or whatever else was driving eurozone tensions.

There has been some relief. Since the European Central Bank (ECB) provided a backstop for eurozone sovereigns during the summer of 2012, markets have gotten some much-needed respite. Since then, fears about an imminent liquidity crisis have been kept at bay, and day-to-day correlations have somewhat moderated.

Nevertheless, the bigger shocks, particularly those stemming from political issues, still drive global markets. The Italian election news in early 2013 is a good example. When the shocking polls from Italy started to trickle down the newswires on February 25, the S&P 500 Index dropped 1.8 percent. It was the biggest single-day drop in the S&P 500 in the first quarter of 2013.

UNSTABLE CAPITAL

Eurozone capital inflows are also crucial for volatility. Investors are erratically putting money into and pulling it out of markets because of uncertainty. This has had obvious implications for eurozone bond and equity markets, but it has also been decisively important in relation to global markets.

For example, historically, European government bonds have always been safe. Pension fund and insurance company money has been sticky and long-term. Many of these investors were known to hold specific government bonds for decades. But in the first half of 2010, their confidence was shaken, and this caused them to rethink their investments. Foreign investors sold off eurozone government bonds in a flurry. Long-term money quickly shortened its term.

In August 2011, when tensions in the eurozone were escalating, investors around the eurozone started selling large amounts of global equities. In the final five months of the year, they repatriated well over $100 billion of cash from sales of foreign equities, with more than $50 billion in August alone. Because of risk aversion, eurozone investors sold all types of risky assets, and this played an important role in driving global equities down more than 15 percent in less than one summer month.

Not a year later, in early summer 2012, eurozone investors fled from previously rock-solid eurozone investments. They dove into AAA-rated safe-haven bonds outside their own region, and this depressed global yields around the world: in the United States, Canada, Australia, Sweden, and Denmark. U.S. Treasury yields dropped dramatically in the first half of 2012 largely because investors were looking for a safe haven after fleeing European positions.

Finally, in early 2013, European investors returned to U.S. equity markets in force. The inflows from the eurozone soared to $100 billion annualized, up dramatically from the previous years. The weak domestic demand in the eurozone made growth assets from outside the region, including those in the United States, relatively more attractive.

The European savings pool is very large, and eurozone assets are prominent in global portfolios too. The combined assets of pension funds and insurance companies in the eurozone add up to more than $10 trillion. Today, these investors are inclined to move more quickly than in the past. They can put funds into and pull them out of investments more nimbly. Fluctuations caused by this hypermovement into and out of the eurozone have significant impacts on global asset prices.

THE POWER OF SOVEREIGN DEFAULT

Sovereign default is another unprecedented threat in the eurozone. Up until 2009, investors thought the idea of a sovereign default in one of the eurozone countries was ludicrous. In fact, European officials continued to claim that Greece was solvent very far into the crisis, only to oversee a full-blown debt restructuring shortly thereafter.

But sovereign defaults have also historically been a source of significant global market volatility. Take the Russian default in 1998, for example. Severe tension in the Russian market in the autumn of 1998 caused turbulent market conditions. One of the largest global hedge funds at the time, Long-Term Capital Management, collapsed as a result.

In this context, it is worth noting that the sovereign bond markets in the eurozone are extremely large relative to the defaults observed in history. Argentina's $132 billion bond restructuring in 2001 held the previous record for the largest sovereign default. Now Greece can claim this infamous title. Its debt restructuring amounted to €206 billion (or $273 billion converted at the currency rate at the time).

In Greece, the circumstances were different from those in past government defaults, however. That some type of default was coming was well signaled. The tension had been mounting over a period of two years. When the actual default became inevitable, it came as no surprise, and it was managed and orderly (combined with capital injections for the Greek banks to keep them afloat). Ironically, the Greek restructuring generated relief because the even worse outcome of disorderly default had been avoided.

But Spain's government debt is five times Greece's, and Italy's is ten times. Orderly debt restructurings of those magnitudes may not be feasible. The bailout required to keep banking systems alive may be too large, even if the country's European partners were willing to step in. Hence, sovereign default may imply a risk to currency convertibility and the commonness of the currency itself. The impact of such a scenario should not be underestimated. This could trigger a banking crisis of a magnitude the world has not seen since the Great Depression.

The risk of a self-fulfilling funding crisis may have abated since the summer of 2012, but the longer-term risk of sovereign default or debt restructuring continues to loom in the background[2]. Even if eurozone markets have calmed since the summer of 2012, it is hard to ignore this risk as long as public debt ratios continue to increase.

As pointed out forcefully by the *Financial Times*'s Martin Wolf, this is particularly dangerous for the eurozone because it doesn't have matching currency and bond markets. Even if the ECB is trying its best, there is no lender of last resort at the national level that can unconditionally support government finance when needed.

Sovereign default risk has also emerged as a key catalyst of violent swings in global currency markets since 2010. Historically, the values of major currencies, such as the dollar, the euro, and the yen, have been driven mainly by growth and monetary policy parameters. But the presence of default risk in the eurozone has changed the fundamentals that drive the euro and made it more vulnerable to risk premiums.

THE EUROZONE'S SIMILARITY TO EMERGING MARKETS

Part of the reason why European markets have become so volatile is that erratic political changes are much more important. Previously, emerging market investors were the experts on politics. They had learned the hard way that politics could trump economics. Now a similar dynamic is in play in the eurozone; indeed, many emerging market investors have started to be more active in the European periphery because yields have jumped and because they know the game.

Politics come into play in relation to asset prices, such as bond prices, when decisions by governments and central banks have the ability to distort the market or meaningfully change the underlying equilibrium. In the world we are now in, European politics matter greatly for asset prices. This is something new.

THE POLITICAL RISK PREMIUM

The importance of politics means that investors in the eurozone need to think about a new concept, which I will call the *political risk premium*. Normally, the overall riskiness of a government bond is linked to country-specific solvency risk. If a country is facing an unsustainable rise in debt, there is an increased risk of default, and as a consequence bond yields will rise. This is generally the way bond pricing works in corporate bond markets and in markets for emerging market government debt. From 2010 to 2012, as it became clear that a default by Greece was a real risk, Greek yields also reflected this dynamic.

However, the eurozone is different today. Crucially, sovereign bond markets are underpinned by a type of cross-border insurance, actual and perceived. Sovereign bond markets in Greece, Portugal, Ireland, and Cyprus are explicitly buttressed, since their funding needs are covered by the European bailout fund. In Italy and Spain, and perhaps elsewhere too, bond markets are implicitly underpinned by the ECB's promise to provide help as needed in the future through government bond purchases.

Spain in the summer of 2012 illustrates the importance of the insurance effect. Before the ECB came to the rescue with a promise of potentially unlimited support, Spanish bonds and spreads versus Germany were trading primarily on the basis of underlying fundamental risk relating to Spain. The Spanish 10-year bond yields reached 7 percent at the time. After the ECB's promise to provide backstop, yields compressed significantly, to a level below 5 percent.

Still, markets are unconvinced that the commitment is a 100 percent guarantee. At 4 to 5 percent, Spanish bonds yields are well below the 7 percent level observed before insurance was provided, but they are still well above German bond yields, which are consistently trading below 2 percent. If there truly were a perceived 100 percent guarantee, the yields would be roughly the same.

The current spread relative to Germany reflects the risk that the insurance will disappear or be ineffective in the future. You can think of the current yield spread between Spanish and German bonds as the product of *the probability that insurance will fail* and *the fundamental spread* that would prevail without insurance. For this reason, bond spreads are influenced by what you could call a political risk premium that captures the risk that cross-border insurance for bonds in the periphery will fail somehow.[3]

Similar to the way stock prices are a function of equity risk premiums and fixed-income instruments are affected by liquidity premiums, eurozone bond markets are now influenced by swings in the political risk premium.

Going forward, questions about political cooperation and cross-border solidarity are crucial. They can spur spikes in the political risk premium and jolt yield spreads. Importantly, volatility in the political risk premium may be even more influential than variation in the domestic fundamentals.

Spikes in the political risk premium can arise in two ways.

First, a breakdown in cooperation, so that the insurance effect disappears entirely, will lead bond spreads to jump back to the level associated with domestic fundamentals.

Second, a change in the "insurance framework," as we have seen in and around Cyprus in early 2013, where some depositors took losses, can cause the insurance effect to be less powerful. In connection with sovereign bond markets, this would happen in the case of a planned debt restructuring that forces losses on bond owners. Bond spreads will need to capture the risk that policy makers may at some point make an active decision to force private-sector creditors to take a haircut. The notion that the insurance may provide only partial coverage is a part of the overall political risk premium, too. It is like an insurance policy where you don't know what the deductible amount is. Such insurance is clearly going to be less valuable.

Importantly, political risk is often binary, like a jump process in physics or statistics. However, investors prefer stability and predictability to random discrete changes. They would like to know: Will there be insurance or not? Will bonds be restructured or not? In reality, an opaque political process determines the outcome. We have seen time and again—in Greece, in Spain, in Cyprus— that this process generates ad hoc outcomes. Investors are likely to be dealing with this unpredictability for years to come until the currency union takes a more final form and the rules of the future euro are set in stone.

POLITICAL EXPLOSIONS

The most important risks for the market are no longer bond auctions, deposit flight, and bank bailouts. Investors have moved away from concerns about imminent funding issues. The concerns are now about fragile political relationships. What political shock could be in store?

Again, a quick flashback in time is instructive. Developments in 2005 provide a template. During 2005, a number of eurozone countries conducted public referenda on a new treaty called the "Treaty Establishing a Constitution for Europe (TCE)." But the TCE was rejected by referenda in both France (55 percent against) and Holland (62 percent against). As a result, the process was put on hold.[4]

Even then, the markets understood the importance of sound legal underpinnings for European institutions. Within a week of the French rejection, the euro was down 3 percent. Importantly, that was during an otherwise very calm global market environment in which equity, bond, and credit markets were moving within narrow ranges. Euro crisis dynamics were simply not in play yet.[5]

In the current situation, where the very viability of the euro project is up for debate and there is an urgent need to reinvent the eurozone, the impact of a failed referendum could be severe. If a constitutional crisis is holding the integration process hostage, this will have dramatic economic and financial market implications. Political risk premiums will spike, and since the recovery in peripheral bond prices since the summer of 2012 has been driven by the insurance effect (which implicitly relies on close cross-country political collegiality), bonds will weaken dramatically.

Because markets are forward looking, even the fear of a failed referendum, such as a bad opinion poll, could potentially be a big market-moving event.

Back in 2005, the euro took a 3 percent hit as a result of a failed public referendum and greater uncertainty about the future of European institutional arrangements. In today's world, where these very arrangements are crucial to the future of Europe, it would be no surprise to see an impact many times that of 2005.

Ironically, the weaker the eurozone becomes, the more influence it has over global markets. Catalysts are increasingly political rather than economic or financial market–related. Unexpected political events in Europe have the potential to move global markets in ways we have not been used to in the past.

HOW DID WE GET HERE?

A complex political process underlies the current effort to reinvent the euro. The process is being driven by the interplay between political constraints within each country rather than by a grand vision for Europe. So far, politicians have shied away from integrating Europe on a more profound level.

But this leaves troubled countries with little room for active macroeconomic policy. Economic adjustment is painfully slow, as can be seen in the historically deep and prolonged recessions in several eurozone countries. The dynamics differ fundamentally from those of past business cycles, and policy makers and market participants have yet to fully realize it.

The euro's future depends on how this scenario plays out. Underfunded countries are required to stick to austerity measures in order to receive continued support from their European partners. But potential political issues are heating up in Greece, Cyprus, Italy, Spain, and Portugal. Economic pain is becoming nearly intolerable, and the promise of recovery remains elusive. Political risks are clearly rising. A public countermovement to spending cuts—a revolt against austerity—could eventually become a huge risk.

The eurozone is based on cooperation among independent countries without a formal political union. This is a process that is fraught with uncertainty fostered by a myriad of political risks. These risks are increasing in line with economic weakness and the eroding credibility of the current policy strategy. Political fragility and the ever-present potential political crisis make the eurozone a source of continued instability.

It is the interplay between these political forces that will determine the direction of the eurozone in the years to come.

A DECISION TREE FOR THE EUROZONE

During the most intense waves of the euro crisis, it appeared that we were close to a market collapse. The most fundamental funding markets—those for banks and governments—were on the cusp of a breakdown. Further deterioration would have precipitated large-scale bank failures and disorderly sovereign default, in the face which the currency would have splintered. We were on the edge of the breakup of the eurozone.

Since then, the European Central Bank (ECB) has assumed a more prominent role as a lender of last resort. With ECB support in place, the risk of a self-fulfilling liquidity crisis has substantially diminished. The safety net provided by common European institutions is providing a backstop. We are now in a form of political equilibrium in which both the core and the periphery generally respect the rules of a game defined during the crisis.

Here's what that means. The core is fulfilling its commitment by providing financial insurance for the weaker countries. This is happening through the European Stability Mechanism for the countries with explicit bailout programs. In addition, the ECB's promise to buy unlimited quantities of sovereign bonds if needed is providing an implicit backstop for Spain, Italy, and potentially others. The weaker countries are holding up their end of the bargain by sticking to certain fiscal austerity measures and structural reform programs demanded by the core.

Since the summer of 2012, this two-way agreement has kept eurozone bond markets in a somewhat more stable state. Despite continued underlying economic weakness and further rises in government debt levels, bond yields in the periphery, from Greece to Italy, have come down. Volatility has moderated, too.

In this fashion, actual and perceived cross-border solidarity has helped to stabilize otherwise vulnerable sovereign markets. But in

15

A Road Map
for the Future Euro

The eurozone is in a transition phase. The old euro, as originally designed, has been abandoned. A new euro, backed by
a more proactive central bank and supported by steps toward
additional integration, is being developed. But the process is moving
slowly and is being stifled by the member countries' reluctance to
commit to a closer political union.

During the transition, the future euro's defining characteristics
will remain uncertain. In coming years, political decisions, often binary in nature, will play a disproportionate role in determining the
fabric of the new version of the currency and the course for European economies and global markets.

There are two main dimensions of political uncertainty.

We do not know whether the peripheral countries will continue
to stick with an austerity strategy. Will Italy be able to pursue further
painful budget cuts in the face of continued disappointing growth?
What about the other countries that are struggling with multiyear
recessions? The strategy is losing credibility, and local politicians are
growing tired of defending policies that are not yielding results.

We do not know the degree to which the core countries are willing to compromise on their economic philosophy in order to save the
euro. Can Germany be converted to believe in permanent transfers
to the rest of the eurozone? Is the Netherlands going to be willing to
give up further sovereignty to make European institutions stronger?
Key principles have already been violated, and the appetite for further bailouts or compromises on quid pro quos is nearly exhausted.

order for this insurance to be valid, continued political commitment from both sides is required. If that commitment fails, from one side or the other, the entire framework will fall apart.

The behavior of the two different groups of countries will determine whether the equilibrium can hold and which specific form it takes. Since 2010, the rules of the game have been defined by a series of political agreements. From a game-theoretic perspective, one can argue that the core countries have defined the rules of the game and that the periphery is next to move. It is now up to the periphery to show its hand.

In the summer of 2012, I wrote a research note called "Forget About Economics." It was during the period when European policy makers were finally realizing that the old structures of the eurozone would not suffice, and that a new structure involving greater cooperation was needed. Some investors thought my angle was a bit strange. The note focused on political indicators: the compositions of eurozone parliaments, trends in opinion polls, and public opinion concerning the euro and European institutions. Indicators of this type may matter the most in the eurozone today because the political process is so crucial to achieving further integration and maintaining a degree of stability. Market participants will have to come around to this new way of approaching investments in Europe. They are used to focusing on economic indicators and balance sheet analysis (the stuff you traditionally learn about when you study business, economics, or finance). But it is now crucial to venture into the political and sociological domain.

Chart 15.1 illustrates the main branches of the Eurozone decision tree.

THE HARD-CURRENCY BRANCH

If the peripheral countries stick to austerity, the long-term adjustment through internal devaluation will eventually bring about economic change. It may take many years, and some government debt restructurings may be needed along the way, but eventually these countries'

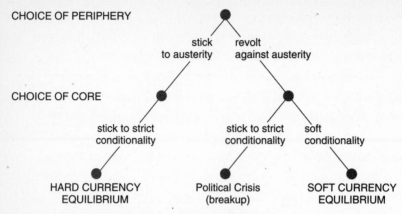

CHOICE OF PERIPHERY

stick   revolt
to austerity   against austerity

CHOICE OF CORE

stick to strict   stick to strict   soft
conditionality   conditionality   conditionality

HARD CURRENCY   Political Crisis   SOFT CURRENCY
EQUILIBRIUM   (breakup)   EQUILIBRIUM

Chart 15.1   The Eurozone Decision Tree

competitiveness will have improved sufficiently to make a difference, as was the case under the gold standard. At that point, more respectable overall growth will return, driven partly by stronger exports and partly by rising confidence. The amount of time this will take will depend on each country's starting point and on the speed of reforms.

If the periphery sticks to austerity, you would expect the core countries to provide sweeteners along the way to keep the process moving. This has already happened in both Ireland and Greece, for example. After sticking to their obligations for a period of time, both countries have received better lending terms and less severe austerity demands.

The hard-currency branch of the decision tree is defined by weak overall eurozone growth for a multiyear period combined with low inflation (and certain pockets of outright deflation). It is an extension of the path we have been on since the summer of 2012. It is likely to involve weakness of the euro against the currencies of key trading partners during the period in which growth is depressed.

The degree of the currency weakness will depend on performance outside the eurozone (currencies are always a relative game). The fall of the euro could be pronounced if U.S. growth recovers further. The growth differential is already very wide (with U.S. growth near 2 percent and eurozone growth still negative in 2013). If U.S.

growth recovers further into 2014, which seems likely, we would be in a situation where there is a historically large growth differential between the world's two largest currency unions, with pronounced implications for asset prices.

On the hard-currency branch, the fall of the euro would be a cyclical type of weakness, comparable to the euro's weakness in the early 2000s, when the euro traded below parity versus the dollar.[1] The weakness would be driven by growth underperformance, relatively easy monetary policy in the region, and capital flows away from the eurozone and toward higher-growth economies elsewhere. Such a pattern could last for a period of some years.

Over time, however, the cyclical conditions in the eurozone economy would normalize and growth would start to recover. After the transition phase, the euro should be able to recover lost ground.[2]

In the hard-currency equilibrium, monetary financing of fiscal deficits in the weaker countries through the European Central Bank would be avoided. There would be no money printing specifically for the purpose of bailing out troubled sovereigns. The peripheral countries would stick to austerity for the long run, and where they were absolutely needed (because of unsustainable debt levels), orderly sovereign debt restructurings would be implemented. Disorderly sovereign defaults and accidental splintering of the currency would be circumvented.

A continuation of relatively conservative monetary policy in the eurozone would also imply that the euro would not suffer any permanent debasement resulting from rising inflation risk. It would remain within its historical range, even if it initially moved toward the weaker end of this range.

On this branch of the eurozone decision tree, a devastating shock to the global financial system would be dodged. Both disruptive sovereign defaults and destabilizing splintering of the euro would be averted. A hard euro resembling Germany's old deutsche mark would be the ultimate outcome. After a period of weakness and uncertainty—albeit potentially quite prolonged—a strong European currency could reemerge.[3]

This branch of the tree would potentially be very painful for millions of European citizens, who will continue to endure the pain from deflationary adjustments during a multiyear transition period. But it would be a path of relative stability from a global financial markets perspective, and to the extent that the equilibrium is stable and valuations are currently depressed by the remaining pricing of tail risk, eurozone equities may also have the potential to rally.

THE POLITICAL CRISIS BRANCH

If the periphery abandons austerity, uncertainty rises dramatically. We are now on an entirely different branch of the eurozone decision tree. On this branch, there are two fundamentally different subbranches. Which subbranch we end up on depends on the core.

The core's next move involves a choice: will it stick to strict conditionality and uncompromising demands on the periphery, or will it give in on some of its conditions?

If the core sticks to its guns, we are in a situation of outright political crisis. The position of the periphery is incompatible with the position of the core. This scenario can quickly morph into economic and financial market crisis.

Ultimately, this is the scenario that can lead to a breakup of the currency union. It has frightening parallels with the breakup of the rublezone about 20 years ago. There are several variants of this scenario (as discussed in Chapters 11 to 13). However, all of them involve the exit of one or more countries from the eurozone, and, for political reasons, most likely the weaker ones. In most of these versions, exit would happen in parallel with some form of disorderly sovereign debt default.

On this branch of the tree, the cross-border insurance provided by the core would become invalid for one or more countries. Political risk premiums would explode. Markets would jump from one price equilibrium to another. Sovereign bond markets in particular would see yields spike dramatically. Government debts would be unsustainable because of much higher yields and negative balance sheet effects (as discussed in Chapter 13). Debt default could happen quickly, either by government choice or through a market breakdown.

The magnitude of the shock would depend on the epicenter of the political earthquake and on the local and regional postcrisis policy response to the eruption.

A political crisis involving a very small country would potentially be manageable, even if it includes exit from the euro (Cyprus would be an example of this). This would be especially true if the crisis is viewed as an isolated case, and if spillover effects to other markets can be contained. A crisis involving a larger eurozone country is an entirely different matter. For example, an exit by Spain would be a different kettle of fish altogether.

A severe political crisis leading to a form of euro breakup involving a large eurozone country would have wide-ranging market implications. It would be a tremendous strain on the eurozone banking system through direct losses. Confidence would be lost. Political risk premiums would spike, not only in the crisis country itself, but more broadly.

This scenario could also include a dramatic short-term decline in the euro. The risk premium on the currency would reach a new crisis high that would drive the euro to new crisis lows versus other global currencies. I have estimated the size of the risk premium on the euro during the crisis using various different models. These models generally come to the conclusion that the peak premium, observed in Q2 2010 and the summer of 2012, was in the area of 15 to 20 percent. Hence, in the face of a bigger shock, such as that related to a sizable country exiting the euro, it would be no surprise to see the remaining euro move 25 to 30 percent lower, or even more in the very short term.

Meanwhile, the combination of disorderly sovereign defaults and outsized near-term euro depreciation would be a dramatic shock to global markets. It would lead to intense pressure on the financial sector globally, and broader global equity markets would probably see pronounced weakness (especially since valuations in some sectors have been getting richer over the last few years). As usual, safe-haven bond markets outside the eurozone would stand to benefit, including the U.S. Treasury market.

Even if the euro has the potential to stabilize over time by regaining status as a hard currency, the short-term effects could be very severe and disruptive.

Then (after the uncertainty has been resolved, exits and defaults have happened, and markets have adjusted—potentially after several quarters of turmoil) the value of the remaining euro may stabilize. Its level could potentially even recover substantially from an initial undershooting. It all depends on the nature of the breakup: which countries are left and which policies are implemented in response to the partial breakup. The euro's long-term characteristic as a hard currency could potentially be preserved if conservative countries remain in control of the remaining eurozone and the ECB.[4]

The political crisis branch of the eurozone decision tree would create the most financial market instability. Depending on the nature of the crisis and the type of splintering, it could produce a very severe financial shock. If large-scale sovereign defaults happen, the short-term impact on global markets will probably be bigger than any of the previous four crisis waves we have observed during 2010-2012. This is especially true because political shifts can happen abruptly, taking markets by surprise. If the exit process is then mismanaged, another full-blown global financial crisis would be a real risk.

To complicate matters, this branch of the decision tree could also put broader European cooperation, including at the European Union level, in jeopardy. The consequences of such a breakdown are far-reaching. It would surely add further to uncertainty and market unease.

THE SOFT-CURRENCY BRANCH

What about the other subbranch of the tree? This is the branch on which the periphery revolts against austerity, but *the core responds by compromising on conditionality* to save the euro and to avoid an explosive political crisis. On this branch, the situation is fundamentally different from both the hard-currency equilibrium and the political crisis branches.[5]

Here, the ECB would provide support for sovereign bond markets in the periphery (through activating the Outright Monetary Transactions [OMT] program). The ECB might even provide monetary support for governments for a sustained period of time. This is the scenario that German central bankers fear most. It is a scenario of potentially "addictive monetary financing," to use Bundesbank president Jens Weidmann's words. Ultimately, it is the scenario that creates heightened inflation risk for the eurozone overall.[6]

Disorderly sovereign default would be avoided. Support for weaker countries would happen through implicit transfers in the form of central bank financing (rather than through fiscal transfers from a eurozone budget). Uncertainty would be less extreme in the short term, compared to the political crisis scenario. There would be no violent spike in the risk premium on the euro, and a near-term collapse of the euro might be avoided. Instead, the risks to the euro would pertain more to the long term.

Eventually, there would be a risk that the ECB would have to support certain eurozone government bond markets permanently through monetary expansion. This risk becomes particularly acute if the presence of the central bank backstop leads to relaxation of fiscal standards and permanently higher deficits. This is the moral hazard effect, which is a source of nightmares in Berlin, The Hague, and Helsinki.

The euro would be vulnerable to a longer-term decline through inflationary debasement. It would turn into a soft currency. Its purchasing power and its value in relation to other currencies would no longer be protected by a conservative central bank.[7] Its fabric would be different from that of the deutsche mark and perhaps more akin to the old Italian lira, which for decades was on a steady weakening trend versus other major currencies.

This soft-currency equilibrium would have less short-term impact on global markets than the political crisis branch. Debasement would happen only gradually over time. It would be a creeping form of weakness, although a clear signal that the ECB was softening its stance on conditions could create a step jump. But while the euro would be facing a long-term decline, both destabilizing sovereign default and the extreme uncertainty surrounding a splintering of the currency would be avoided. Finally, near-term growth could also potentially be stronger. Because of this, this branch could be relatively favorable for global risk assets and for assets in the eurozone periphery. A somewhat higher inflation level in the region could even avert some of the cost of deflationary adjustment, allowing internal devaluation to happen at a lower cost.

Meanwhile, certain other eurozone assets would be under pressure. For example, the value of core eurozone fixed-income investments (for foreign investors) would decline as a result of both currency depreciation and a repricing of expectations for future interest rates. German bonds in particular could be a very bad investment for investors, especially foreign investors, who would face both losses resulting from currency depreciation and losses resulting from rising interest rates (related to rising long-term inflation expectations).

On this branch of the tree, the fallout from abandoning austerity means a softer euro.[8] The long-term trend for the euro would be fundamentally different from that on the other branches. Over time, the value of the euro would erode, and it would be expected to break out of its historical range to the weak side versus currencies with lower inflation risks. It would fall in value, and potentially by a substantial amount over time. But other growth-related assets and export-oriented sectors could potentially benefit if the nominal exchange rate overshoots (creating real depreciation).

The peripheral countries are generally still sticking to the austerity strategy and the European Central Bank has so far not activated its new bond buying program (OMT). Hence, we are not yet on the soft-currency branch of the tree. But the rhetoric of European monetary policy makers is starting to soften on the margin. In July 2013, ECB president Draghi announced that Eurozone interest rates would be kept low for 'an extended period' in an attempt to send a stronger signal that monetary policy would be kept easy in the future[9]. Pronounced and persistent economic weakness in the eurozone is gradually softening the ECB.

A FOURTH WAY: PROACTIVE TRANSFERS OR EXIT

In theory, there is another option: a fourth branch of the tree, characterized by proactive choice by the strongest eurozone country, Germany (perhaps in coordination with other creditor countries).

If meaningful further integration cannot be achieved and if a soft-currency equilibrium cannot be agreed upon, the result would be that the eurozone remains an incomplete monetary union indefinitely and that growth will continue to suffer. This would be a situation of increasing political fragility and vulnerability to repeated crises.

To escape this deadlock, a temporary policy of ad hoc bilateral transfers could be a way to jolt the peripheral economies out of recession, turn around political sentiment, and overcome the rigidity involved in decision making at the EU and eurozone levels. Transfers from the strong hands could take the form of special support for the unemployed, cross-border investment programs, direct bank capital injections, or proactive debt forgiveness. Regardless of the specific form, the purpose would be to provide active growth support when and where it is needed the most, and to provide a catalyst for a change in political sentiment. It could be a valuable down payment on Europe's future, facilitating both economic recovery and a greater sense of European unity.

How the political situation in Germany plays out following this year's crucial election may determine whether there is any hope for such a mini-Marshall Plan.

If such a scheme of proactive bilateral transfers is politically impossible, the economically optimal economic solution may be the exit of strong countries from the euro. Again, Germany is the best example (as mentioned in Chapter 13). But such a radical path seems almost inconceivable politically. It would require a phenomenal turn in political sentiment, a seismic shift within Europe's political center.

History shows that real policy change tends to happen only during crises. The fear of the unknown is so great that a bold but uncertain path is embraced head-on only when the alternative is intolerable.

WEIGHING THE PROBABILITIES

The decision tree is a stylized version of reality. It has three main branches: a hard-currency branch, a political crisis branch, and a soft-currency branch (the fourth branch of radical change is mainly theoretical at this point and I don't attach a high probability to it).

The tree describes only the final outcomes at the end of the three main branches, not the dynamics along the path (or other policy dimensions complementing fiscal austerity, such as structural reform). Markets will not wait for the end result before reacting, however. It is the nature of markets to incorporate new information and new risks as soon as they are anticipated. Even a small risk of ending up on the political crisis branch of the tree can have an outsized impact on asset prices well before the final outcome is known with certainty. Changes in the political risk premium have the potential to generate market volatility long before outcomes are known with certainty.

Right now, it may seem that we are on the hard-currency path, with enough effort being focused on fiscal consolidation in the periphery to avert outright political tension or the need for monetary financing of deficits. But there is significant jump risk.

Opposition to austerity is gathering momentum. In April, new Italian prime minister Enrico Letta said to the *Financial Times*: "Europe's policy of austerity is no longer sufficient." More generally, austerity fatigue is spreading in the periphery, and perhaps in France too, calling into question how long painful reforms can be sustained.

Meanwhile, the risk of a political crisis triggered by a failed referendum on a new EU treaty is perhaps already starting to rise. In the spring, German finance minister Wolfgang Schäuble talked about the need for a change in the EU treaty to push through the important parts of the banking union. A treaty change would involve risky public referenda in a number of countries. Finally, early elections in Spain, Greece, or Portugal could put the centrist euro-friendly consensus in question.

There are many different potential catalysts for a change to a different branch, and such a change could happen abruptly. Even if each individual risk may seem small, their joint weight is very significant. This is a consequence of a currency union based on cooperation among 17 independent countries, each with its own political processes, culture, and history. Investors should think about the outlook in a probabilistic fashion, even if we currently seem to be moving on the hard-currency branch.

And this is where the challenge lies. Because the political risks are binary, it is very difficult to quantify the probability of ending up on the political crisis branch (and to pinpoint which specific version of it). Nevertheless, it would be foolish to ignore these contingencies.

BOND STRATEGY: THE RISK OF DEBT RESTRUCTURING

With regard to fixed-income investments in the eurozone, the political risk premium is the key. And even on the hard-currency branch of the tree, the political risk factor is crucial.

If significant further eurozone integration cannot be achieved, there will be no economic mechanism to compensate for lack of monetary flexibility in the short to medium term. In that case, it is likely that peripheral countries will remain stuck in a low-growth deflationary trap for years. The economic dynamics will be similar to those of the gold standard, but the negative effects will be worse because debt levels are much higher in the eurozone today. This will in itself be a drag on growth-sensitive assets in those countries.

More important, persistent low growth may necessitate active debt restructuring for sovereigns (and for other sectors, where possible) to bring debt levels back to sustainable levels. This can happen even in the absence of a political crisis, simply as a function of economic necessity and the limits of cross-border funding arrangements.

The lesson from both the Latin American debt crisis in the 1980s and the German reparations payments in the interwar period is that at some point, respectable growth is not feasible without debt reduction. The specific threshold above which the debt level will be a drag on growth is hard to define precisely (as Professors Reinhart and Rogoff have learned the hard way[10]). But I would personally argue that several eurozone countries are probably above that threshold, given their extreme levels of overall external debt. Importantly, as long as growth in Portugal, Ireland, Greece, and Spain is lacking, this long-term risk will continue to rise.

Hence, a policy of active debt reduction may eventually be needed. While this may be the right solution from a macroeconomic perspective, it would produce losses for private creditors (and potentially official-sector creditors, too). But it may be what is needed in order to break away from subpar growth and deteriorating political dynamics, and to set the stage for future prosperity.

Eurozone bond markets have been rallying significantly since the summer of 2012 because of the insurance effect and positive market momentum (as well as the lack of yield in global fixed-income markets broadly). But the insurance effect can evaporate for many different reasons, including a political decision to go down the route of orderly restructuring.

Investors should be on the alert and not be fooled by the relative market calm observed since the summer of 2012. There is a difference between bond yields that are consistent with fundamentals and yields that have been artificially pushed lower as a result of insurance from the core. Political risk premiums declined as investors got comfortable with the improved backstop infrastructure. But current peripheral bond yields may not take fully into account the future risk of active debt restructuring.

In July 2013, government bond yields in Portugal quickly spiked to around 8 percent on the back of the resignation of a few key government ministers and general uncertainty about the stability of Portugal's governing coalition. In May 2013, the same bonds were trading at a yield just above 5 percent. It is just one example of how the political risk premium holds the key to asset price moves in the eurozone.

People do not buy fire insurance because they think there is going to be a fire. Similarly, investors should take the risk scenario into account, even if they don't regard it as the central case. Asset prices are likely to continue to reflect the mix of possible scenarios (although there may be occasional periods of excessive relaxation), and understanding the politics is key to calibrating the probabilities.

Solidarity between eurozone countries and the provision of bailout funding is likely to be a temporary mechanism to buy time, not an indefinite tool for sustaining unsustainable debts. Hence, there may still be a time to sell certain eurozone bond markets as a result of the remaining restructuring risk.

THE FUTURE VALUE OF THE EURO

In the current environment, where cross-border agreements have the power to dominate the domestic fundamentals in the eurozone, the risk of breakdown in the political equilibrium is the single most important factor. Therefore, swings in the political risk premium are now the primary driver of eurozone assets, from bonds to equities, and, as we have seen in recent years, this matters greatly for global markets, too.

While there are several possible paths, it is notable that many of the different paths involve euro weakness, at least in the shorter term. Hence, from a probabilistic perspective, a fall in the euro's value is one of the clearest conclusions.

During the euro crisis, there were many moments when the euro seemed imminently doomed. However, I am proud to say that during 2010–2012, when those moments occurred rather frequently, I never had a parity (or below parity) forecast for the euro. I am not claiming to have been right all the time, but I avoided that mistake. However, just because the euro has been trading largely between 1.20 and 1.40 to the dollar over the last three years does not mean that that range will hold forever. Crucially, the outlook for the dollar is changing, as the underlying growth trend in the U.S. economy seems to be improving into 2014. This will be a key factor allowing the euro to break out to the downside (ultimately to the benefit of the eurozone economies, in both the core and the periphery).

THINK NEW

To understand European markets and to manage investments proactively, investors need to rethink the role of politics and societal pressures. Poverty is increasing in Greece. The homeless population is growing in Spain and Ireland. An entire generation of new entrants into the labor market is facing dire prospects in Italy and Portugal. Go to London and young graduates from southern Europe will serve you in restaurants and cafés. There are just no opportunities for them at home.

In addition to economic indicators and financial market statistics, investors should monitor opinion polls, public sentiment surveys, and the broader political pulse of the various eurozone countries. Trends in public opinion may be more important than hard economic indicators in coming years.

In stable times, currency unions live quiet lives. As long as the common monetary policy system functions smoothly, nobody deliberates about it or questions it. That has been the case in the United States for decades, and it was the situation during the euro's honeymoon years. During those years, everybody blissfully avoided thinking about the common currency's potential weaknesses.

In times of crisis, however, currency unions can turn into pressure cookers. They can exacerbate existing imbalances and ignite dramatic economic and financial market turmoil. Moreover, currency unions have the potential to catalyze irreconcilable political tensions. At that point, an explosive breakup is a risk.

The future of the euro remains uncertain. It is in the hands of the region's officials and voters. A failed referendum on a new EU treaty, for example, could put us on an entirely new path.

For now, policy makers are determined to preserve the euro and to gradually rebuild the institutional structures underpinning it. While financial markets have calmed, the economic and social cost of an incomplete and dysfunctional currency union continues to accumulate, and progress toward improving its structure is slow.

The people on the streets are feeling the pain, and their voice is getting louder. Whether political fragility will morph into outright political crisis remains to be seen. European policy makers are only now realizing the extent of the recessionary impulse created by their current policy strategy. It will take time to change the policy mix, and it will be hard to win back public trust, especially in those economies that are suffering the most from slow deflationary adjustment.

It would be foolish to dismiss the possibility of severe political tension, given the unprecedented nature of the current crisis, the vulnerability of the system, and the multiplicative nature of the political risk at hand.

Political considerations were the prime motivation for the euro from its birth, and politics will remain the driving force for years to come. Markets are no longer in free fall, but confidence in the European project has been dramatically shaken, and the euro itself has fallen from grace. Europe's next crisis will be political and will have significant implications for global markets. Investors and savers should act accordingly.

Afterword

In the spring of 2013, I attended a conference in Berlin that had been arranged by the Institute of International Finance. Jörg Asmussen, the German representative on the European Central Bank's executive board, gave a speech during lunch. It was delivered in a downbeat German tone (although the language was English), but the message was in fact rather upbeat.

Mr. Asmussen provided an outline of the advantages of the new euro, the reinvented version of the currency that had been created through a series of institutional reforms in recent years. He called it EMU 2.0, and he strongly recommended that European Union countries in Central and Eastern Europe join the new and improved currency as soon as possible.

ANOTHER PREMATURE CELEBRATION

The speech reminded me of Joaquin Almunia's upbeat comments during the 10-year anniversary celebration for the euro in 2009. Again, there was a one-sided focus on the benefits of the euro, with little attention being given to the costs. The glasses were perhaps not quite as rose-colored as Mr. Almunia's had been four years earlier. The shadow of the crisis had created at least a little humility, after all. But the broad perspective was the same: the underlying political drive to empower the euro and expand its reach was undeterred.

One thing that Mr. Asmussen entirely ignored was the potential fiscal cost associated with bailing out fellow eurozone member countries though the European bailout fund or through the European Central Bank itself. New members of the eurozone would probably have to pay part of the bill. But this hidden cost was not a part of the speech. Instead, it ended with the following conclusion:

> [The eurozone] is here to stay. It will survive this crisis, it will emerge from it stronger and more countries will join the euro in the future.

STRENGTHS AND WEAKNESSES IN EUROPEAN INTEGRATION

The key question is what a stronger eurozone really means. A currency's success cannot be measured simply by its value. The euro's success should not be judged solely on the basis of its price against the dollar, or against any other currency. The verdict should ultimately be based on the currency's ability to deliver on the economic, political, and social objectives of its citizens. Can the euro ultimately make people's lives better?

The European Union and the previous incarnations of European supranational cooperation can validly claim significant long-term success. Efforts to integrate Europe over the last 60 years have paid off in terms of increased trade, better cooperation, and more political stability in the region.

The integration of Central and Eastern European countries into the European Union after the end of the Cold War was perhaps the best example of how the cross-border integration process has supported the building of democracy and provided a foundation for lasting peace. For these reasons, the EU was a worthy recipient of the Nobel Peace Prize in 2012. But the European Union, not the eurozone, deserves the credit for those achievements.

What about the eurozone? Based on economic performance during its first 15 years of existence, the euro has failed to deliver economic prosperity for large groups of the region's citizens.

Moreover, the euro is increasingly putting core European values at risk. Income levels within the eurozone are diverging. Social safety nets are under pressure from austerity. Living standards for the unemployed and the elderly are deteriorating in many countries. Finally, trust in democratic institutions is declining. Local policy makers are facing record low approval ratings, while European institutions are viewed with ever-increasing skepticism in more and more countries. This democratic deficit is now one of the euro's key weaknesses.

It is ironic that while European institutions have been a force for building democracy on the fringes of Europe, the eurozone—the symbol and the crowning achievement of European integration—now risks undermining democratic principles at the core of the European continent. The euro crisis may even serve to ignite political extremism in both the eurozone periphery and the core itself, sowing the seeds for political crisis in the future.

EUROPE'S DILEMMA

To complete the monetary union, more integration is needed. To create a genuine and stable currency union without severe internal divergence, more sharing of resources is needed. A common eurozone budget, eurobonds, and common deposit insurance are some of the key ways of facilitating cross-border transfers to weaker regions.

Politically, achieving such a new equilibrium with greater resource pooling is the key challenge ahead. The eurozone is a highly unusual construct: a currency union without a political union. Further integration requires political buy-in from all member countries. At this point, the economic need for further integration is clashing with public sentiment, which is increasingly opposed to handing over additional functions to European officials in Brussels and Frankfurt.

This fundamental dilemma explains why finding a solution to the euro crisis has been so slow. The U.S. template of fast economic integration from more than 80 years ago in response to the Great

Depression is not feasible in Europe because of the absence of a political union. This quandary is set to get even worse in the coming years as growth in the region continues to disappoint. Broken policy promises and fading hope for a better future are denting the credibility of the European integration project in the eyes of voters.

EMBRACING RADICAL CHANGE

Europe is facing a big choice between more and less integration. The current in-between solution of limited integration is failing to deliver results for the citizens of many eurozone countries. To break the deadlock, brave policies that embrace radical change are needed.

Bilateral ad hoc transfers from strong member countries, particularly Germany, could play a crucial rule in turning around both growth dynamics and political sentiment in the periphery. Such a proactive policy step—a mini-Marshall Plan—could act as a bridge to more institutionalized eurozone transfer mechanisms in the future. While this would be controversial, it would be a sound investment in Europe's future.

More proactive policy from the European Central Bank could help too. Inflation is already slipping below target. The risk of persistent deflation (and therefore too high real borrowing cost) is rising. The eurozone is not Germany. The eurozone is struggling to cope with conservative monetary policy and a hard currency resembling the D-mark. The monetary policy stance needs to be softened further, at least temporarily. This is necessary to moderate the pain associated with an extremely challenging economic transition in the periphery and to counter a deflationary bias in the aggregate.

But proactive macroeconomic policy alone will not be sufficient. Policy makers also need to pursue greater transparency and accountability to regain their credibility and initiative more broadly. They need to be honest and realistic about the region's economic prospects and what is needed to overcome the current malaise. They need to put the key facts on the table and ask voters for a mandate for further integration. This is the only path to greater European unity, sustained solidarity, and overall prosperity. You win back trust through honesty; not by repeating old lies.

Policy makers need to overcome the fears that are holding back decisive policy change: fears of a breakup itself, of losing face, or of confronting public sentiment head on. They need to put the question of more or less Europe directly to voters in elections and public referenda in the next few years.

The leaders who will be remembered positively will be those who make visionary decisions and take bold action for the benefits of their citizens, not those who stick to the current script.

Only through closer integration can the current institutional weaknesses of the euro be overcome. But without clear public buy-in, such integration goes against the basic democratic principles that are central to European cultures.

If the public support is there, it is feasible to move ahead at a faster speed and build a real currency union, with elements of more powerful resource sharing embedded in it. This is how to build a strong currency, not in monetary terms, but along the dimensions that matter to the citizens of the eurozone. A euro supported by institutions that have a stronger capacity to deal with regional crisis dynamics and country-specific economic weakness is needed.

If the public support is *not* there, the logical solution is to move back to more independent monetary policies. This would allow economic adjustment through exchange rates to happen fairly quickly, rather than through a decade-long process of painful deflation. There would be large transition costs, but there would potentially be a long-term gain from allowing monetary and exchange-rate policy to reflect persistent structural differences at the country level. This outcome would also be more consistent with current public opinion and therefore in line with European democratic ideals

Any form of breakup of the euro is highly controversial politically; an entire political class has invested immense amounts of political capital in preserving the common currency. These people will not give up the fight easily, that is for sure. But if true reinvention of the euro is politically impossible and the euro cannot deliver on core European values, what is there to fight for?

Data Appendix:
The Breakdown of Eurozone Debts

Charts A.1 and A.2 show proprietary estimates of foreign law external liabilities for 11 eurozone countries. The numbers are broken down into public-sector (government) exposure and private-sector exposure. These numbers are derived through a bottom-up approach, looking at literally hundreds of thousands of different bonds, one by one, and then aggregating the numbers. The details of the method is outlined in "Rethinking the European monetary union" (by Nordvig, Jens and Nick Firoozye).

These tables give a sense of which external debts would be problematic in an exit or a full-blown breakup scenario because they would stay in their original currency (the euro) and therefore would become harder to repay if the new domestic currency is weaker. Chart A.1 focuses on the gross liabilities only. Chart A.2 tries to account for the offset that may be provided by foreign currency asset positions abroad.

Chart A.1 Breakdown of Gross Relevant External Liabilities (% of GDP)

	Austria	Belgium	Finland	France	Germany	Greece	Ireland	Italy	Netherlands	Portugal	Spain
Public position	20%	17%	11%	11%	8%	109%	100%	16%	2%	66%	23%
Central bank	11%	14%	1%	8%	2%	49%	77%	12%	0%	36%	16%
General government	9%	3%	10%	4%	6%	61%	23%	3%	2%	30%	6%
Private position	59%	69%	105%	48%	25%	20%	72%	33%	108%	73%	56%
Bank	44%	50%	84%	36%	19%	16%	24%	21%	87%	48%	34%
Non-bank	16%	19%	21%	11%	6%	4%	49%	12%	21%	25%	22%
Total relevant external liabilities	**80%**	**86%**	**116%**	**59%**	**33%**	**130%**	**172%**	**49%**	**110%**	**139%**	**78%**

Source: "Rethinking the European monetary union"

Chart A.2 Adjusted Net Relevant External Positions Using Partial Weighting of Assets (% of GDP)

	Austria	Belgium	Finland	France	Germany	Greece	Ireland	Italy	Netherlands	Portugal	Spain
Net relevant external position	−2%	34%	−34%	13%	42%	−92%	−73%	−20%	8%	−80%	−50%
Private position	9%	49%	−48%	21%	33%	13%	20%	−8%	−4%	−22%	−31%
Assets	68%	118%	57%	68%	58%	34%	92%	25%	103%	51%	25%
Liabilities	59%	69%	105%	48%	25%	20%	72%	33%	108%	73%	56%
Public position	−10%	−15%	13%	−8%	9%	−106%	−93%	−12%	12%	−57%	−19%
Assets	10%	2%	24%	4%	17%	4%	6%	4%	15%	8%	4%
Liabilities	20%	17%	11%	11%	8%	109%	100%	16%	2%	66%	23%

Source: "Rethinking the European monetary union"

Bibliography

Altafaj, Amadeu. "Brussels Says There's No Way for Eurozone Member to Abandon Common Currency." *Eurotribune*, September 8, 2011.

Athanassiou, Phoebus. "Withdrawal and Expulsion from the EU and EMU: Some Reflections." European Central Bank, ECB Legal Working Paper No. 10, December 2009.

Aussilloux, Vincent, and Lionel Fontagne. "What Benefits from Completing the Single Market?" Centre d'Etudes Prospectives et d'Informations Internationales, *La Lettre du CEPII*, December 2011.

Baig, Taimur, and Ilan Goldfajn. "Monetary Policy in the Aftermath of Currency Crises: The Case of Asia." International Monetary Fund, December 1998.

Bawlf, Patrick, and Dominic O'Kane. "Global Guide to Corporate Bankruptcy." Fixed Income Research, Nomura Securities, July 2010.

Bayoumi, Tamim, and Barry Eichengreen. "Shocking Aspects of European Monetary Unification." National Bureau of Economic Research, NBER Working Paper No. 3949, January 1992.

Bayoumi, Tamim, Richard Harmsen, and Jarkko Turunen. "Eurozone Export Performance and Competitiveness." International Monetary Fund, IMF Working Paper No. WP/11/140, June 2011.

Bernanke, Ben, and Harold James. "The Gold Standard, Deflation, and Financial Crisis in the Great Depression: An International Comparison." In National Bureau of Economic Research, *Financial Markets and Financial Crises*," 1991.

Bofinger, Peter, Lars P. Feld, Wolfgang Franz, Christoph M. Schmidt, and Beatrice Weder di Mauro. "A European Redemption Pact." VOX, November 2011.

Boltho, Andrea, and Barry Eichengreen. "The Economic Impact of European Integration." Centre for Economic Policy Research, Discussion Paper No. 6820, May 2008.

Bordo, Michael D. "The Euro Needs a Fiscal Union: Some Lessons from History." Shadow Open Market Committee, Rutgers University, October 2010.

Bordo, Michael D., and Lars Jonung. "The Future of EMU: What Does the History of Monetary Union Tell Us?" National Bureau of Economic Research, NBER Working Paper No. 7365, September 1999.

Broll, Udo, and Jack E. Wahl. "Mitigation of Foreign Direct Investment Risk and Hedging." *Frontiers in Finance and Economics 7*, no. 1 (April 2010): 21–33.

Buiter, Willem. "Can Central Banks Go Broke?" Centre for Economic Policy Research, CEPR Policy Insight No. 24, May 2008.

Cavallo, Michele, Kate Kisselev, Fabrizio Perri, and Nouriel Roubini. "Exchange Rate Overshooting and the Costs of Floating." Federal Reserve Bank of San Francisco Working Paper, May 2005.

Céspedes, Luis Felipe. "Financial Frictions and Real Devaluations." Central Bank of Chile Working Paper No. 318, 2005.

Chinn, Menzie and Jeffrey Frankel. "Will the Euro Eventually Surpass the Dollar as Leading International Reserve Currency?", in *G7 Current Account Imbalances: Sustainability and Adjustment*, University of Chicago Press, May 2007.

Clifford Chance LLP. "The Eurozone Crisis and Derivatives." Briefing Note, January 2012.

Dalton, John W., and Claudia Helene Dziobek. "Central Bank Losses and Experiences in Selected Countries." International Monetary Fund, IMF Working Paper WP/05/72, April 2005.

Darvas, Zsolt. "Competitiveness Adjustment in Euro-Area Periphery." Bruegel, April 2012.

Davis, Kevin E. "The Concept of Legal Uncertainty: Definition and Measurement." New York University School of Law, Working Paper Series, November 2011.

Dedek, Oldrich. *The Break-up of Czechoslovakia: An In-Depth Economic Analysis.* Aldershot, U.K.: Avebury, 1996.

Dor, Eric. "Leaving the Eurozone: A User's Guide." IESEG School of Management, Lille Catholic University, IESEG Working Paper No. 2011-ECO-06, October 2011.

————. "The Cost of a Greek Euro Exit for Spain." IESEG School of Management, Lille Catholic University, May 2012.

Duisenberg, Willem F. "The Past and Future of European Integration: A Central Banker's Perspective." International Monetary Fund, IMF 1999 Per Jacobsson Lecture, September 26, 1999.

Eichengreen, Barry. "The Break-up of the Eurozone." National Bureau of Economic Research, NBER Working Paper No. 13391, September 2007.

————. "Is Europe an Optimum Currency Area?" National Bureau of Economic Research, NBER Working Paper No. 3579, January 1991.

————. "Was the Euro a Mistake?" VOX, January 2009.

European Central Bank. "Financial Integration in Europe." April 2012.

European Commission. "European Cohesion Policy in Greece." 2009. Available at ec.europa.eu.

————. "European Competitiveness Report 2011." Commission Staff Working Document SEC(2011) 1188, 2011.

Frankel, Jeffrey A. "Contractionary Currency Crashes in Developing Countries." International Monetary Fund, Fifth Mundell-Fleming Lecture, IMF Annual Research Conference, November 2004.

Frankel, Jeffrey, and Andrew Rose. "Is EMU More Justifiable ex Post than ex Ante?" *European Economic Review* 41, no. 3–5 (May 1997): 753–760.

Fisher, Irving. "The Debt-Deflation Theory of Great Depressions." *Econometrica* 1, no. 4 (1933): 337.

Gathmann, Florian, and Philipp Wittrock. "More Power to Brussels?" *Der Spiegel*, August 10, 2012.

"Germany and the EMU." *Economist*, February 12, 1999.

Goldstein, Morris, and Philip Turner. "Controlling Currency Mismatches in Emerging Markets." Peterson Institute for International Economics, April 2004.

Gros, Daniel, and Felix Roth. "Do Germans Support the Euro?" Centre for European Policy Studies, CEPS Working Paper, December 2011.

Halac, Marina, Sergio L. Schmukler, Eduardo Fernández, and Ugo Panizza. "Distributional Effects of Crises: The Financial Channel." *Economía* 5, no. 1 (Fall 2004).

Herndon, Thomas, Michael Ash and Robert Pollin, "Does High Public Debt Consistently Stifle Economic Growth? A Critique of Reinhart and Rogoff", PERI Working Paper 322, April 2013.

Keynes, John Maynard. *A Tract on Monetary Reform*. London: Macmillan, 1924.

Koo, Richard. *Balance Sheet Recession: Japan's Struggle with Uncharted Economics and Its Global Implications*." New York: Wiley, 2001.

Krugman, Paul. "Lessons of Massachusetts for EMU." In *Adjustment and Growth in the European Monetary Union*, edited by Francisco S. Torres and Francesco Giavazzi. New York: Cambridge University Press, 1993, pp. 241–261.

Kydland, F., and E. Prescott. "Rules Rather than Discretion: The Inconsistency of Optimal Plans." *Journal of Political Economy* 85 (1977): 473–490.

Lane, Philip, and Jay Shambaugh. "Financial Exchange Rates and International Currency Exposures." IIIS Discussion Paper No. 229, September 2007.

March, David. *The Euro*. New Haven, CT: Yale University Press, 2009.

Nitsch, Volker. "Have a Break, Have a ... National Currency: When Do Monetary Unions Fall Apart?" CESifo Working Paper No. 1113, January 2004.

Nordvig, Jens. "Currency Risk in a Eurozone Break-up: Valuing Potential New National Currencies." Nomura Securities Fixed Income Strategy, December 2011.

———. "Currency Risk in the Eurozone: Accounting for Break-up and Redenomination Risk." Nomura FX Strategy, Nomura Securities, January 2012.

———. "Preparing for a Greek Eurozone Exit: Part II." Nomura FX Strategy, Nomura Securities, May 2012.

———. "Preparing for a Greek Eurozone Exit: Part III." Nomura FX Strategy, Nomura Securities, May 2012.

———. "Forget About Economics," Nomura FX Strategy, Nomura Securities, June 22, 2012.

Nordvig, Jens, Ylva Cederholm, and Yujiro Goto, "Eurozone March Capital Flows." Nomura FX Strategy, Nomura Securities, May 2012.

Nordvig, Jens and Nick Firoozye, "Rethinking the European monetary union." Paper written for the Wolfson Economics Prize, June 2012.

Nordvig, Jens, Charles St-Arnauld, and Nick Firoozye, "Currency Risk in a Eurozone Break-up—Legal Aspects." Fixed Income Strategy Special Topic, Nomura Securities, November 2011.

Pastor, Lubos, and Pietro Veronesi. "Political Uncertainty and Risk Premia." National Bureau of Economic Research, NBER Working Paper Series No. 17464, September 2011.

Piodi, Franco. "From the Schuman Declaration to the Birth of the ECSC: The Role of Jean Monnet." Cardoc Journals, no. 6, May 2010.

Price, D. H. *Schuman or Monnet? The Real Architect of Europe*. Brussels: Bron Communications, 2003.

Proctor, Charles. *Mann on the Legal Aspect of Money*, 6th ed. New York: Oxford University Press, 2005.

———. "The Greek Crisis and the Euro—a Tipping Point?" Client Advisory, Edwards Angell Palmer & Dodge, June 2011.

———. "The Euro—Fragmentation and the Financial markets." *Capital Markets Law Journal* 6, no. 1 (January 2011): 5–28.

Reinhart, Carmen, and Kenneth Rogoff, *This Time is Different: Eight Centuries of Financial Folly*, Princeton University Press, July 2011.

Rhodes, David, and Daniel Stelter, "What Next? Where Next? What to Expect and How to Prepare." Collateral Damage Series, January 2012.

Rodrik, Dani. *The Globalization Paradox*." New York: Norton, 2012.

Rose, Andrew. "Checking Out: Exits from Currency Unions." Haas School of Business (Draft), University of California, Berkeley, December 2006.

Scott, Hal S. "When the Euro Falls Apart." Working paper, Program on International Financial Systems, Harvard Law School, 1998.

———. "When the Euro Falls Apart—a Sequel." Working paper, Program on International Financial Systems, Harvard Law School, January 2011.

Sinn, Hans-Werner, and Timo Wollmershaeuser. "Target Loans, Current Account Balances and Capital Flows: The ECB's Rescue Facility." National Bureau of Economic Research, NBER Working Paper No. 17626, November 2011.

Slaughter and May LLP. "Euro Break-up/Fragmentation: Impact on Financial Documentation." December 2011.

Steininger, Michael. "Auf wiedersehen, Euro?" *Christian Science Monitor*, April 15, 2013.

Takagi, Shinji, Mototsugu Shintani, and Tetsuro Okamoto. "Measuring the Economic Impact of Monetary Union: The Case of Okinawa." Vanderbilt University Working Paper No. 03-W15, July 2003.

Taylor, Alan M. "The Great Leveraging." Bank for International Settlements conference material, July 2012.

Tett, Gillian. "Banks Bet on a Fractured Europe." *Financial Times*, May 25, 2012.

Towbin, Pascal, and Sebastian Weber. "Limits of Floating Exchange Rates: The Role of Foreign Currency Debt and Import Structure." International Monetary Fund, IMF Working Paper 11/42, February 2011.

Trichet, Jean-Claude. "Address at the Ceremony to Mark the 10th Anniversary of the European Central Bank and the European System of Central Banks." European Central Bank, June 2008.

Weiss, Uri. "The Regressive Effect of Legal Uncertainty." Faculty Paper 30, Tel Aviv University Law School, 2005.

Wolf, Martin. "Why the Euro Crisis Is Not Yet Over." *Financial Times*, February 19, 2013.

Notes

CHAPTER 2

1. Quoted from *Schuman or Monnet? The Real Architect of Europe,* (Brussels: Bron Communications, 2003).

2. Quoted from *From the Schuman Declaration to the Birth of the ECSC: The Role of Jean Monnet,* Cardoc Journals, no. 6, May 2010.

3. For this reason, the EU was awarded the Nobel Peace Prize in Oslo in December 2012. The prize committee judged that the EU's positive achievement as a long-term builder of peace warranted recognition, even in the face of a significant ongoing economic crisis.

4. Greece did not undergo the intense scrutiny that was imposed on applicant countries in Central and Eastern Europe, which had previously been under Soviet rule, before their entry into the EU in 2004 and 2007. Greece's fast track into the EU was a function of its geostrategic position and its NATO membership.

5. According to the rules of the Bretton Woods system (formalized in the IMF's Articles of Agreement), member countries could change their exchange rate's central parity value only with IMF approval, which was contingent on the IMF's assessment that the country's balance of payments was in a "fundamental disequilibrium."

6. Ironically, after decades of pro-market reforms, European leaders have recently reverted to such sentiment, projecting frustration in the direction of undefined evil speculators who were unjustly manipulating various European markets. This time around, the condemnation is not so much of currency traders as of CDS and bond traders, who have pushed yields higher "against fundamentals" (this was the initial story in Greece, at least). The notion of a financial transaction tax, which is still slated for implementation during 2014, is another example of a newfound anti-market sentiment within EU policy circles.

7. There is no official statement or transcript that directly confirms these events. But it is the conclusion of David Marsh, who has researched the topic in great detail and conducted hundreds of personal interviews with European leaders and officials, as presented in the book *The Euro: The Politics of the New Global Currency* (New Haven, CT: Yale University Press, 2009).

8. This quote is taken from Marsh, *The Euro.*

9. They remain out to this day because they have technically not satisfied the entry criteria. But this is really just a political decision, and following the euro crisis, there is no political support for entry within either the Swedish government or the electorate.

10. In 1984, then prime minister Margaret Thatcher famously negotiated a significant rebate of 65 percent on the United Kingdom's contribution to the EU budget. And this was just one example of the United Kingdom's reluctance to fully participate in the European integration process.

11. See, for example, Daniel Gros and Felix Roth, "Do Germans Support the Euro?," CPES WORKING PAPER No. 359, December 2011.

12. See, for example, Barry Eichengreen, "Is Europe an Optimum Currency Area?," NBER Working Paper 3579, 1991.

13. While many of the costs of giving up currency flexibility were anticipated, there were also a number of economic effects that came as a surprise and were all generally negative. These were crisis effects that had previously not been relevant for developed markets. Unfortunately, this oversight may have profound consequences for the eurozone for many years to come.

14. See "Germany and the EMU," *Economist,* February 12, 1999.

15. This quote is from a *Der Spiegel* article from May 2012, based on previously secret government documents.

CHAPTER 3

1. In later years, AIB would go on to incur massive losses–€2.3 billion in 2009 and €10.4 billion in 2010, an unenviable record in Irish corporate history.

2. It should be noted that some of the growth was due to the many multinational companies expanding their production in Ireland, partly as a function of Ireland's low corporate tax rate. Hence, even if Irish production increased dramatically, not all of the income accrued to Irish residents. The increase in the gross domestic income was less impressive than the increase in the gross domestic product.

3. See for example, the European Commission paper on "European Cohesion Policy in Greece.", 2009.

4. Many East German monetary assets, such as cash and deposits up to a certain limit, were converted at a 1:1 exchange rate for political reasons. The 1:1 conversions took place even when the East German mark had been trading much lower than the West German equivalent in the free market.

5. Some used the term *Great Moderation* to describe the more stable business cycle and the lower volatility in financial markets.

CHAPTER 4

1. The former communist countries in Eastern Europe were the only recent examples of default in the European region. Poland defaulted in 1981, and Ukraine defaulted in both 1998 and 2000. But these defaults were too small to have major spillover effects on the global financial system.

2. In reality, the fund's effective lending capacity was substantially lower than €440 billion. This was because the fund was permitted to lend out only a certain proportion of the amounts guaranteed by eurozone governments. As a result, its effective lending capacity was around €250 billion. This figure was later expanded in various rounds, as policy makers realized that €250 billion was insufficient.

3. The total outstanding Italian government debt was near €2 trillion by the end of 2011, similar to the nominal amount of outstanding government debt in Germany. In relation to domestic GDP, Italy's debt-to-GDP ratio was around 125 percent, whereas the ratio was around 90 percent in Germany.

4. Eurozone banks and the countries associated with the euro are very closely interconnected. This link has many dimensions. First, sovereign bonds are the preferred form of collateral for various types of bank funding, including funding from the ECB. Second, banks are implicitly supported by the perception that in a crisis situation, troubled banking institutions will be recapitalized through government intervention.

5. While traders and brokers were busy digesting the morning's economic releases, I took note of this new degree of volatility and conveyed its significance for other asset markets to trading heads and risk managers. Within a few hours, many of the trading desks in the fixed-income division had tweaked their trading setups so that real-time information about movements in key European bank stocks would feed into the day-to-day market-making and risk management functions. This was the first time that sovereign bond traders had to take their cue from the performance of specific bank stocks. But given the size of the institutions that were in trouble and the interconnectedness of the overall system, it would have been foolish to ignore the banks in the current environment.

6. There are essentially two ways to improve capital ratios: either raise equity or sell assets. But since there were no forced capital injections from public sources (as was the case through the TARP process in the United States in 2009), and since no private capital was available given market conditions, this left sales of bank assets as the only remaining option. This bank deleveraging process, in turn, reinforced the negative market dynamics, putting additional downward pressure on asset prices as a result of the supply of securities from bank sellers.

7. The second Greek bailout amounted to additional funding for Greece of €130 billion, of which €28 billion came from the International Monetary Fund.

8. The tension between the federal government and the regions was also visible in relation to the Spanish banking crisis. Each region had run its own savings banks (the so-called *cajas*), which had been designed to promote regional investment. The management of these large regional institutions was highly political, involving local politicians and even representatives from the church.

9. The capital flight was also reflected in the buildup of so-called TARGET2 balances between the eurozone countries' individual central banks through the ECB.

10. The video of Draghi's speech (from July 26, 2012) is provided by UKTIWeb on YouTube: http://www.youtube.com/watch?v=hMBI50FXDps

11. This feature of the original euro was enshrined in the EU treaty (Article 127). But in the face of severe market tension, there was sufficient political will to circumvent this legal provision.

CHAPTER 5

1. Another less-known example of a durable currency union is the CFA franc zone in Africa, which includes 14 African countries linked to the currency of France (initially the French franc and now the euro).

2. In fact, there were three currencies in existence during that period. On the Pacific Coast, the official currency remained linked to gold. Even after the end of the Civil War, both greenbacks (by then the currency of both the North and the South) and so-called yellowbacks backed by gold (with an exchange rate that floated relative to the greenbacks) circulated. In 1879, the currency union was finally reestablished, and the greenback once again became the only currency of the entire United States.

3. The Baltic countries (Estonia, Latvia, and Lithuania) were different. They moved actively to create their own separate currencies as part of a broader process of independence from the former USSR and Russia.

4. The size of the cost of giving up flexibility depends on a number of factors. The work by Nobel Prize–winning economist Robert Mundell and other economists who have elaborated on his work have focused on the following factors as the key determinants of the cost of giving up monetary independence:

   a. It depends on the degree to which a country is hit by idiosyncratic shocks (that is, country-specific shocks), rather than shocks that are common to the entire currency union.

   b. It depends on the degree to which labor is mobile within the currency union.

   c. It depends on the degree to which prices and wages are sticky within the currency union.

   d. It depends on the degree to which a federal budget is capable of making cross-border transfers to smooth out the impact of shocks at the country (state) level.

CHAPTER 6

1. The number of eurozone member countries is set to expand to 18 in January 2014, when Latvia is scheduled to join. The number of EU member countries increased to 28 in July 2013, when Croatia joined the European Union.

2. The weakness of the insurance systems in individual countries had been exposed during the crisis. Would deposit insurance be worth anything if the country providing the insurance was itself bankrupt? This was a major concern in Greece during 2011 and 2012, and it later became a pressing issue in Cyprus.

3. The four crisis waves of the euro crisis are outlinked in Chapter 4. The treaty for the Fiscal Compact was signed in March 2012 by all EU countries except the United Kingdom and the Czech Republic.

4. The Fiscal Compact further cements the notion of fiscal conservatism by putting limits on nominal and cyclically adjusted fiscal deficits. For example, the structural

deficit (the deficit adjusted for the effect of weak growth) is not supposed to exceed 0.5 percent in countries with debt levels above 60 percent of GDP.

5. In addition, there were the usual disagreements about the use of funds. The French, as they have been for years, were adamant that subsidies to European (that is, French) farmers continue largely unchanged, while southern and Eastern European member countries have been calling for larger so-called cohesion funds (cross-border transfers aimed at stimulating growth in countries with lower income levels). The European Commission proposal, which involved a sizable budget increase, had a similar flavor, with larger amounts of funds earmarked for cross-border infrastructure investments.

6. The euro was supposed to be the currency of the European Union, but the United Kingdom and Denmark have formally opted out, and Sweden has effectively done the same (although formally there is no such agreement). Meanwhile, a number of Eastern European countries are having second thoughts about joining. This creates an institutional mess. The key European institutions were set up to cater for the 28 EU countries, while only 17 of those countries have adopted the euro. There is an increasing tension here.

CHAPTER 7

1. In his 1924 book *A Tract on Monetary Reform*, Keynes's key line was: "In truth, the gold standard is already a barbarous relic."

2. In Europe, the working class was able to secure a degree of political influence earlier on. For example, various Social Democratic parties were founded during the final years of the nineteenth century.

3. Using economics terminology, one would say that the Phillips curve, which expresses the relationship between inflation rates and unemployment, was relatively steep. The fact that central banks were fairly independent at the time also played a role here.

4. In economics terms, the *sacrifice ratio*, defined as the increase in unemployment necessary to achieve a 1 percent decline in inflation, had worsened. The deteriorating trade-off between price declines and unemployment came both from the changed structure of labor markets and from less independent central banks. This is an example of the so-called commitment problem of central banking, as described by F. Kydland and E. Prescott in "Rules Rather than Discretion: The Inconsistency of Optimal Plans" (*Journal of Political Economy.* 85: 473–490 [1977]). Lack of ability to commit, caused by lack of independence, increases the cost of disinflation. The sacrifice ratio had increased, and the political ability to tolerate economic pain had decreased. The system failed. It proved too costly to undertake deflationary adjustment to reestablish the prewar exchange rates to gold.

5. The post-World War II monetary system tried to learn from this experience. The Bretton Woods system, which was devised at an intergovernmental conference in 1944, was designed to avoid the rigidities and economic costs associated with the gold standard's inflexibility. This system was in place from 1945 to 1971, and even if the specific system has formally ended, many of the basic principles of monetary policy on which it was based remain valid today.

6. Only three of the countries in the eurozone (Germany, France, and Italy) are big enough to be part of the G20.

7. There is an inherent coordination problem similar to the often-debated "deflationary bias" in the Bretton Woods system, which also derived from an asymmetric approach to handling balance of payments imbalances, and similar to the lack of policy coordination during the interwar attempt to revive the gold standard.

CHAPTER 8

1. High emigration, as we typically see in the United States, is one way to overcome high regional unemployment. In the eurozone, however, labor mobility has historically been lower. In recent years, there has been some evidence in the direction of greater flexibility. In the absence of a fiscal union, however, this creates potential demographic and fiscal issues at home (given that there is no central eurozone budget to make "counter-transfers").

2. My colleague Richard Koo has written extensively about the downward economic spiral that can result from tight fiscal policy during a period of private-sector debt reduction. He calls this dynamic a *balance sheet recession*. This is described in detail in his book *Balance Sheet Recession: Japan's Struggle with Uncharted Economics and Its Global Implications* (New York: Wiley, 2001).

3. Non-standard tools, such as forward guidance on interest rates and balance sheet expansion (quantitative easing) still have potential to deliver additional easing, however.

4. In theory, all that is needed is lower inflation than in a country's trading partners. But since inflation in major eurozone countries such as Germany and the Netherlands is very low, there is not much room for internal devaluation in the peripheral economies without outright price declines. We do not have broad-based deflation in the entire eurozone, at least not yet. But the weakest countries in the eurozone have lower inflation than the average, and certain sectors within those economies have been experiencing deflationary dynamics during the crisis years. Hence, the cost of deflation is highly relevant for the weakest economies and sectors in the eurozone. There are clear deflationary trends in some key sectors in Ireland, Greece, Portugal, and Spain, and to a lesser degree in Italy, although rising consumption taxes are masking falls in underlying prices in some cases.

5. Back in 1933, economist Irving Fisher famously described the debt-deflation dynamics in the context of the collapse of the financial system during the Great Depression. Since then, Ben Bernanke has also written about distributional aspects of deflation. This work was done quite a while ago, when Mr. Bernanke was an academic, and it was not specific to the eurozone.

6. See for example, Alan M. Taylor's BIS conference paper "The Great Leveraging," from July 2012.

7. Both suppressed wage growth and rising productivity should serve to reduce production cost per unit. Linked to this, many economists are paying close attention to trends

in statistics on unit labor cost (ULC). There have indeed been notable improvements on this front, especially in Ireland and to some degree in Greece. These changes should mean that some GIIPS countries will be more competitive (or at least less uncompetitive) than they have been in the past.

8. During those years, all eurozone equity markets generally followed a common trend, with differences mostly being determined by the sector composition of indexes, rather than by country-specific macro developments. Hence, it mattered more whether the index had a high weighting in financials or in energy than which country you were looking at.

9. This is one of the reasons why Mr. Hollande's approval rating has dropped to an extraordinarily low level of just 27 percent less than a year into his presidency.

CHAPTER 9

1. The coalition initially consisted of New Democracy, PASOK, and the smaller Democratic Left Party. However, the Democratic Left withdrew from the coalition in June 2013 after the controversial closure of the state television broadcaster, leaving a two-party coalition with a slim majority in parliament.

2. These specific figures are taken from an opinion poll carried out by the firm Public Issue for Kathimerini and Skai, as reported by ekathimerini.com in February 2013. Other polls published in early 2013 have shown broadly similar trends.

3. This quote is from the *Financial Times*. In addition, ahead of the presidential election in 2012, Marine Le Pen stated: "Today, we are trying to save the euro at any cost, but at what cost? I do not want my people to be forced, like the Irish, to lower the minimum wage by 12%, to reduce family allowances, to lower unemployment, to lower the remuneration of civil servants. If that is the price which must be paid to save the euro, well then I say that is better to leave Europe and better to leave the euro," according to euractiv.com.

4. It should be noted that it did less well in local elections in 2012.

5. Mr. Grillo's movement (he refuses to call it a party) is based entirely on grassroots support and direct communication with supporters through social media.

6. Opposition has been more stable in Italy (31 percent) and France (27 percent). In the north, opposition is still a clear minority and not increasing.

7. Interestingly, France is one of the countries with the strongest view that taxation should be a national issue (74 percent).

8. In Portugal, the election loss of the center left Socialist Party in June 2011 led to a majority coalition government between the centrist Social Democratic Party and the center right People's Party. The policy path remained largely intact. In Spain, the Socialists, who had governed Spain since 2004, lost the election following a dramatic rise in unemployment during the crisis. The center right Popular Party gained an absolute majority in parliament. It was a big shift, but policies—including efforts to contain budget deficits in accordance with EU guidance—remained largely unaffected.

9. This trend in itself has many drivers, including less powerful unions, the impact of globalization, and the fall of communism. One reason is linked to a less uniform labor voice: While strike activity has increased in Greece, Portugal, and Spain, the impact has been limited. One reason is that the strikes are not as broad-based as they were in the past. There has been disagreement between different unions in both Spain and Portugal, meaning that only certain unions have participated. Another factor playing into this is that unionization has been in a declining trend for decades. These trends can be linked to the broader debate about globalization. In an increasingly integrated global economy, as Dani Rodrik (in *The Globalization Paradox* [New York: Norton, 2012) and others have pointed out, there is a fundamental tension between maintaining local social support systems, globalization, and democracy. This is part of the explanation why the attack on the prized social systems is not leading to the same violent protest that many predicted. In a way, the unions have become a part of the established center, and the confrontation is not between capital and labor, but between the establishment (including unions) and the outsiders, such as the unemployed youth. But this is probably not something that the social democratic parties are willing to be too explicit about.

10. Ironically, one of the euro's strengths lies in its unprecedented nature. While this has led to unexpected costs, it also works as glue. The fact that there are no precedents for a euro breakup means that the fear of the unknown can live on, and it is this fear, the anxiety associated with real change, that is creating a commitment to stick with it.

11. The other parties joined up as coalitions, and those coalitions (both on the left and on the right) got more votes than the Five Star Movement.

12. See for example, "Auf wiedersehen, Euro," *Christian Science Monitor,* April 15, 2013.

13. The bailout involved Monte dei Paschi di Siena, the world's oldest surviving bank.

14. The beauty of the Outright Monetary Transactions (OMT) system so far has been that its mere existence has calmed markets, as discussed in chapter 4.

15. The question of whether an OMT for France is politically possible is taboo. It may not seem a relevant question now, but French debt dynamics are worsening. It could become a real issue in the future.

16. Ewald Engelen, a professor of finance at the University of Amsterdam and one of the petition's sponsors, said that its goal was to block the government from expanding EU powers unless it could demonstrate popular legitimacy. "The EU is undergoing radical changes that call out for new treaties. But they are being pursued without treaty change, because the European elite is scared as hell [that voters would reject it]," Mr. Engelen said to the *Financial Times* on March 6, 2013.

17. See, for example, "More Power to Brussels?," *Der Spiegel,* August 10, 2012.

18. In 2006, 40 percent of French Eurobarometer respondents said that they tended to trust the EU. This has now dropped to 34 percent.

19. Scotland is to hold a referendum on independence from the United Kingdom in the autumn of 2014. Catalonia, one of the largest economic regions in Spain, accounting

for 20 percent of output, is planning its own referendum on independence, also slated for 2014. Finally, UK prime minister David Cameron has promised that should he be reelected, the United Kingdom will have a referendum on EU membership by 2017. According to recent opinion polls, only one-third of the U.K. electorate is currently in favor of EU membership.

20. He has recently been reflecting on European politics in a series of interviews with *Der Spiegel.* As a retired politician, he can be frank about what needs to be done, with no need to protect his ability to be reelected.

21. The specific quote here is taken from the Financial Times, June 21, 2013

CHAPTER 10

1. There was no common central bank until the creation of the Federal Reserve System, which came into effect only in 1914.

2. In the two largest banks, deposits greater than €100,000 have been frozen and will be partially paid out only over time. Within the second largest bank, Cyprus Popular, large depositors are expected to lose around 80 percent of their money. Within the largest bank, Bank of Cyprus, large depositors are expected to lose 30 to 50 percent of their money. For now, deposits are frozen, and they will be paid out only gradually, in line with how the banks perform.

3. In the United States, the central clearing is done through the so-called Interdistrict Settlement Account. This is an arcane technical element of the Federal Reserve System that very few people generally know about. In the eurozone, the central clearing is done through the so-called TARGET2 system, which is administered by the European Central Bank in Frankfurt. In both cases, the central banks guarantee continuous clearing at par between bank balances in different parts of the common currency area. In theory, there is no limit on how large outstanding clearing balances can become, since central banks have the ability to create their own liquidity (although there might be institutional or political limits to such cross-border liquidity injections).

4. This was more by accident than by design, since the nonconvertibility was imposed on Ukraine from the outside, leaving it no time to plan for a more comprehensive currency switch. In fact, a new currency regime was formalized only much later in the form of a new currency law approved in parliament, spelling out the characteristics of the new legal tender.

5. There have, however, been fears about the safety of bank deposits in the United States since 2008. This fear has been reflected in rising prices for gold, especially during 2008-2010. This is the case even though no insured depositor in the United States has ever lost money since the creation of the FDIC.

6. In Cyprus, this was very nearly the case in March 2013, as there were unresolved solvency issues within the key banks. It was also very nearly the case in Greece in May 2012, when it was unclear whether government policy would be compatible with continuing the bailout program, which underpinned government finance.

CHAPTER 11

1. The degree to which companies and banks have prepared for the scenario also matters. A breakup scenario that comes as a total surprise is one issue. A breakup against which certain precautions have been taken is another. By now, most major institutions have gone through comprehensive risk management exercises to put contingency plans in place. For this reason, the impact of a breakup would be very different today from the situation in early 2010, when it would have taken many institutions by surprise.

2. For a detailed description of all major aspects of the Czechoslovak currency separation, see Oldrich Dedek, *The Break-up of Czechoslovakia: An In-Depth Economic Analysis* (Aldershot, U.K.: Avebury, 1996).

3. The worries about extreme and destabilizing capital movement project the idea of efficient market concepts onto deposits. But this idea often does not capture the true behavior of depositors. In an efficient market, speculators are supposed to react immediately to any new information, and to move huge amounts of capital almost instantly to reflect profit opportunities and risk of loss. Some financial instruments, such as government bonds, which are owned predominantly by institutional investors, might react very violently to new information, as we have seen repeatedly during 2010 to 2012. Institutional deposits might also move. But retail deposits are different. They are held because they might be needed for transactions. And the holders may not have access to multiple bank accounts. They may not be able to move capital around quickly, especially not internationally.

4. In Cyprus, the major banks were left undercapitalized and vulnerable for months. When this was combined with a heated debate about either taxing or simply confiscating deposits on a large scale, it was an effective way to completely undermine any confidence in the banks.

5. Mr. Soares has not commented explicitly on exit from the euro. But it is hard to imagine that active default would be compatible with continued eurozone membership.

CHAPTER 12

1. The ECB felt unable to fully backstop sovereign bond markets. The European bailout fund, at the time called the European Financial Stability Facility (EFSF), had far too little capacity to support fragile bond markets in Spain and Italy. It was designed to take care of "smaller" problems in Greece, Ireland, and Portugal. Meanwhile, during the third quarter of 2011, the ECB had even scaled back its bond purchases and essentially left the markets alone. This all happened while Jean-Claude Trichet was the ECB president, that is, before Mario Draghi had announced the much more powerful Outright Monetary Transactions (OMT) program for sovereign bond market intervention.

2. Quoted from Bloomberg News.

3. The Greek parliament approved a law including so-called collective action clauses (CACs) in Greek law bonds. The CACs allowed a debt restructuring to happen by a

majority decision, essentially allowing the government to force through a debt restructuring for all investors, even the ones who did not explicitly agree to the deal.

4. The details of this idea are specified in the Wolfson Economics Prize paper coauthored with Nick Firoozye. The paper is called "Rethinking the European monetary union," and it is available on *http://www.policyexchange.org.uk* and on JensNordvig.com.

CHAPTER 13

1. Much has been written about the so-called Marshall-Lerner condition: the condition under which currency depreciation causes the trade balance to improve. It basically has to do with how responsive export and import volumes are to prices. In addition, there is the issue of whether nominal depreciation of the exchange rate will be neutralized by rising inflation. The answer will partly depend on the policy regime: the ability of new independent central banks to control inflation. In the context of eurozone countries, however, given that there is plenty of spare capacity after multiple years of weak growth, there seems a good possibility of avoiding excessive inflation.

2. For more detail on how to estimate potential currency moves in a breakup scenario see Appendix III in "Rethinking the European monetary union," available on policyexchange.org.uk or JensNordvig.com.

3. The so-called IS-LM model, which is a part of most undergraduate economics courses, is an example of that.

4. This is as opposed to emerging market countries, where borrowing often takes place in dollars.

5. To be specific, in Italy's case, the low foreign currency exposure in an exit derives from two sources. First, the Italian government issues almost all its debt under local laws, with the result that it can potentially be redenominated into a new Italian currency. Second, the private sector in Italy simply does not borrow a lot from the rest of the world. In addition, Italy has not yet borrowed through the European Central Bank (ECB) or the IMF, and its TARGET2 liabilities to the ECB are smaller than those in the other peripheral countries.

6. It is also worth putting debt levels into perspective. While Italy's debt of around 130 percent of GDP is very high by European standards (the average is 90 percent), it is not nearly as high as Japan's, which exceeds 240 percent of GDP. Whether Italy's debts are unsustainable depends on real growth, inflation, and funding cost. But if negative balance sheet effects are minor, it is not inevitable that exit from the currency union will make debts any more unsustainable than they are now. In fact, if growth recovers over time, it could be the opposite. In relation to government debt sustainability, having an independent currency and a central bank that is willing to provide backstop can make all the difference.

7. Little detailed analysis of the implications of breakup has been done, and a lot of the analysis that has been done fails to properly take into account the binding legal constraints involved in the process. The cost-benefit analysis is complex, but it is possible to quantify the key effects to get a sense of their importance. Some of the conclusions

from this type of analysis are politically controversial and at times collide with conventional wisdom too. But in an extreme crisis, these are nevertheless the relevant considerations and lessons to draw from.

8. One very complex issue would be how to split assets and liabilities on the ECB balance sheet between Germany and the remaining eurozone.

9. It is currently not possible to hedge such currency exposure, as there is no market for country-specific FX hedging. Such a market could potentially be set up using nondeliverable forward contracts, similar to the way currencies trade in many emerging markets.

10. As always, it depends on which country you look at. Bond spreads relative to Germany have compressed significantly in countries such as Spain, Italy and Ireland. Meanwhile, government bond yields remain high in both Greece and Portugal, embedding a significant premium for risk of default still.

CHAPTER 14

1. The markets that are perceived as being the safest, including the German and U.S. bond markets, have rallied on safe-haven inflows every time tension in the eurozone has escalated. Meanwhile, riskier assets, such as equities and high-yield bonds, have sold off during those periods.

2. Public debt ratios continue to rise (due to a combination of weak growth, remaining fiscal deficits and relatively high funding cost). Hence, it is clearly too early to say that debt dynamics have become sustainable. In addition, from a longer-term perspective, it is worth noting that demographics are deteriorating in many parts of Europe. This is putting downward pressure on potential growth in many eurozone countries and creating a further challenge for debt sustainability in the longer term.

3. The actual yield spread of eurozone government bonds over German bonds reflects a combination of two separate factors.

First, the country-specific fundamentals (fundamental spread).

This is the spread that would prevail without any insurance effect if bond prices were determined by a country's own fundamentals alone.

Second, the probability that insurance will fail (political risk premium).

This probability will depend on political considerations. If countries were entirely on their own, it would be 100 percent. If insurance were fully effective, the probability would be 0 percent, and yields would converge to the level seen in Germany.

This can be written as:

Yield spread = (political risk premium) x (fundamental spread)

The actual yield spread reflects both the probability that insurance fails and the fundamental spread that would prevail in the scenario without insurance, based on country-specific factors.

4. European leaders called it a "period of reflection." However, the reflection did not last long. The leaders eventually pushed through many of the same provisions in the Lisbon Treaty, which was ratified a few years later. Since the Lisbon Treaty was done as an amendment to existing treaties, it required a referendum in only a few countries. And when Ireland rejected the treaty in 2008, it was asked to vote again in 2009. This was the one time in history that public anti-integration sentiment (some would call it anti-European sentiment) managed to stall the European integration process, even if only for some time.

5. For example, the Greek credit default swap (CDS) spread, which is a measure of implied default risk, widened only marginally from 13 bp, to 19 bp, an example of how different the market environment was at the time. In today's world, where the Greek CDS spread is near 4,000 bp in early 2013, the minuscule increase seems laughable.

CHAPTER 15

1. The euro generally traded below parity to the dollar from early 2000 to mid-2002, and it reached a record low of 0.8272 on October 25, 2000.

2. In fact, after a period of deflation, the long-term equilibrium levels may even be higher than those of the past. This follows from the basic assumption that real exchange rates are mean-reverting over the long run. Therefore, deflation should translate into (nominal) exchange-rate strength over the long run, at least in theory.

3. However, the issue of internal imbalances as a function of asymmetric shocks could well recur in the future if no fiscal union has been established.

4. This all assumes that policies are put in place to stabilize the remaining core of the eurozone so as to avoid a full-blown breakup, which would mean that the euro would cease to exist. However, given the cataclysmic consequences of a full-blown breakup, it seems likely that such measures would indeed be taken.

5. It is worth noting that this type of equilibrium could also come about though the core voluntarily deciding to impose a path of less austerity on the periphery. In reality, the decisions of the periphery and the core happen simultaneously. Hence, the soft-currency branch of the tree could come about through more actively allowing it to materialize.

6. One question on the soft-currency branch of the tree is whether abandoning austerity will actually require monetary financing of deficits. If you believe that abandoning austerity will generate such a strong growth boost that fiscal deficits will not widen, this may not be the case. In the end, it is likely to depend on the type of fiscal loosening, the interplay with structural reforms, and the nature of external factors (such as global growth). It is perhaps conceivable that monetary financing would not be needed, but it is certainty an increasing risk in an environment of looser fiscal policy.

7. Economists call this a situation of fiscal dominance because monetary policy is determined by fiscal needs, rather than by the (currently) more conventional objective of price stability.

8. The exception is perhaps the extreme version in which inflationary dynamics spin out of control. In that situation, we could potentially see a splintering of the euro, driven by Germany's refusal to accept higher inflation and thereby undermining the wealth of its savers. There is a reason why the Germans are demanding conditionality. Their fear of inflation is great, and they are unlikely to compromise on conditionality to a degree that allows inflation risks to rise very substantially. Hence, there would be an inflation threshold where we would switch from the soft-currency branch to the political crisis branch. This would be one way to a disorderly exit of the strong.

9. This was a clear departure from the European Central Bank's previous philosophy of 'never precommitting', which was in place from 1999 to July 2013.

10. In an influencial book, *This Time Is Different: Eight Centuries of Financial Folly*, Carmen Reinhart and Kenneth Rogoff argued that there was a certain threshold for government debt above which growth would tend to be negative. This finding has since been found to be faulty and partly the result of coding errors. This is documented in a paper by Herndon, Ash and Pollin: "Does High Public Debt Consistently Stifle Economic Growth? A Critique of Reinhart and Rogoff", published through the Political Economy Research Institute.

Index

Note: Boldface numbers indicate illustrations.

A

Agenda 2010 (Germany), 43, 115
Aggregate growth vs. country-
    specific, 46–47
Almunia, Joaquin, 5, 221
Alternative for Deutschland
    (AfD), 134
Anastasiades, Nicos, 10
Anger, public displays of,
    126–127
Anglo Irish Bank (AIB), 37
Anti-establishment
    weakness, 131
Argentina, default by, 52, 130,
    163–164, 173, 188, 197
Asian crisis, 179–180
Asian Tiger, 36
Australia, 196
Austria, 61
Austro-Hungarian Empire, 166
Austro-Hungarian Empire currency
    union, 76

B

Backlash from bailouts, 135–137
Bailouts, 6–7, 221
Balance sheet effect, 179, 180–182
Banco Santander, 35–36
Bank of England, 102–103

Banking regulation, 8–9, 18, 93–95.
    See also European Central Bank
    (ECB)
    deflation and, 113–114
    deposit/capital flight, 157–158
    euro crisis and, 60–62
    Greece, 157–158
    nationalism vs. 86–88
    US, 144–146
Banking union, 85–90
Bankruptcies, 114
Barroso, Jose Manuel, 84
Bavarian Christian Social Union, 65
Belgian Central Bank, 154
Belgium, 4, 14, 154
    euro crisis and, 60
    GDP vs. debt in, 30
Berlin Wall, 23
Berlusconi, Silvio, 58, 62, 129
BH Option Trust, 163
Bloomberg, 54, 99
BMW, 43
BNP Paribas, 60
bond markets, 47, 67–68, 88–89, 95,
    164–165, 193, 196, 215–217
    euro crisis and, 53, 55–59, 63
    eurobonds, 8
    political risk premium and,
    198–202, 216–217

Brazil, 45

Breakdown of Eurozone debt, 227, **228**

breakup of the eurozone, xvii–xviii, 10, 64–69, 81–82, 83, 141, 153–162
analysis of, 176–177
Asian crisis and 179–180
balance sheet effect and, 179, 180–182
cost of, 160–162
Cyprus and, 148–149, 154, 158, 159, 175, 185
Czech example of, 156–157
debt overhang effects and, 178–179
deposit/capital flight and, 157–158
ECU-2 and, 173–174
end of euro and, 164–165, 169–170
European Central Bank (ECB) and, 153, 159
fiscal union and, 84
France, 182–183, 185
Germany and, 175, 176, 183–186
Greece and, 155, 157–158, 176–178, 181, 184, 185
Holland, 183–184
house on fire analogy and, 160–162
Ireland and, 181
Italy and, 177, 182–183
legal issues of, 167–169
legal warfare and, 163–164, 172–173
likelihood of, 214–215
litigation/legal warfare and, 163–164, 172–173
market implications of, 185–186
mechanics and implications of, 141

mini-Marshall Plan vs., 224
policy response and, 158–159
Portugal and, 177, 178, 181, 184, 185
possibility of, 154–156, 160–162
proactive economic policies vs., 224
proactive transfers and, 213–214
redenomination of currency and, 170–172, 173–174
repercussions of, 165–167
Spain and, 177, 181
strong vs. weak countries and, effects of exit, 183–184
trade effects after, 177–178
unintended, 149–151
worst-case scenario in, 163–174
"zombie" euros and, 169–170, 172

Bretton Woods currency control system, 19–20

Brown, Gordon, 26

Budget regulation, 8–9, 40, 90–92. *See also* Fiscal union

Bundesbank, 29, 33–34

Business Insider, 170

C

Canada, 80, 196

Capital flight, 157–158

Capital, instability of, 195–196

Capitalism and the gold standard, 101

Celtic Tiger, 36–38. *See also* Ireland

Central Bank of Cyprus, 135

Central Bank of Russia, 80, 147, 148

Central Europe, x, 23, 47, 222

Central parity rates, 19

Central Statistics Office Ireland, 37

Centrist movements, 128–130,
  134–135
China, 42
Chinn, Menzie, 48
Christian Democratic Union (CDU),
  128–129, 130, 134
Churchill, Winston, 102–103
Civil War, US, 77, 143, 145
Coene, Luc, 154
Cold War, 17, 23, 222
Common market, EU, x, 18, 81
Communism, 23
Confidustria, 6
Constitutional crisis, 137–139
Contract law, 167
Contract, frustration of, 169, 172
Convergence optimism, 40
Convergence vs. divergence, deflation
  and, 118–120
Cost of deflationary policy, 111–114
Costs of implementing the euro/
  eurozone, 28–29
Credibility gap, 120–121
Credit ratings, 54
Credit risk, 170
Crises waves, xv. *See also* Euro crisis
Criteria of economic convergence,
  29–30, 45
Culture, 9, 41
Currency, 205–208, 210–213
  Bretton Woods system and, 19–20
  central parity rates in, 19
  control of, 19
  convertibility of, 146–151
  "currency snake" and, 21
  debasement of, 211–212
  definition of, 3–4

deutsche mark (D-mark)
  and, 19–20
devaluation of, 19, 21
ECU-2 as, 173–174
euro vs. US dollar, 48
European Exchange Rate
  Mechanism (ERM) and, 21, 59
exchange rates for, 4, 19, 20–22
floating value of, 20–22
francs in, 19
"gnomes of Zurich" and, 19
gold standard for, 99–107.
  See also Gold standard
international law and, 168–169
legal issues concerning, 167–169
Maastricht Treaty and, 24–25
money vs., 3–4
post war years and, 18
post-breakup valuations of,
  177–178
pound and, 20, 21
purpose of, 3–4
redenomination and, 170–172,
  173–174
valuation of, 4, 19
yen and, 20, 48
Currency risk, 170
"Currency snake," 21
Currency unions, 75–82
  advantages of, 81
  banking union and, 85–90
  breakup of, 81–82
  common markets and, 81
  examples of, 76
  fiscal flexibility of, 75–76
  fiscal union and, 84
  history of, 76

Currency unions, (*Continued*)
optimal currency areas and, 80–81
Soviet Union, 76, 79–80, 82
Swiss Confederation, 76
United States, 76–79, 82
US Civil War and, 77
Current account deficits, 44–46
Customs, 15
Cyprus, xviii, 6, 10, 120, 200, 202
bailout of, 134–135, 136
banking crisis in, 86–88, 146
breakup and, 154, 158, 159,
161, 175, 185
convertibility of currency
and, 149–150
currency crisis in, 148–149
euro crisis and, 70
exit from eurozone by, 10
gross domestic product (GDP)
in, 111
near breakup experience in,
148–149
Czech Republic, 43, 143, 156–157
Czechoslovak currency union, 76
Czechoslovakia, 143, 156–157, 166

D
DAX, 119
DDR. *See* East Germany
Debasement, 211–212
Debt, xv, 7, 30, 39, 45, 50
balance sheet effect and,
179, 180–182
breakdown of eurozone, 227, **228**
deflation and, 113–114
overhang effects and, 178–179
PIIGS countries and, 41, 44

restructuring, 215–217
sovereign default and, 196–198
Decision tree for Eurozone,
204–219, **206**
hard currency branch in, 205–208
proactive transfers and, 213–214
probabilities and, 214–215
soft currency branch in, 210–213
Declining support for EU,
127–128, **127**
defaults, 7, 47, 52, 64, 188, 196–198
euro crisis and, 63
sovereign, 196–198
Deflation, xvii, 74, 99, 105, 109–121
banking systems and, 113–114
bankruptcies and, 114
convergence vs. divergence as
result of, 118–120
cost of deflationary policy and,
111–114
credibility gap and, 120–121
debt levels and, 113–114
Eurozone growth crisis and,
117–118, **118**
exports vs., 115–117
fading faith in the EU and, 121
in Germany, 115–117
gold standard and, 112–113
in Greece, 116
hardest impact of, 113–114
"hit em while they're down effect"
and, 112
inadequate pessimism leading to,
110–111
interest rates and, 111
internal devaluation, 112
in Ireland, 116

in Italy, 116
monetary expansion vs., 114
policy constraints and errors
leading to, 109–110
in Portugal, 116
in Spain, 116
unemployment and, 109–110, 119
Delors Report, 22
Delors, Jacques, 22
Democracy and economic
integration, 16–17, 25–26
Demonstrations, 126–127, 133–134
Denmark, 16, 25, 138, 196
Deposit/capital flight, 157–158
Deutsche mark (D-mark), 19–20, 21,
23–24, 27
Devaluation of currency, 19, 21
Devaluation, internal, 105, 112
Dexia bank, 60
Dobrindt, Alexander, 65
Dollar. See US dollar
Draghi, Mario, 62–63, 69–70, 84,
99–100, 149, 212

E
East Germany (DDR), 14, 23–24
Eastern Europe, x, 22–23, 47, 79, 222
Economic and Monetary Union
(EMU), 22, 26
Economic convergence, 29–30, 40, 45
Economic crisis, xv
Economic development, 16
Economic growth, 34, 40
aggregate level vs. country-specific,
46–47
convergence of, 40
deflation and, 117–118, **118**

in Germany, 42–44
in Greece and, 38–39
in Ireland and, 36–38
in Italy, 42
in Spain and, 35–36
economic integration in Europe, ix–x,
xv, xvii, 7–8. See also Currency
unions 1950-2014, 17, **17**
banking regulation and, 18
banking union and, 85–90
criteria of economic convergence
for, 29–30, 40, 45
currency unions and, 75–82
customs and, 15
deflation and, convergence vs.
divergence and, 118–120
democracy and, 16–17, 25–26
European Central Bank (ECB)
and, 86, 87, 93–95. See also
European Central Bank (ECB)
European Coal and Steel
Community (ECSC) and, 14–15
European Economic Community
(EEC) and, 15–16
Fiscal Compact and, 91
fiscal union and, 90–92
gradualism in pursuit of, 94–95
increased, 83
lack of centralized fiscal policy
and, 8
Maastricht Treaty and, 24–25
more or less, 75–82
opposition to, 84
polarization of political stances vs.,
123–124
political realities and, 10–11, 83–97
political union and, 92

economic integration in Europe,
   (*Continued*)
  realpolitik and, 83–97
  restructuring of Eurozone and,
   96–97
  reversal of, 7
  Single European Act and, 18
  Stability and Growth Pact and, 91
  strengths vs. weaknesses of,
   222–223
  tariffs and, 15
  theory vs. practice in, 85
  voter apathy toward, 9
Economics of exits, 175–189
Economist, 176
ECU-2, 173–174
Eichengreen, Barry, 155
Eisenhower, Dwight D., 14
Emerging markets and Eurozone, 198
Escudo, 21
EUobserver, 49
Euro
  costs of implementing, 28–29
  countries invited to
   participate in, 29
  creation of, 4
  ECU-2 and, 173–174
  end of, 164–165, 169–170
  euroskepticism and, 26–31
  exchange rates and, 28–29
  flawed basis of, 7–8
  future value of, 217–218
  German reunification
   and, 23–24
  history of, 13–31
  "honeymoon period" of, 35–40
  infrastructure behind, 8–9

  international law and, 168–169
  lack of centralized fiscal policy
   behind, 8
  launch of, 25, 33–34
  legal issues concerning, 167–169
  Maastricht Treaty and, 24–25
  optimism concerning, 40
  policy changes affecting, 71
  politics of, 10–11, 13
  post-breakup valuation of,
   177–178, **178**
  propaganda campaign to support
   launch of, 27–28
  redenomination and, 170–174
  reforming the infrastructure of,
   8–10
  splintering of, 143–151
  success of, 4
  tenth anniversary of, premature
   celebration for, 4–5, 49
  US dollar vs., 5, 33, 48, 53, 56
  yen vs., 53, 56
  "zombie", 169–170, 172
Euro crisis, 9–10, 49–72, 83
  persistence of, 97
  restructuring of Eurozone
   and, 96–97
  sovereign default and, 196–198
  banks react to, 60–62
  in Belgium, 60
  bond markets and, 53, 55–59, 63,
   67–68, 67
  breakup of EU and, 64–69
  credit ratings and, 54
  in Cyprus, 70
  defaults and, 52, 63–64
  Dexia bank and, 60

European Central Bank (ECB) and, 54, 57–59, 62–71

European Financial Stability Facility (EFSF) and, 68, 88

European Stability Mechanism (ESM) and, 88

fall of original euro in, 71

fourth wave in, 64–69

in France, 59, 60, 62

future waves in, 71–72

in Germany and, 62, 64–65, 71

in Greece and, 49–54, 64–66, 71

Grexit and, 65–66, 69, 157

interest rates and, 57

International Monetary Fund and, 53–54, 56

in Ireland, 55–57, 68

in Italy in, 57–59, 62, 63, 70

Japanese yen vs. euro in, 56

market stabilization near end of, 70

Outright Monetary Transactions (OMT) and, 70

in Portugal, 56–57, 68

press coverage of, 65, **65**

recovery from, 63

second wave in, 54–57

in Spain in, 56–58, 63, 66, 69, 70–72

stock markets in, 60–63

structural change in Eurozone prompted by, 69–70

third wave in, 57–63

United States policy and, 49, 61

US dollar vs. euro in, 56

Eurobarometer, 127–128, **127**

Eurobonds, 8

Eurogroup, 84, 176

European Banking Authority, 60

European Capital of Culture, 41

European Central Bank (ECB), xv, 7–8, 9, 10, 29, 33–34, 36, 47, 82, 84, 128, 135, 136–137, 149, 173, 195, 205, 210, 211, 212, 221, 224

bailouts and, 136

breakup and, 153, 159

convertibility of currency and, 150–151

Cypriot currency crisis and, 148–149

euro crisis and, 54, 57–59, 62–71

European integration and, 86, 87, 93–95

gold standard and, 99–100, 106

Outright Monetary Transactions (OMT) and, 70

restructuring of Eurozone and, 96–97

European Coal and Steel Community (ECSC), 14–15

European Commission, 18, 22, 40, 71, 84, 92, 111, 118, 127

European Constitution, 138, 201

European Council, 84, 90

European Court of Justice, 18

European Economic Community (EEC), 15–16, 20, 25, 161

European Exchange Rate Mechanism (ERM), 21, 59

European Financial Stability Facility (EFSF), 68, 88, 125

European Monetary Institute, 29

European Parliament, 18

European Stability Mechanism (ESM), 88, 125, 205

European Union (EU), x–xi, 4, 17,
  25, 85, 222
  constitutional crisis and, 137–139
  declining support for,
    127–128, **127**
  fading faith in, 121
  gross domestic product
    (GDP) of, 105, 135
  imbalances among member
    nations in. *See* Imbalance
Euroskepticism, 26–31, 124–128, 138
Eurozone growth crisis, 117–118, **118**
Evolution of the euro/eurozone, xv
Exchange rates, 4, 19–22,
    28–29, 33, 39
  convertibility of currency and,
    146–151
  "currency snake" and, 21
  currency splintering and, 143–151
  European Exchange Rate
    Mechanism (ERM) and, 21, 59
  floating values of currency and,
    20–22
  franc vs. deutsche mark, 21–22, **22**
  gold standard and, 103–104
Exits, economics of, 175–189.
    See also Breakup
Exports, deflation and, 115–117

F
Fading faith in the EU, 121
Federal Reserve System, 57, 144–146
Federal Deposit Insurance Corporation
    (FDIC), 85–86, 90, 145
Federal Reserve Act of 1913, US, 78
Fektor, Maria, 61
Fianna Fail, 129

Financial Services Authority, 171
Financial Times, 154, 170, 198
Fine Gael, 129
Finland, 95, 125, 136
Firoozye, Nick, 170, 227
Fiscal Compact, 91, 104
Fiscal union, 84, 90–92, 104–107
Fitch Ratings, 39
Five Star Movement
    (M5S), 125, 133
Flawed basis for euro's
    creation, 7–8
Floating value of currencies, 20–22
Foreign investment, 195–196
Fox News, 125
Franc, French, 19, 21–22, **22**
Franc, Swiss, 194
France, 7, 14, 24, 40, 41, 44, 83, 92,
    105, 120, 135, 138, 139, 154,
    188, 201
  breakup and, 182–183, 185
  euro crisis and, 59, 60, 62
  exports and, 117
  floating value of currencies
    and, 20–22
  franc and, 21
  politics of, 125
  post war years in, 13–14
  unemployment in, 121
Franco, Francisco, 16
Frankel, Jeffrey, 48
Friedman, Milton, 28, 188
Frustration of contract, 169, 172
Future euro crisis, 71–72, 71
Future of the euro/eurozone,
    xviii, 191
Future value of euro, 217–218

G

Geithner, Tim, 61

General Electric, 18

German Christian Democratic
    Union (CDU), 115 '

Germany, xv, xviii, 5, 7, 14, 23–24, 29,
    30, 31, 36, 40–44, 58, 59, 68, 83,
    92, 94, 95, 105, 137, 138, 139,
    158, 187–188, 203, 215, 224
    1950s–1960s in, 15
    Agenda 2010 and, reforms, 115
    banking regulation in, 86, 89, 90,
        93–94
    bond markets and, 199
    breakup and, 10, 159, 175, 176,
        183–186
    budget regulation/fiscal
        union and, 91
    deflation and, 115–117
    deutsche mark (D-mark) and, 19–27
    economic growth in, 42–44
    euro and euroskepticism in, 27, 31
    euro crisis and, 62, 64–65, 71
    floating value of currencies and,
        20–22
    Greece euro crisis and, 53
    gross domestic product (GDP) of,
        40, 57, 116
    inflation in, 46
    politics of, 128–129, 130, 134
    post war years in, 13–14
    proactive transfers and, 213–214
    reforms urged by, 42–44
    reparations following
        WWI by, 216
    reunification of, 23–24, 188
    unemployment in, 119, 121

"Gnomes of Zurich", 19

Gold standard, xvii, 73–74,
    99–107, 188
    capitalism and, 101
    classical version of, 101
    deflation and, 112–113
    European Central Bank (ECB)
        and, 99–100, 106
    exchange rates and,
        103–104
    Fiscal Compact and, 104
    fiscal union and, 104–107
    Great Depression and, 103
    Group of 20 (G20) and, 104
    history of, 100–102
    interest rates and, 100–102
    internal devaluation and,
        105, 112
    involuntary acceptance of,
        in Europe, 104–107
    mechanics of, 100
    operation of, 100–102
    problems with, 102–104
    Stability and Growth Pact
        and, 104–105
    United Kingdom and, 102
    United States, 100
    US ends, 20

Goldman Sachs, 34, 47

Gorbachev, Mikhail, 24, 79

Gosbank, 79

Governing law, 167

Gradualism in pursuit of
    increased European integration,
    94–95, 94

Great Depression, 79, 82, 86, 103,
    145, 197

Greece, xv, xviii, 4– 6, 7, 40, 41, 47,
58, 59, 83, 92, 95, 124, 135, 154,
160, 195, 202, 215, 216, 218
bailout of, 136
banking regulations and,
86, 157–158
bond markets and, 199, 200
breakup and, 155, 157–158, 161,
176, 177, 178, 181, 184, 185
convertibility of currency and,
149–150
credit ratings for, 39, 50
current account deficits
of, 44–46
debt restructuring in, 63, 169
debts and deficits in, 50–54
declining support for EU in, 128
default by, 7, 197, 199, 200
deflation and, 116
economic crisis in, 5–6, 7
economic growth in, 38–39
economic recovery in, 110
EEC membership by, 16, 17
euro crisis and, 49–54, 64–66, 71
exit from eurozone by, 10
exports and, 117
failure to meet economic
convergence criteria by, 30
fast-tracking into EEC of, 17
Germany's response to euro
crisis in, 53
Grexit and, 65–66, 69, 157
gross domestic product (GDP)
of, 40, 45, 46, 50, 110–111, 181
inflation in, 45
International Monetary Fund and,
53–54

Japanese response to euro crisis in,
51–52, **52**
New Democracy party in, 64, 69,
123–124, 130
PASOK political party in, 50, 64,
123–124, 130
politics of, 64–69, 123–126,
130, 154
support for, in euro crisis, 53–54
SYRIZA Party in, 64, 65–66,
68–69, 124, 154
Turkey vs., 17
unemployment in, 119
Grexit, 65–66, 157
Grillo, Beppe, 125, 138
Gross domestic product (GDP), 30, 34
Asian countries, 179–180
bank credit level vs., 114
convergence of, 40
current account deficits and, 44–46
Cyprus, 111
EU, 92, 105, 135
Eurozone debt vs., **228**
Germany, 40, 57, 116
Greece, 39, 40, 45, 46, 50,
110–111, 181
growth of, 40
Ireland, 37, 40, 45, 56, 181
Portugal, 40, 45, 181
Spain, 36, 40, 45, 67, 89, 181
United States, 78
Group of 20 (G20), 104

H
Hard currency branch, decision tree
for Eurozone, 205–208
Hedge funds, 193, 197

History of the euro, x–xi, xv, 13–31
"Hit em while they're down effect,"
    deflation and, 112
Holland. *See* Netherlands
Hollande, François, 120
"Honeymoon period" of euro, 35–40
Hoover, Herbert, 82
Housing market and real estate,
    7, 36, 37, 55, 83, 112
Hungary, 43
Hunger, 6
Hyperinflation, 93–94

I

IBEX, 119
Imbalance in individual economies,
    xv, xviii, 6, 8, 28–29, 25, 44
    current account deficits and, 44–46
    PIIGS countries and, 44
Income levels, convergence of, 40
Indonesia, 179–180, 181
Inflation, 33–34, 45–46, 93–94
Infrastructure of euro/eurozone, 8–10
Infrastructure, physical, 120
Integration. *See* Economic
    integration in Europe
Interest rate risk, 170
Interest rates, 4–5, 36, 37–38, 57
    deflation and, 111
    euro crisis and, 57
    gold standard and, 100–102
Internal devaluation, 105, 112
International Business Time, 61
International law, 168–169
International Monetary Fund (IMF),
    19, 53–54, 56, 90, 110, 118, 124,
    157, 179–180

Investment risk, 41, 47
Investment strategies, xviii, 191,
    203–219
    decision tree for Eurozone in,
    204–219, **206**
Involuntary gold standard in Europe,
    104–107
Ireland, 7, 36–38, 40, 41, 58, 59, 83,
    88, 95, 138, 216, 218
    bailout of, 136
    banking regulation in, 86
    bond markets and, 55
    breakup and, 161, 181
    deflation and, 116
    economic growth in, 36–38
    EEC membership by, 16
    euro crisis and, 55–57, 68
    exports and, 117
    gross domestic product (GDP)
    of, 40, 45, 56, 181
    housing market collapse in, 55
    inflation in, 45
    International Monetary Fund
    and, 56
    politics of, 129
    pound of, 21
Italy, 5, 6, 7, 14, 47, 68, 95, 135, 138,
    193, 195, 202, 203, 218
    banking regulation in, 86
    bond markets in, 164–165
    breakup and, 10, 161, 177,
    182–183
    default by, 197
    deflation and, 116
    economic crisis in, 6
    economic growth in, 42,
    117–118, **118**

Italy, (*Continued*)
euro crisis and, 57–59, 62, 63, 70
exports and, 117
GDP vs. debt in, 30
lira and, 21
negative growth in, 9
politics of, 125, 129, 133
unemployment in, 121

J

Japan, 20, 48, 50
deflation and, monetary expansion in, 114
Greece euro crisis and, 51–52, **52**
JPMorgan Chase, 60
Juncker, Jean-Claude, 84, 159

K

Keynes, John Maynard, 100
Knickerbocker Trust, 144
Kohl, Helmut, 23, 24, 27, 29, 31
Krugman, Paul, 29

L

La Stampa newspaper, 21
Labour Party, Ireland, 129
Lack of centralized fiscal policy, 8
Latin American debt crisis, 216
Latin currency union, 76
Launch of the euro, 25, 33–34
Le Pen, Marine, 125
Legal aspects of breakup, xviii, 167–169
Legal jurisdiction, 167
Legal warfare, 163–164, 172–173
Lehman Brothers, 60, 85–86
Letta, Enrico, 214–215
Lira, 21

Lisbon Treaty, 138
Litigation and breakup, 163–164, 172–173
Long-Term Capital Management, 197
Luxembourg, 14, 18, 159

M

Maastricht Treaty, 24–25, 29–30, 45, 138
Madrid protests, 6
Market complacency, 47
Market implications of breakup, 185–186
Market, EU. see Common market, EU
Merkel, Angela, 6, 53, 58, 62, 65, 89, 90, 129, 130, 134, 159, 165, 176
MF Global, 193–194
Mini-Marshall Plan, 213–214, 213
Mitterrand, François, 23–24
Money, 3–4. *See also* Currency
Monnet, Jean, 14–15, 14
Monti, Mario, 21, 62, 129, 165
Moody's, 39
Mundell, Robert, 80–81

N

National Front, France, 125
National Statistics Institute, 114
Nationalism in banking regulation, 86–88
Negative growth, 9
Netherlands (Holland), 14, 30, 41, 68, 83, 95, 138, 140, 201, 203
banking regulation in, 86
breakup and, 183–184
politics of, 125

New Democracy party, Greece, 64, 69, 123–123, 130
New York Clearing House, 144, 147
New York Times, 121
Nixon, Richard, 19, 188
Nomura Securities, x, 50, 166
Orphanides, Athanastos, 134
Outright Monetary Transactions (OMT), 70, 211, 212

P
Papandreou, George, 154
Party for Freedom, 125
PASOK political party, Greece, 50, 64, 123–124, 130
Peseta, 21
PIIGS countries, 41, 44
Poland, 61
Polarization of politics, 123–124
Political risk premium, 198–202, 216–217
Political union in Europe, xv, xvii, 92
Political utopia, 139–140
Politics, political realities, 9–11, 13, 74, 83–97, 200–202, 208–210
  anti-establishment weakness and, 131
  backlash from bailouts and, 135–137
  centrist movements and, 128–130, 134–135
  constitutional crisis and, 137–139
  euroskepticism, 124–126, 128
  polarization in, 123–124
  political risk premium and, 198–202
  political utopia and, 139–140
  protests, strikes, demonstrations and, 126–127, 133–134
  public anger and, 126–127
  referenda and, 137–139, 201
  revolt from within and, 134–135
  stability of financial markets and, 132–133
  status quo and, 130–131
  trust in European institutions declines, 127–128
Portugal, 7, 40, 41, 47, 58, 59, 95, 202, 215, 216, 218
  bailout of, 136
  bond markets in, 217
  breakup and, 161, 177, 178, 181, 184, 185
  current account deficits and, 44–46
  declining support for EU in, 128
  deflation and, 116
  EEC membership by, 16, 17
  escudo and, 21
  euro crisis and, 56–57, 68
  exports and, 117
  gross domestic product (GDP) of, 40, 45, 181
  inflation in, 45
  politics of, 126
  unemployment in, 121
Portugal, Ireland, Italy, Greece, Spain (PIIGS). *See* PIIGS countries, 41
Post war years, 14–16
Pound sterling, 4, 20, 21
Pound, Irish, 21
Premature celebrations, 4–5, 49
Proactive economic policies, 224
Proactive transfers, 213–214
Probabilities, 214–215
Project Bond/Project Bond Initiative, 120

Project Syndicate, 184

Propaganda campaign to support
euro's launch, 27–28

Protests, 126–127

Purpose of currency, 3–4

R

Real estate. *See* Housing market
and real estate

Realpolitics and European
integration, 73, 83–97. *See also*
Politics, political realities

Recession, 5, 7, 49, 102, 105, 106,
135, 203

Redenomination of euro/currency,
170–174

Redenomination risk, 171

Referenda, 137–139, 201

Reforming the euro/eurozone, 8–10

Regulation of business practices, 18

Regulatory frameworks, 47

Restructuring of debt, 215–217

Restructuring of Eurozone, 96–97

Reunification of Germany, 23–24, 188

Reuters, 54, 89

Risk, 170, 171, 198–202, 216–217

Roosevelt, Franklin D., 82

Rosler, Philipp, 159

Rublezone, 76, 79–80, 82,
137, 150, 188

Russia, 52, 79–80, 86, 147, 148, 150,
188, 197. *See also* Soviet Union

S

S&P 500 Index, 194–195

Salamanca, 41

Sarkozy, Nicolas, 58, 62, 154, 165

Scandinavian currency union, 76

Schauble, Wolfgang, 64, 121,
138, 215

Schroder, Gerhard, 31, 43, 139

Schuman, Robert, 14

Scotland, 139

Single European Act, 18

Slovakia, 136, 143, 156–157

Soares, Mario, 161

Social Democratic Party, 130

Social Security Act of 1935,
US, 78

Socialist Party, France, 135

Societe Generale, 60

Soini, Timo, 125

Soros, George, 184

South Korea, 45, 179–180

Sovereign default, 196–198

Soviet Union, 14, 23, 24, 76,
78–82, 188

Spain, xv, 5, 6, 7, 36, 40, 41, 47, 58,
68, 83, 92, 95, 100, 114, 135,
138, 139, 160, 202, 215, 216, 218
bailout of, 88–89, 136
banking regulation in, 86, 88–89
bankruptcies in, 114
bond market in, 59, 88–89,
164–165, 199, 200
breakup and, 10, 67, 161,
177, 181
budget problems in, 66–67
convertibility of currency
and, 149
declining support for EU
in, 128
default by, 197, 199, 200
deflation and, 116

economic crisis in, 6
economic growth in, 34–36,
    117–118, **118**
EEC membership by, 16, 17
euro crisis and, 56–59, 63, 66,
    69, 70–72
exports from, 116
gross domestic product (GDP)
    and, 40, 45, 67, 89, 181
inflation in, 45
negative growth in, 9
peseta and, 21
politics of, 126–127
unemployment in, 6, 119, 121
Splintering currency, 143–151
    convertibility of currency and,
        146–151
    Cyprus and, near breakup
        experience in, 148–149
    Czech example of, 143
    unintended breakups
        and, 149–151
St-Arnaud, Charles, 170
Stability and Growth Pact,
    91, 104–105
Stability of financial markets,
    132–133
Status quo, politics of, 130–131
Stock markets, 60–62, 63, 119,
    194–195
Strengths vs. weaknesses of
    integration, 222–223
Strikes, 126–127, 133–134
Structural change in Eurozone,
    euro crisis and, 69–70
Suicide rates, 6
Sweden, 27, 103, 138, 196

Swiss Confederation, currency
    union of, 76
Swiss franc, 194
Switzerland, 19, 76
SYRIZA Party, Greece, 64, 65–66,
    68–69, 124, 154
Tajikistan, 80
Tariffs, 14, 15
Telegraph, 159
Thailand, 179–180, 181
Thatcher, Margaret, 24, 26
Trade effects after breakup, 177–178
Treaty Establishing a Constitution
    for Europe (TCE), 201
Treaty of Rome, 15, 18
Treaty on the Functioning of the
    European Union, 94
Trichet, Jean-Claude, 25, 49, 62, 153
Troubled Asset Relief Program
    (TARP), 88, 89
True Finns, 125
Trust and confidence in EU, 9, 71
Tsipras, Alexis, 64
Turkey, 17, 45
U.S. Treasury bonds, 196
Ukraine, 80, 147, 148, 150, 188
UN Economic Commission for
    Europe, 36
Unemployment, x, 6, 101, 102,
    109–110, 119
Union of Soviet Socialist Republics
    (USSR). *See* Soviet Union, 79
United Kingdom, x, 14, 21, 24, 86,
    92, 139, 171, 193
    EEC membership by, 16
    euro and euroskepticism in, 26–27
    gold standard and, 102

United States, 5, 8, 14, 34, 36, 57, 83,
    88, 93, 112, 114, 193, 196, 218
  banking regulation in, 85–90,
    144–146
  currency union of, 76, 77–79, 82
  euro crisis and, 49, 61
  gold standard in, 20, 100
  gross domestic product
    (GDP) of, 78
"United States of Europe," xv
University of Bocconi, 21
University of California,
    Berkeley, 155
US dollar, 53, 56, 76, 77–79,
    144–146
  deutsche mark (D-mark)
    and, 19–20
  euro exchange rate for, 5, 33, 48
  franc and, 19
Value of currency, 4
Vanity Fair, 58
Volkswagen, 15, 43
Von Rompuy, Herman, 84, 85, 89,
    90, 92

W
Wages, deflation and, 112
Wall Street Journal, 149, 170
Weidmann, Jens, 211
West Germany, 14. *See also* Germany
Wilders, Geert, 125
Wolf, Martin, 198
Wolfson Economics Prize, x,
    171–172, 171
World Economic Outlook (IMF), 110
World Financial Center, 53
World War I, 100, 102
World War II, 13, 18, 78, 96,
    106, 160, 187
Worst-case scenario, 163–174.
    See also Breakup

Y
Yen, 20, 53, 56
Youth unemployment, 6, 118, 218
Yugoslavia, x

Z
Zombie euros, 169–170, 172

About the Author

Jens Jakob Nordvig began his finance career at Goldman Sachs in London in 2001. He eventually went on to lead the global currency strategy group before joining the hedge fund Bridgewater Associates. Currently, Nordvig is the head of currency strategy and fixed-income research for Nomura Securities. Over the past two years, throughout the worst of the European financial crisis, Nordvig was the ranked as the number one currency strategist by *Institutional Investor.**

In 2012, he received international recognition as a finalist in the Wolfson Economics Prize competition for his lead authorship of "Rethinking the European monetary union," an essay on the future of the eurozone.

Nordvig's work has been published in the *Financial Times*. He is frequently quoted in the *Wall Street Journal*, the *New York Times*, *Bloomberg Businessweek*, and the *Economist* and is a regular contributor to CNBC, Bloomberg TV, and other international news channels.

Nordvig studied economics at the University of Aarhus. At the age of 28, he was the coauthor of a book called Matematik og økonomi (*Mathematics and Economics*).

Nordvig grew up in Denmark in a town with the nickname City of Smiles. He enjoys yoga and is a surprisingly good golfer. He currently resides on New York City's Upper West Side with his wife, who is studying to be a neurologist.

* All-America Fixed-Income Research Team Ranking, 2011 and 2012.